VINES OF CLARITY

VINES OF CLARITY

SUFFER UNTO GREATNESS

Alexander Griffin

Cat & Crow Publishing

First published by Cat & Crow Publishing 2021

Copyright © 2021 by Alexander Griffin

All rights reserved. No part of this publication may be reproduced, stored or transmitted in any form or by any means, electronic, mechanical, photocopying, recording, scanning, or otherwise without written permission from the publisher. It is illegal to copy this book, post it to a website, or distribute it by any other means without permission.

Alexander Griffin asserts the moral right to be identified as the author of this work.

Alexander Griffin has no responsibility for the persistence or accuracy of URLs for external or third-party Internet Websites referred to in this publication and does not guarantee that any content on such Websites is, or will remain, accurate or appropriate.

First edition

ISBN: 978-1-7368384-0-2
ISBN: 978-1-7368384-1-9

Contents

Dedication vii
Forward ix

Heroism & Tragedy ... 1
Magic & Energy ... 3
Feminine & Masculine ... 5
Novelty & Repetition ... 8
Idealism & Nihilism ... 11
Individual & Collective ... 14
God & Eternity ... 21
Beauty & Potentiality ... 28
Transformation & Transcendence ... 35
Truth & Reality ... 46
Death & Dreams ... 57
Love & Appreciation ... 69
Knowledge & The Unknown ... 80
Ideas & Thoughts ... 93

Science & Philosophy	106
History & Future	121
Abuse & Insanity	135
Nature & Psychedelics	159
Humans & Aliens	180
Values & Morality	209
Will & Consciousness	246
Mind & Cosmos	278
Politics & Religion	311
Art & Technology	364
Society & Childhood	412
Greatness & Suffering	507
Notes	533
Bibliography	537

I dedicate this book to my children, my family, my ancestors, my future descendants, and the billions of brothers and sisters of Earth I have yet to meet.

Forward

This is a book for great minds who aspire to become greater minds. This is a book for great minds who do not yet know they are great and free minds who do not yet know they are free. This is a book for minds whose only biases are that of truth, consciousness, and freedom; a book for those minds who no longer will allow themselves to be weakened, deceived, underappreciated, and enslaved. This is a book for the individual and the higher potentiality of the human species. This is a book that is never to be read only once or twice.

This is a book dedicated to open-ended creativity, transformation, and clarity. If anything communicated within this book breeds new thoughts in new minds, those thoughts deserve to be shared with the world. Watch the ideas multiply, complexify and empower. This is a book of ideas that honor ideas, old and new. The purpose of this book is to stretch, strengthen and liberate the mind, consciousness, and imagination of its readers. This book supports the honest and loving search for higher potentiality. It supports the eternal chase of the infinite mystery, using every possible resource.

This book is never to be taught as a religious doctrine. It is never to be forced onto anyone, especially children. It is never to be made illegal or forbidden. It is meant to be deeply pondered and discussed with miraculous honesty. This book was created to heal the world, define the world, empower the world and refine the world. Those who read this book well will not be the same people who opened it.

This book is offered as a mind-refining guide for all who have the bottomless hunger for goodness, greatness, and truth. Within these pages, you will notice the organic development of my thoughts. This book contains a decade of thought. It is a guide on how to wield the sword of trauma after pulling it from one's own heart. All traumatic experiences must be overcome by being creatively and lovingly utilized.

This book is a sanctuary for great solitary minds and a blacksmith for the common public mind. This book is my sermon on the mountain. It is a drug; a tool; a technology. My goal is to inspire new thoughts and ideas in unexpected ways and to influence the spread of self-empowerment and self-expression. May each thought find a home, further branching out in the minds of new inspired readers.

I left my thought-work in the order that I wrote them in order to show their organic development, like watching long coiling vines of growing clarity. This work is unfinished in the sense that you, the reader, can use these thoughts to influence your own work, in whatever art medium that may be. I have taken great care of my thoughts and have ensured that they each are given center stage so that they can each be appreciated and expounded upon individually, as all thoughts deserve. I cannot control where my thoughts will land or what impact each will have over time, but my hope is that they will travel far and wide, improving the minds and lives of every reader.

May this book cleanse every reader's mind of abusive and parasitic indoctrinated beliefs. This is not a closed doctrine but an open guide for the creation and refinement of greatness. This book is an open tap from which anyone can drink and quench their thirst for the honest search for clarity. May the vines of clarity grow on.

To the readers who feel the urge to close my book: keep reading, or as Churchill was attributed, "If you find yourself in hell, keep going!"[1]

My preference for the aphorism as a writing style is fueled by the same desire as Friedrich Nietzsche, who said, "…it is my ambition to say in ten sentences what everyone else says in a whole book,—what everyone else does *not* say in a whole book."[2]

I would have never written this book without suffering enough to need to create it in order to overcome my suffering.

Heroism & Tragedy

1. The most successful hero inspires new heroes.

2. Bad things happen because we exist in a time before their prevention.

3. The hero: one who takes advantage of trauma and suffering by refining oneself with them.

4. Pity: the degrading arch-nemesis of the hero.

5. **The Tragedy Of Heroism**

Every hero is tortured and only finds happiness in improving the world that bore them by letting their world drain them of their energy, thoughts, and blood.

6. **The Tragedien**

To think and live as a Tragedien, one must never forget the hell of history, the dark and tragic roots of our potential paradise, so that one can nourish and empower one's mind and the minds of others in order to help create the future of our loftiest dreams. One must never shy away from any traumatic experience of the past, present, or future. One must become proud of one's scars and disgusted with self-pity and the pity for others. The practice of pity for others is often unproductive, disempowering, and enables the practice and spread of self-pity. For the more you pity someone, the more they pity themselves, in turn, making them more pitiful.

7. The Connection Between Comedy And Tragedy

Comedy and tragedy: information that is failed to be predicted until it is too late to stop oneself from either laughing or crying.

8. The Origin Of Heroes And Saviors

There are creations only a certain mind can create, problems only a certain mind can discover, solutions only a certain mind can solve.

Magic & Energy

1. Magic originates from the overwhelming underdog.

2. **The Reality Of Magic**

Technology continues to prove that magic is real.

3. The necessary release of creative energy is similar to the necessary release of emotional and sexual energy.

4. **A Law Of Energy**

All energy that is not spent on creation ends up spent on destruction.

5. **What Is Magic?**

A new power never before predicted, comprehended, or created. The further into the past you go from the moment it is born, the less possible it is of being predicted. When something magical becomes understood, it ceases to be magic to those who understand it, though it will always be magic, and to those who have yet to be able to predict, comprehend or create it, it is seen for what it truly is: magic that is capable of completely replacing the ugly sufferings of reality with the greatest creations of mind. Technology and its growth is a prime example of magic. For new technology begins as a new thought and grows into unique possibilities, opportunities, and potentialities.

6. For magic to be created, a mixture of things that almost did not happen and things that were never supposed to happen is needed.

7. Magic: a creation that cannot be predicted.

8. All art is magic.

Feminine & Masculine

1. The Masculine Spirit
    Focus
    Impatience
    Rigidity
    Confrontation
    Accumulation
    Determination
    Daring

The Feminine Spirit
    Appreciation
    Patience
    Flexibility
    Expression
    Preservation
    Surrender
    Safe

2. Slow And Steady Wins The Race

Men spend the first act of a relationship fighting to start it and sustain it until they exhaust themselves while women conserve their energy for the acts ahead when men have used up all of their energy and women have been more conservative with their use of energy. Is this partly why men tend to die before women?

3. **Genders: A Balancing Act**

Both genders and their unique qualities are necessary for the harmonious balance of the human species.

4. **The Paradox Of Women**

Women tend to be more transparent than men in their expressions but also tend to have a higher capacity to deceive than men.

5. The subconscious mind represents the feminine and its nurturing and revelatory nature.

6. Men and women are both incomplete without each other, and both rarely accept this truth.

7. What do women tend to find most attractive in men? Passionate and impatient willpower.

What do men tend to find most attractive in women? Calm and patient willpower.

8. Women: defenders, healers, organizers, planners, and preservers.

9. Women are more cutthroat than men but are better able to hide their poison under their delicate and dainty petals.

10. The Impossible Expectations Of Men And Women

The ideal woman: confident but not too confident; independent but not too independent.

The ideal man: daring but not too daring; gives attention but not too much attention.

Novelty & Repetition

1. Chaos sacrifices order for the unique.

2. Mixture: inevitable and infinite.

3. **Repetition: A Service To Novelty**

You cannot be novel without sacrificing repetition, if only for a moment.

4. **Have Faith In Weakness And Ignorance**

Weakness and ignorance should never be assumed to always remain weak and ignorant. For there is nothing allowed to remain the same for long, not even the weakest and most ignorant lifeform.

5. Uniqueness cannot occur or thrive without the freedom of transformation.

6. Complexity grows with uniqueness.

Uniqueness grows with complexity.

7. The Permanence Of Change

Change: consistently constant.

8. There Is Death In Sameness And Life In Novelty

There is temporality in sameness and permanence in novelty.

9. There is no greatness without novelty.

Terence McKenna said, "My faith is novelty will win. It is winning or we wouldn't be here."[3]

10. Prove Your Uniqueness

No one else has a mind exactly like yours. Prove this by utilizing and expressing your uniqueness of mind while you are still living.

11. All healing and regeneration is novel.

All healers and regenerators are novel.

12. Anything novel and strange wears the mask of the elusive and confounding jester bearing astonishing alien gifts, profoundly intricate, unpredictable in their complexity, and joyously nuanced in their revelatory expressions. They contradict current understanding like sneaky elvish teachers of a distant potential future with a childlike eagerness to share their knowledge and their mysterious creations with the most curious and courageous minds they encounter.

13. The Enemies Of Novelty

Beliefs and their systems are generally opposed to novelty. For their most loyal believers pray harder for the end of the world the more new knowledge, technologies, and possibilities are created.

14. A new glitch is like a new genetic mutation, as unforeseeable as a new idea or technology.

15. The urge to procreate is the urge to combine.

16. **The Most Liberating And Clarifying Epiphany**

Novelty is created, not discovered.

17. Repetition: a resource for novelty.

Idealism & Nihilism

1. I consider myself an idealist when confronted with the endless mysteries and changes of cosmic existence.

2. In life, we can either focus on the motivation of optimism or we can become victims of disempowering pessimism.

3. Nihilism: a defeatist attitude towards existence.

4. Two minds fighting to the death, one with passion, love, virtue, and high standards of value and thought, the other mind is only fueled by survival. The more purposeful and passionate mind is more likely to outlast the more indifferent mind.

5. **Nihilists: The Most Open-Minded?**

Nihilism: preparation by the exhausted and aimless for something new and timeless to revive themselves with.

"Actually, every major growth is accompanied by a tremendous crumbling and passing away: suffering, the symptoms of decline belong in the times of tremendous advances; every fruitful and powerful movement of humanity has also created at the same time a nihilistic movement. It could be the sign of a crucial and most essential growth, of the transition to new conditions of existence, that the most extreme forms of pessimism, genuine nihilism, would come into the world. This I have comprehended." - Friedrich Nietzsche[4]

6. Nihilism is as easy and useless as answering every problem with God.

7. A village of educated nihilists is just as useless and stubborn as a village of uneducated idealists.

8. Ideas have brought us more clarity, happiness, and technology than nihilism ever can. For we have built and achieved more out of our dreams than our doubts about our dreams.

9. **We Were Not Put Here To Give Up And Surrender To Our Universe**

We have not become what we have become by giving up. Pretending like we have not been born into a mystery of magnificently puzzling proportions is the typical defeatist attitude of a nihilist.

10. Life: an ongoing battle between nihilism and idealism, pessimism and optimism.

11. Nihilists push idealists to create.

Idealists push nihilists to create.

12. Nihilist: a failed idealist.

13. **Nihilists Think As If There Is No Future**

Nihilism has its uses in dealing with the past, but when dealing with the future, it is useless.

14. Technology is an enemy of nihilism and an ally to idealism.

15. The skeptic and the nihilist sharpen the linguistic blade of the idealist, causing their thoughts, ideas, and arguments to become more durable and more damaging to their rejecters.

16. Anarchy has the same problem as atheism and nihilism. It is more concerned with resentment, revenge, and tearing things down than with the unbiased, creative and idealistic aftermath.

17. **A New Spring Is Nigh**

Winter represents nihilism.

Spring represents idealism.

18. To become a great idealist one must first experience becoming a nihilist.

Individual & Collective

1. **Stuck In A Dilemma**

To want people to always have the freedom to believe what they want to believe but also to want people to be able to think with their own God-given minds rather than depend on anyone or anything else to think for them. We were created as individuals, not as robots.

2. The collective can be altered by individual intention.

3. Although many will try, no one can take away your individual importance and potentiality.

4. **The Purpose Of Self**

No plan or purpose given outside of oneself is worth more than the creative and intellectual potential of oneself.

5. **Memorializing Experiences And Epiphanies**

The individual and the collective would benefit greatly from the practice of writing down not only personal confounding experiences but also personal epiphanies, no matter how small or large, throughout one's life.

6. You, as a unique individual, can help forge the universe and the planet you have found yourself in through the perpetual act of creative thought.

7. You are a valuable point of view.

8. If you are sensitive enough to others, you can feel the tug-of-war match between what someone expects you to say and what you want to say, between what the collective expects and what the individual desires.

9. Individually, everyone represents a personalized reflection to everyone. People tend to utilize the closest people around them to either boost their self-esteem or to disempower themselves. People hate and love themselves with the tool of other people, and if what they see of themselves in and from certain people is too revealing, they are likely to move on from using them at all.

10. **A Major Source Of Our Prevalent Psychological Agony (The Poisoning Of The Independent Individual)**

The life of our more familiar past has been pulled out from under us. Our ancestors were more open to our necessary symbiosis with ego-taming and mind-refining plant and fungal life. We are not adapting well to the relatively recent drastic changes caused by the growing governments and systems surrounding us, which treat us as peripheral automatons. Our continuously stolen independence is bringing about a collective feeling of purposelessness, the side-effect being mass mental anguish and anxiety.

11. Pride: necessary for individuality.

12. **A Realization For Endless Confidence**

There has never and will never be another you in your totality of unique potentiality.

13. Controlling others is a lazy form of self-control.

14. **Trusting The Individual Over The Collective**

All the collective wants is their beliefs, their money, and their toys. All higher values of the individual, like love, family, art, knowledge, independence, and truth, are treated as lower values.

It was George Carlin who said, "I love people as I meet them one by one. People are just wonderful as individuals. You see the whole universe in their eyes if you look carefully. But as soon as they begin to group, as soon as they begin to clot when there are five of them or ten or even groups as small as two, they begin to change. They sacrifice the beauty of the individual for the sake of the group."[5]

15. One cannot be offended without having one's perceived identity threatened.

16. The collective cannot remain free without the individual remaining free.

17. **The Spell Of Solitude**

The benefit of solitude is not just the accompanying peace and quiet but the enhanced passion, expression, and creativity that comes with a hidden longing to love and be loved and to communicate with others one's pain and wonder while under the spell of solitude.

18. The Values Of The Individual

Self-awareness
Self-expression
Self-dependence
Self-love
Self-empowerment
Self-teaching
Freedom
Peace
Solitude
Mastery
Transcendence
Passion
Honesty
Intuition
Experimentation
Uniqueness
Knowledge
Thoughts
Ideas
Questions
Clarity
Technology
Mystery
Discovery
Art
Exercise
Diet
Rest

Dialogue and debate
Mind-freeing plants and fungi.

19. There is no powerful collective without powerful individuals.

20. The majority represents the follower and is best utilized as a follower. The individual represents the leader and is best utilized as a leader.

21. **A Majority Of Free Individuals**

Can the divide between the majority and the individual be erased by the creation of a majority of strong, creative, intelligent, and leading individuals?

22. **The School Of M.E. (My Education)**

Practice learning, thinking, and creating alone.

23. **The Individual Versus The Collective**

How do we remedy the dividing imbalance between the needs and freedom of the individual and the needs and freedom of the collective?

24. The empowered free-thinking individual is always a problem to the state, no matter how peaceful they are.

25. We can only unite when we can think and act as free individuals.

26. **Solving Problems Yourself**

Do not assume that someone else will solve a problem you find.

27. The war for individual freedom is a battle between those who prefer to be controlled by others and those who prefer to be in control of themselves.

28. The focus of the individual is more beneficial and of more significance to both the individual and the collective than the focus of the mere collective.

29. **The Shared Blind-Spot Between The Individual And The Collective**

An individual perspective is never a complete view of a collective and a collective perspective is never a complete view of an individual.

30. When the individual is forgotten, the collective must remind their government who the real King is or risk further enslavement.

31. If you feel repulsed and terrified when you fight for your freedom then you have already been conditioned into slavery.

32. **The Individual: More Valuable Than The Collective**

Without great and lasting individuals, there cannot be a great and lasting collective.

33. The collective is equal to the sum of its individuals.

34. Throughout human history, choosing the collective over the individual has obliterated both.

35. The people represent the freedom of the individual.

The state represents the enslavement of the collective.

36. Individualist: a person who is dependent on themselves.

Collectivist: a person who is dependent on anyone or anything but themselves.

37. **The Illusion Of The Collective**

There is no collective, no matter how fervently governments ignore the individuals that make up a collective. Only the individual is real. Whatever happens to a collective is happening to individuals, all of whom are different.

38. The individual is more valuable than the universal. For the individual creates and defines the universal.

God & Eternity

1. Defending God From Religion

How many people are pushed by a religion away from God and the belief in something greater than oneself? I will always defend God, greatness, and the individual from all closed belief-systems.

2. God Has Given Us The Ability To Become Gods And Create Heaven

I believe in something greater than human beings. I believe in something greater than human reality. I believe we can become greater beings and create a greater world while we are still alive rather than waiting until we die or waiting for God to do it for us.

3. Unless God is evil, no omniscient, omnipotent, omnipresent, and omnibenevolent God would trust human beings with its message to them, especially if successfully communicating that message accurately without being edited meant the difference between eternal paradise and eternal hell.

4. All cycles mimic and express infinity.

5. Atheism: like an ugly divorce that comes with an intolerable amount of bias and resentment.

6. Many people put more faith in their beliefs than themselves, but what use does God have for believers who do not believe in themselves?

7. Every God is limited by the religions in which they influence.

8. Perhaps the God of Eden tried to warn us of the tempting and poisonous belief-systems we would cultivate, fall ill to and divide over.

9. God: relative to its believer.

10. Whatever created us is part of us. For there is nothing created that is apart from its creator.

11. **Permission To Become Gods**

The ancient Greeks were honest and prideful enough to openly create and be inspired by gods who represented different pieces of human nature. Because of this, they made the idea of becoming gods more realistic, giving even the poorest of minds the confidence and courage to think and act like Godly versions of themselves. For Napoleon rightly stated, "The human race is governed by its imagination."[6]

12. **The Dreamers: The Truly Living**

A dreamer is someone closer to spirituality than the religious people who never think for themselves or use their own God-granted imagination. How could that ever be misconstrued as being spiritual or Godly? Would not God be a thinking God? Would not God be a dreamer?

13. Belief in God: the belief that one will eventually become one with God.

14. The Origin Of The Almighty

What if a long history of suffering, adequately utilized, is the only way to become a God? What if the only way for God to have existed was for it to endure millions of years of pain, adapting to evil by becoming powerfully good?

15. Infinity: One (The Echo Of One)

Are all numbers after one echoes of one? All numbers after one exist only for human practicalities. One is all that exists. For one represents infinity.

16. The Recipe For God

    Energy and information.
    Space and time.
    Light and mind.
    Pain and consciousness.
    Knowledge and technology.

17. God: Eternal Greatness

I believe in greatness.

18. God's Philosophy

Believe in your mind and its powers. This is no doubt a philosophy God would adhere to. Surely, God would not be dependent on any of its creations for anything it could not do better itself, nor would it limit their thinking and their mental and technological development towards becoming closer to being one with it, unless God prefers to be surrounded by thoughtless fools. For the purpose of being human is to live, think and become godly, despite the story of the banishment of Lucifer from heaven that was used and is still used to keep people as controllable as possible by keeping them in fear and ensuring that they live and operate without thoughts and decisions of their own.

19. **The Three Scars Of God**

Error, chaos, and distortion.

20. **Novelty: Infinite (Infinity: Novel)**

Eternity: the infinite combinations of novelty.

21. Will God turn its back on those who did not cultivate their own higher potentiality and those who did not create new works and refine their own beauty? Those who did not turn their life into a unique work of art, freeing themselves like a precious undying jewel uncovered from its dark womb, inspiring and strengthening all who behold it and all who appreciate it. What of those who ignored the cries of their own planet and their own people? Will they be forgiven?

22. **Eternal Things**

Knowledge, creation, and greatness.

Truth, novelty, and love.

23. **G.O.D.**

Greatness overcomes death.

24. **The Godly Self**

A prayer to your greater self is a prayer to God.

A prayer to God is a prayer to your greater self.

25. God represents infinite potentiality, possibility, and sublimity.

26. God: infinity.

27. **God: Creative Language (God Speaks Creation)**

At the beginning of the Bible, language is the creator of all things: "In the beginning was the word and the word was with God and the word was God."[7] The first creation this linguistic God decides to speak into existence is light by saying, "Let there be light."[8]

28. Having faith in God is having faith in eternal love, eternal mystery, eternal beauty, and eternal greatness. It was Soren Kierkegaard who taught us that faith is reserved for the strongest of spirits.

29. **From One To Infinity: Eternal Reflections**

One mirror plus one mirror equals infinite mirrors.

30. God is loving and merciful if you so choose. God is hateful and cruel if you so choose.

31. Some people use God to escape themselves.

32. The Great Beyond

God: the beyond.

33. God wants its creations empowered. What use would God have for weak and disempowered human beings?

34. God will never be as human, as hateful, as vindictive, or as unforgiving as people want God to be. The truth is that we have not become Godly enough to comprehend what God is.

35. God: An Infinite Attractor (Climbing God's Trail)

We are part of an endlessly ascending trail of Godhood where the most strong, enduring, willful, loving, thoughtful, and creative beings are eternally pulled towards God. This is why we were able to become what we have become. It is up to us whether or not we continue to climb.

36. God: mystery everlasting.

37. God: the incomprehensible.

38. God: infinite love and appreciation.

39. God: eternal refinement.

40. A Godly State Of Being

Heaven: being able to laugh at one's previous levels of development, with the joy, pride, appreciation, and confidence a parent has for their child.

41. To be Godly is to have endless love for eternal refinement.

42. **God Is Not Dead**

Because of religion, people are often too resentful of God to be able to interpret the belief in God as the pursuit of a greater self and a greater reality of which God would be proud.

43. Love is more important than belief when it comes to God and heaven. For one can believe without action and growth but one cannot love without action and growth.

44. We are disgustingly dishonest creatures who argue and divide over what name to call God. God has become more alien to us but we are capable of becoming more similar to God.

Beauty & Potentiality

1. Seek, examine and appreciate the creativity and potential in everyone you meet. Nothing is more tragic than unrealized and forgotten potential.

2. Do not allow destroyed potential to destroy your potential.

3. **The Duality Of Potentiality**
Darkness – Light
Rest – Motion
Cold – Heat
Contraction – Expansion
Division – Unity
Stagnancy – Progress
Unrealized – Realized

4. There exist potential hunters who impulsively end potential, but there also exist potential creators and preservers.

5. Wasted time and energy is lost potentiality.

6. The place before life and after death rejects closure. It is living and breathing unknown potentiality.

7. Look for the beauty in others, and you will be rewarded with a more beautiful world.

8. **We Are Players Of Potentiality**
Each of us can help build a bridge towards higher potentiality.

9. **No Shell Remains Un-cracked**
Incubate becoming.
Hatch open potential.

10. We are Earth children playing in the dream fields of our higher potential.

11. Surrender to your higher potentiality.

12. Trust your own mind and have faith in its higher potential.

13. **The Beautiful**
The contradicting qualities of beauty:
Consistent and unpredictable.
Inviting and intimidating.
Strong and malleable.
Complex and simple.
Futuristic and ancient.
Alien and nostalgic.
Endures and transcends.

The non contradicting qualities of beauty:
Stable
Symmetrical
Communicates
Connects

Strengthens
Complexifies

14. The Blessing Of Ugliness
The more people you physically attract, the more difficult it is to find someone who loves you for more than your physical attraction.

15. The Necessity Of Higher Potentiality For Higher Powers Of Necessity
All life calls upon the power of necessity, unconsciously willing into existence higher forms of their own potentiality, and the greater the mind of a life-form, the more extraordinary the effects of the power of necessity. For with higher potentiality comes higher powers of necessity.

16. Infinite Potentiality
There is no such thing as permanent nothingness, only infinite potentiality.

17. Beauty: The Appearance Of Truth
We can only expect to find the appearance of truth, which is none other than beauty, artistically, mathematically, and technologically.

18. Beauty: the attraction of power.

19. Everything which exists was once nothing but potentiality.

20. My mind is but an eggshell for the yolk of unknown potentiality.

21. Beauty: Truth Dressed With New And Refined Combinations Of Potentialities Of Ever-Increasing Complexity

Beauty: complexifying combinations of novel potentiality.

22. Beauty: Reflections Of Eternity Peeking Through Dresses Of Temporality

Like the brief afterglow of a shooting star, sometimes the beautiful is that which lasts the least amount of time and demands the eyes, ears, and minds of all spectators to open wide, so as to permit the beautiful to reveal the eternity that shines underneath all things dressed in temporality.

23. The Higher The Difficulty, The Higher The Potentiality

The higher potentiality of a thing cannot be found without a higher difficulty of growth and existence.

24. Triangulating Our Higher Potential

From every angle possible, using every piece of knowledge I collect, every fact I utilize, and every new insight I formulate, I aim for our higher potential state of becoming; I aim for the higher potentiality of all things healing, loving, and empowering.

25. Potentiality is always greater than actuality, but only if one is willing and ready to fly above the actual.

26. Universal Beauty (The Universal Translation Of Beauty)

It is possible that beauty is universal, that what is beautiful on another planet would be beautiful to us on this planet, however far away and however different in appearance and mental power they are. We would only have to try to understand them, and if we were successful we would find the connection between all objects, creations, symbols, and definitions of beauty. For beauty is connected to truth, if beauty is universal. This would confirm Plato's intuition of the good, the true, and the beautiful being connected. What is the good? Being constructive with one's mind for the empowerment of oneself and one's species. The good is what you find if you follow and preserve beauty. For to follow and preserve beauty is to follow and preserve truth.

27. Beauty: The Complex And The Novel
Complexity needs stability and must fight ugliness in all its disorderly forms in order to obtain it, preserve it and build upon it with ever grander forms of beauty and novelty.

28. The most beautiful thing would be that which cannot be retraced.

29. Beauty: The Unbelievable
The most beautiful is the most difficult to believe.

30. Beauty: both delicately and disastrously formed.

31. Potentiality: created, not discovered.

32. The greater potentiality of all things never tires of seeking a greater vehicle of expression.

33. Beauty: gracefully extreme.

34. We are born equipped with boundless potentiality.

35. Beauty: rare, unique, and transformative empowerment.

36. All greater potentiality waits to exist.

37. The Thing-In-Itself: The Potentiality Of A Thing

The thing-in-itself is the lower and higher potentiality of a thing, along with its perpetually changing power, uses, materials, and appearances. An example would be the development from our significantly simpler ocean-dwelling form into the complex, space-wandering, water, land, and air-dominating form we know as a human being. We are now more what we are than we ever were before. For we are what we can become.

38. From simple forms to complex forms, all things are lower and higher representations of potentiality.

39. Alchemy represents the infinite transformational potential of mixture combinations.

40. The beautiful is connected to the strange.
The strange is connected to the beautiful.

41. Beauty: Always Alien; Never Stagnant

The future development and beauty of the human mind, the cosmos, and technology are unpredictable to their past and, therefore, always alien and never stagnant.

42. There Is No Greatness Without Love And Beauty

There is no beauty without greatness.
There is no greatness without beauty.
There is no beauty without love.
There is no love without beauty.

43. There exist infinite levels of potential advancement for all life.

44. Beauty: the love of mystery.

45. Greater beauty and potentiality are created, not discovered.

46. The beautiful: the Godly.

47. Beauty is intimidating because of how powerful it can be, regardless of how loving it can be.

48. Love and beauty: healing and empowering.

49. In nature, beauty is used to continue life, whether through nourishment, motivation, or procreation.

50. **Beauty: Conscious And Unconscious Pride**

A flower is not modest about its beauty.

51. Beauty mesmerizes so that greater beauty can be inspired into existence without distractions.

52. In the presence of astounding beauty, one is on the verge of transformation if one is strong enough.

53. Lower levels of mind cannot comprehend higher levels of beauty so it is translated as monstrous and horrifying. Like angels from an unimaginable realm, lower levels of mind cannot so much as peek at their beauty.

54. **I Believe In The Greater Potential Of People**

There are too many people in this world who hate themselves or are apathetic about their greater potential and too many people who benefit from people hating themselves or treating their greater potential apathetically.

Transformation & Transcendence

1. Change: unnoticed death; unnoticed creation.

2. When the container of life reaches its transporting limit, life becomes a new order of being?

3. Sometimes having our faults insulted is the only way to be persuaded to remove them.

4. Every moment is a time for growth and refinement.

5. Inhale being. Exhale becoming.

6. Everything prepares, and everything becomes.

As Plato said, "Nothing ever is, everything is becoming."[9]

7. Our purpose is to transcend our limitations.

8. Penetrate reality.
Consume information.
Embrace becoming.

9. There is no closure in becoming.

10. Being: the tail.
Becoming: the head.

11. The Diet Of Complexity
In order to continue upgrading, every new upgrade eats previous simpler upgrades.

12. We are the dancing shadows in the hyper-genetic egg of self-becoming.

13. It is important to remember that people are capable of changing from the time you first meet them and from the time you last saw them.

14. Turn Thy Mind From Lead Into Gold
We should improve our minds at least as often as we improve our appearance. What good is beauty without a pristine mirror?

15. All being survives to become.

16. Those who know themselves well enough and care enough about their own potentiality are ready to venture into uncharted avenues of thought and freedom.

17. A Transformative Environment
Surround yourself with great ideas and great art.

18. All eggs are prepared to be depleted by their growing inhabitants so that the egg may be exited and the inhabitant made anew.

19. All things are prototypes of their own greater potentiality.

20. Make yourself necessary to your universe.

21. **Leaving The Human Cocoon**
It is inevitable that we will become more machine, so we must make the preservation of our greatest talents and traits a priority as we build stronger shells around our soft and vulnerable caterpillar-like bodies and brains so that when we take flight from the human cocoon, we will leave behind our weakest traits and bring along with us our strongest traits and creations of thought.

22. Life is steadily incomplete.

23. We know not what higher expressions of love and bliss could be, nor can our minds as they currently are, comprehend them.

24. **A State Of Rapturous Resolve**
Invigoration: a representation of higher being.

25. **The Advancement From Simple Resolution To Higher Complex Forms Of Resolution**
The more communication advances in a species, the less ambiguous, difficult, and destructive the communication. If debate is a more complex version of physically fighting, then what could be a more complex version of debate?

26. There is no power without complexity.

27. **The Aim Of Existence: Survive To Complexify**
Survival: a stepping stone for a higher, more necessary value: complexity.

28. Simplicity, if disturbed, as a human's mind is occasionally disturbed and altered by traumatic experiences, can sometimes uncontrollably become more complex.

29. Those beyond a boundary can better understand and describe those underneath that boundary than those underneath that boundary can understand and describe those beyond that boundary.

30. I forgive myself for the past versions of me that have tried to overcome my existence, and, as a result, I allow myself to ascend higher than ever before.

31. **Resistance Creates Power**
The stronger the force of resistance, the more power is created.

32. **The Difficulty Of Existence**
Why has the creator or creators made existence so difficult for all living things? It is because the more difficult the test, the more powerful the participants must become in order to pass.

33. **The Eagerness Of A Tired Mind (Strengthening One's Mind)**
Like a weight-lifter whose muscle-tissue fibers connect during sleep, strengthening the muscles, a tired intellectually-exercised mind becomes exhausted from the weight of new information, curiosities, and problems collected throughout the day which are organized and stored during sleep, lightening its load, in preparation of more information from another day of mind-work.

34. **Finitude: A Lower Representation Of Eternity**
Mortality: a lower representation of immortality.

35. The Power Of Necessity: Used For The Preservation Of Complexity And Novelty

Nature changes and complexifies out of necessity. Animals unwittingly use this power of necessity to complexify and preserve themselves by becoming stronger, more colorful, more daring, more energetic, and more awe-inducing.

36. A Mantra For Survival And Growth

I love myself.
I love everyone.
I forgive myself.
I forgive everyone.

Chanting this either inside or outside one's head can cause one to realize that there is a weight that is shed. For if we do not love ourselves and we do not forgive ourselves for hurting others or from being hurt by others we will consciously or unconsciously harm ourselves, sabotaging our own life and our potential growth.

37. The Growth Of The Fruit Is Equal In Importance As The Fruit

Every task is just as important as the end result.

38. The Entertainment Of Progress (Leveling Up)

What attracts us most about video games is the exaggerated and accelerated sense of progress and transformation they offer of which is more difficult to obtain in the real world but always possible with enough willpower, as well as more rewarding.

39. Self-Devouring (Self-Overcoming)

The great eternal self has infinite hunger for self-refinement, symbolized by Ouroboros, the snake with a taste for eternal self-becoming.

40. Surpassing Our Masters
The reason we have masters of thought is for us to become masters of thought ourselves, not to remain pupils. For all masters are meant to be surpassed.

41. Two Roads To Success
Some people become successful because they are more ambitious than they are intelligent, more relentless than they are creative, more resourceful than they are talented.

42. Become less predictable creatively and lovingly.

43. Fear, Tragedy, And Greatness
One cannot become greater without tossing aside one's fears along with the lies one tells oneself to calm and avoid those fears. One cannot become greater without accepting and utilizing the tragic nature of our human universe, as much as we accept and utilize its glorious nature.

44. Using Obstacles To Climb Over Obstacles
Turn every obstacle in your way into a piece of your ladder.

45. Advance And Appreciate Yourself
Advance and appreciate yourself until you never want to be someone else.

46. All Gods were once believers who became that which they believed in.

47. The Motivating Illusion Of Finish Lines

Crossing a finish line is a penetration that causes the finish line to become pregnant by the victor, bearing a long line of new and further finish lines.

48. One Must First Accept What One Is Before One Can Become Greater Than One Is

People are afraid of what they are and of what they could become.

49. What Stops Most People From Becoming Greater?

One's perception of self-value of which is usually inherited and hindered by one's government, culture, family, and religion but can and should be created and determined by oneself.

50. Gods Must First Live As Beasts

The greater we become, the less human we become. For the less human we become, the less animal we become.

51. Find what you are good at so that you may become great at it.

52. One has become a God when one becomes unfathomable to one's perceiver(s).

53. Wombs And Cocoons

Language has not finished tumbling about inside its cocoon. Neither have we.

54. With Great Power Comes Great Possibility

The greater the power of a mind-form, the more possibility it is capable of creating.

55. Times Of Danger (Great Risks Unlock Great Rewards Or Great Punishments)

Times of danger are the best and the worst times for exploration, creation, and transformation. Danger provides the push needed for the acceptance of new knowledge and the new creations made possible by new knowledge, but if one is too daring, one can lose all creative progress thus far achieved. For if one is too careless, too greedy, too impatient, or too confident, danger also provides new opportunities for error, misery, degradation, and death.

56. If you have nothing honest to share, it is in the best interest of all that continues to overcome and improve for you to keep shut that lying hole embedded in your face.

57. **Creating What We Pray For And Becoming What We Pray To**
Priests became doctors.
Prayer became medical technology.

58. **New Orders Of Being**
We are part of something that never stops transforming, as life never stops evolving.

59. Refinement: infinite.

60. Some people do not think they deserve to refine themselves.

61. **Thy Brain Is A Cocoon**
The imagination is the brain's ghostly butterfly. With sufficient time and energy, it tears through its material chrysalis. It begins to flap its freshly developed wings, changing the landscape of reality by adding new colors of iridescent possibilities.

62. What is most healthy? The least wasteful.

63. The Self-Permission Of Life To Transcend Towards Greater Places And Greater Forms Of Being

Roots lengthen and strengthen overtime until they receive permission to break the veil of cold dirt and enter the blessed realm of light, warmth, and air.

64. Disorder: A Resource For Exponential Order

A certain amount of disorder is necessary for order to sustain its own existence and to increasingly strengthen. For disorder is a resource for order to develop even more orderly, until what was once considered mere disorder is later discovered to have been a resource the entire time for the most reality-refining minds, cures, technologies, and discoveries.

65. The Tranquility Of Purging Sickness

Those quiet fleeting moments after vomiting where one feels the surrounding air get cooler as it touches the sweat that has accumulated on one's buzzing body. One feels, for a short time, renewed and rejuvenated by the passing of sickness. For one feels more appreciative, more hopeful, and even more healthy than one did before one became ill.

66. All illnesses reward their hosts when the hosts manage to remove them.

67. There is no highest state of being, only infinitely higher states of being.

68. The Blind Grow Towards The Ripening Glow

Growth always begins in darkness and ripens in brightness.

69. The Transformative Snake

The symbol of the snake was once a symbol of wisdom and transformation that was reduced to a symbol of chaos and deceit.

70. Self-Actualization

Sometimes we have to temporarily hate ourselves in order to permanently change things we hate about ourselves.

71. The beautiful thing about starting over is that one always finds something new that one missed. For starting over is paramount to the creation and discovery of something new and improved.

72. Every advancement is a rebirth.

73. Heaven And Hell

Heaven and hell are symbols that can be used for either refining or degrading oneself. They are symbols of the optimistic and blissful future or the pessimistic and painful past.

74. Perfection Eternally Perfects

Even the most intelligent can become more intelligent. Even the strongest can become stronger. For there is no end to perfection.

75. To become greater, become creatively and lovingly unpredictable.

76. The vines believe that the blocking fence is one of them. They refuse to let it get in their way of growth towards the light of clarity.

77. Train your mind like a bodybuilder trains their body. Think and read often so that your imagination and intuition can be strengthened.

78. Train and refine your peak state by entering it more often. Cannabis is a useful tool for this.

79. Every day that is used in order to build oneself mentally and physically is a day conquered.

80. Weakness needs to be challenged. It does not need to be overly shielded from the storms of life.

Truth & Reality

1. Everything we know of that exists has different degrees of similarity. We describe many things as euphoric but fail to compare euphoria to anything known to us. A reality could be created where euphoria is a permanent state of being.

2. No amount of scientific understanding can hide the reality of magic.

3. Existence: an unresolved state of being.

4. The truth is in potentiality.

5. To express love is to express truth.

6. The utterly bizarre situation we find ourselves in, being birthed into this universe, onto this planet, surrounded by other bewildered faces.

7. Our reality adapts to our imagination.

8. Truth does not come from reality but from the edge of reality.

9. The tide of expectation further hints to us, through observation and experience, that we each take part in co-creating reality. A person's expectations collide with the expectations of those they come into contact with, causing fortunate or unfortunate things to occur around them and to them by way of a shared psychological interference with reality.

10. **Three Ways Of Responding To Reality**
People either confront reality (Science and Philosophy), flee from reality (Western Religion), or passively accept reality (Eastern Religion).

11. Reality: made of dreams.

12. **New Realities For New Minds**
The potential brightness of light, to an eye, represents the potential ascension of a mind. Many accounts of psychedelic and near-death experiences speak of more vibrant colors and a light brighter than our human eyes can allow. We are locked in a reality that can only be escaped, however temporarily, through the synthesis of old and new information as well as extreme altered states of mind. For we are never completely trapped.

13. **Reality Is Mental**
We continue to manifest our ideas and surround ourselves with them.

14. **Truth: Found Through Experience And Error**
The difficulty of being increases the closer one gets to the errors of falsehood. The difficulty of being decreases the closer one gets to the truth.

15. Truth: untangled information.
Untruth: tangled information.

16. **Honesty: Separates The Strong From The Weak**
Power cannot be sustained without the sustained honesty of self and others.

17. Truth: infinite potentiality.

18. The advancement of technology: confirmation of being on the right path, towards truth.

19. **The Supreme Adaptation Of Truth**
Truth: the most adaptable to change.

20. Reality: the relationship between the observer and the observed.

21. **Addicts In Denial**
What you habitually do to deal with your reality is an addiction no different than any other addiction, and the stressful response of having any of these daily rituals threatened or removed confirms this.

22. We all live in our own private mental asylums, which play our favorite music and offer us our favorite drugs.

23. The reality of simpler life forms is connected to the reality of more complex life forms.

24. **The Imagination: More Powerful Than Reality**
In the main, what is reality but a life-refining stream of seemingly endless problems which attract thinking and self-reflecting minds

to create seemingly endless solutions that only the imagination can provide?

25. The Different Sides Of Our Relationship With Truth

One side pretends not to care. One side denies it. One side is too ignorant to care. One side is actively searching for the truth, while another side live their lives believing they already know the truth.

26. Reality can only be changed by changing the mind that perceives it.

27. The psychedelic reality: a non-human reality which we translate into a human reality?

28. Truth: immortal novelty; eternal transformation.

29. Face Reality To Cope With Reality

Let us not forget that some drugs help us face our reality and ourselves. They are tools of clarity. For a perpetually unperturbed mind is like unperturbed water: it becomes unclear, unhealthy, unconstructive, and uninhabitable.

30. What Is Truth? That Which Is Healing (Truth Heals, Falsity Kills)

What is good? That which is healing. What is beautiful? That which is healing. What is love? That which is healing. What is art? That which is healing. What is stability? What is nature? What is useful? What is necessary? That which is healing.

31. Reality: created, not discovered.

32. Truth: novel potentiality.

33. The high from certain drugs is a potential state of perpetual being.

34. Truth Should Not Be Based On Our Identities But On Truth

People tend to care more about their identities than they do the truth.

35. To Perceive Is To Create (Perception Is Creation)

Reality is made of ideas created by the mind(s) perceiving and translating it.

36. Truth remains uncertain so long as all things known continue to change?

37. There Is Truth In Understanding

To understand is to move closer to truth.

38. If one does not have loyalty for the pursuit of truth, rather than settling for beliefs, one will be content with prematurely ending one's pursuit of truth.

39. Anger Makes Way For Truth

How much anger is necessary for battling and defeating our weaknesses, our delusions, and our avoidance of both.

40. The Strangeness Of Truth

If the universe and the awareness of the universe are not strange to you, then you are looking in the wrong direction for truth.

41. Truth: the constant creation of unique and transcendent potentiality.

42. There is greatness in truth.

There is truth in greatness.

43. Truth: self-transcendence.

44. Great honesty requires great courage.

45. **The Greater The Mind, The Greater The Truth**
Is the truth discovered or created? Every religion is a created truth that is disguised as belief and faith. Every value-system was created by people who could never foresee how influential, whether constructively or destructively, it would become in the future when millions of people follow and defend it as the truth.

46. The artist creates truth, whether that truth is poor, average, or great, whether it is honest or dishonest, whether it is healthy or unhealthy and whether it is empowering or disempowering. If that truth is indoctrinated and unquestioned enough, it becomes a religious belief and is taught to children as truth that they must spread and defend, even in adulthood.

47. **Truth And Reality Are Not Confined To One Conscious Species On One Planet**
If something is not universal, can it be true? Can it be real? For the limits of a perceiving life form and a civilization of perceiving life forms are not equal to the limits of universal truth and reality.

48. **Visual Truth: More Difficult To Suppress Than Audible Truth (Visual Footprints: More Lasting Than Audible Footprints)**
It was Georg Lichtenberg who said, "What a blessing it would be if we could close and open our ears as easily as our eyes!"[10] The rea-

son why we never developed the ability to close our ears when we do not want to hear a truth the same way we can close our eyes when we do not want to see a truth is that we can just as easily deceive ourselves that we might have mistaken what we heard, but it is more difficult to deny what we have seen. We do not trust our ears as much as we trust our eyes. For it is more difficult to suppress visual truth than audible truth.

49. **Truth And Knowledge Are Eternal**
It frustrates us that we can still be considered ignorant, no matter how much our species knows. This is what influenced Socrates to be ordered to face a premature death. For some people think that if they kill someone who is speaking the truth they will have also killed the truth, but truth can no more be killed than knowledge can be killed.

50. **The Truth: Always Fresh**
The truth can handle endless scrutiny because it endlessly refines itself anew, adapting to new knowledge freely, gracefully, and seamlessly.

51. Lies cannot withstand free speculation for long.

52. We are suffering from the result of dramatically different realities simultaneously being lived and perpetuated. These are the reality tunnels, coined by Robert Anton Wilson, that become entangled, causing ambiguity, division, disorder, and mayhem for everyone.

53. A greater mind with a greater imagination is capable of creating a greater reality.

54. Reality: a dream that is paused during sleep when the unconscious mind awakens and runs amok in a field of unpredictable visions.

55. Any truth that makes people feel that they are losing control is less likely to be believed.

56. Truth: alien greatness.

57. Those who focus on the beyond focus on truth.

58. Those who aim their minds towards universal greatness aim their minds towards universal truth.

59. As reality changes, truth changes.
As truth changes, reality changes.

60. **Truth: The Enduring Greatness Of Eternal Transformation**
The truth is what always remains, no matter what kind of change occurs. For truth is not dead or stagnant. It is alive and transformative. It always lives because it always transforms by creatively enduring the ever-sculpting universe, which forever chisels away at its creations with water, wind, and fire; love, pain, and death.

61. Truth: infinite novel creation.

62. Dishonesty and delusion are weaknesses.

63. **The Middle-Man**
If you want to start a fire, you must combine the correct materials and use them the correct way, during the correct environmental conditions. If you want to change the state of water, you must add or reduce heat. Why is there always a middle-man between our

minds and our reality, between what we imagine and what we create? Does there have to be a middle-man?

64. We know how little people care about the truth by how little they appreciate people who speak more truth than falsity.

65. **The Paradox Of Truth**
Truth: both never changing and ever-changing.

66. The truth silences dishonest people who want to forget it and keep it from spreading. The truth makes honest people want to remember it and spread it to as many people as they can.

67. Speak the truth now, for there is no guarantee anyone else will speak it for you when you are gone.

68. **Dreamality**
There is no reality without dreams.

69. The truth should always be demanded by the people.

70. Reality: a dream-stream.

71. Any truth that causes people to feel like they are losing control is less likely to be believed.

72. Always search for the truth and always demand the truth from those who use the truth against us.

73. Those who are still searching for the truth contradict themselves more often. Those who believe they have the truth never search for the truth, and so their answers are unchanging and never contradictory.

74. The truth can set you free to become greater or it can weaken and enslave you by potentially rendering you too afraid to accept it, overcome it and utilize it.

75. Reality Is Created On The Fly
The universe does not know what will happen next. It is just as lost about the future as we are. This gives credence to Idealism, optimism, and purpose. For the future is created, not discovered, and with it, new possibilities.

76. The possible must always be speculated, or it may never become actual.

77. All doors lead to new places with new doors.

78. Truth Requires An Outside Perspective
When looking for the truth, it is not only more effective but more necessary to see things from the outside looking in rather than from the inside looking out.

79. Truth: embedded in the strange and the elusive.

80. Truth: A Mixture (The Alchemical Nature Of Truth)
Truth: a mixture of attraction and repulsion; creation and destruction; error and certainty; habit and novelty; cause and effect; internal and external.

81. What is real is what is possible.

82. Truth: a prerequisite for novel creation.
Novel creation: a prerequisite for truth.

83. The future is more true than the past.

84. The problem we have with truth is that we tend to expect it to please or entertain us on a whim. This is the same problem we have with God.

85. The abstract represents the incomprehensible.

Death & Dreams

1. Death: the unknown cave behind the waterfall.

2. Dreams: the informational casino of the subconscious mind.

3. The subconscious mind speaks through dreams to influence the conscious decryption of its messages.

4. Fire does not cease existing once it is extinguished. It pauses patiently until the next spark.

5. Death collects and transforms energy.

6. **Death: A Process**
All processes lead to new processes.

7. Death is to life as dreams are to sleep?

8. Dreams: creators and reminders of what is possible.

9. Like a bright dead star, the end is an illuminating illusion.

10. Since there is more to life than death, is it possible that there is more to death than the absence of life?

11. The study of anything is the study of everything. The study of anything is the simultaneous study of its opposite. Is the study of life also the study of death? Is death a continuation of life?

12. The more you know, the more your dreams have to work with to become seamless with your reality.

13. **Becoming The Shape Of The Afterlife Container**
We come from the ocean,
Grow in prepared wombs.
Like water through a sunken ship,
We leak through mortal tombs.

14. As Carl Jung taught us, dreams can either save or destroy us, depending on how we react to them.

15. It is unfitting in a resourceful universe and planet that such a complex and accumulative process as birth would be abruptly and forever extinguished by such a simple process as death.

16. If life is a download, is death an upload?

17. The higher the intelligence of an animal, the louder they react to death.

18. **Death: The Fire Under Our Feet**
Life does not require death to occur, but death, like pain, depends on the living and works best as a motivational catalyst towards becoming, and as life advances, death is increasingly rejected and disempowered. For all that is revealed to be unnecessary invites itself to be separated from what is necessary.

19. **The Ancestor Spirits Of Near-Death Experiences**
Why do near-death experiences often feature deceased family more than living family, even if living family is the last thing the experiencer saw and was comforted by?

20. **A Necklace Of Temporary Illusions Around The Neck Of Eternity**
Could death, that which the illusion of pain exists for, not also be an illusion?

21. **Death: Unknown Growth**
As a tree grows by unseen roots to bear new fruit in the future, death causes unseen growth in the living, technology being the fruit that grows to unknown and unpredictable proportions, exponentially enhancing the power of its wielders.

22. How often do we remember the experiences of our dreams when we think we are remembering an experience from our past?

23. The only way forward is through dreams.

24. **The Future Orientation Of Dreams**
Dreams are more concerned with the future than they are with the past or the present. Dreams are more about solving problems than consuming problems. They are more about learning than remembering. This is why information we do not realize we are learning often shows up in our dreams as the focal point when it was overlooked as useless information while we are awake. For dreams are more about the creation of the future by consuming memories, both old and new, than they are about the recreation of memories.

25\. **Reality: Secondary To Dreams**
Why do dreams change our reality more than reality changes our dreams?

26\. Prepare your child for this life. Let them prepare themselves for the afterlife.

27\. Where there is death, life is sure to follow.

28\. **Playing Death's Instrument**
Pain: death's instrument that, when played for too long, lulls its listener to one final sleep. This is why some people worship pain. It is an attempt to play death's instrument on one's own, thereby stealing control from death.

29\. One can be both unafraid of death and reject it simultaneously.

30\. **The Conservation Of The Conscious Mind**
Trees die and return to life because something is preserved, whether by seed or by code. Where does something as unique and complex, something as full of knowledge and experience as our minds go when there is no adequate seed or code to conserve and replicate it? Another place beyond life that is necessary to exist for the conservation of the unique mind of the individual?

31\. **From The Expansion Of The Growing Cocoon Of Life To The Rupture Of The Cocoon Into The Bright Unknown**
Is life the cocoon phase and death the tearing through of the cocoon?

32\. **The Light At The End Of Life**
When matter is fully consumed by fire, white becomes its color.

When all heat dissipates, whiteness dominates. For the end of heat is the end of life and the end of life is the end of darkness.

33. Death urges life to become conscious by having to face it repeatedly in the form of danger, pain, sickness, old age, and the loss of family and friends. We have become conscious in order to face death without acting like panicking apes as soon as we see our reflection in it.

34. The True Self: The Subconscious Mind
What knows us more intimately than our dreams?

35. An eternal paradise is all that could justify existence. An eternal state of bliss that requires temporary suffering is all that could justify all suffering.

36. The disappearance of a mind does not prove its non-existence anymore than an extinguished fire proves that fire no longer exists.

37. All unconscious dream activity is a release, like an overly-satisfied volcano.

38. The End Of A River: The Eternal Waterfall
A temporary river must pass around immovable mountains before the river becomes an endless waterfall, sustaining movement, sound, pressure, and energy. The death of a river turns out to be the birth of a triumphant waterfall. For all rivers are strengthened and made eternal by leaving their waterfalls' edge.

39. The Bright Side Of Death
Coolness has nothing to change to but heat. For all that is frozen is preserved and prepared to be thawed.

40. The end of one's life might simply share the same outcome as leaving the edge of one's understanding.

41. Professional Dreamers

It is likely that we experience more in our dreams than our waking reality. For we are not professionals at living but at dreaming, our very job being to dream.

42. Life: the flower that grows towards the light.
Death: the seed that grows from darkness.

43. A Dream Beyond The Dreams Of Life And Sleep

Since sleep is a temporary death, is death a temporary sleep?

44. At some point in life, all people are traumatized and permanently altered with the realization that everyone we have ever known will pass away into the great unknown.

45. Death: The Ignorance Of Becoming

A butterfly requires the self-sacrifice of a caterpillar. Here, we see the possibility that death is not the end for our cocooned minds. For we are just as ignorant as the caterpillar, oblivious to its next existence of becoming a flying marvel when it dies.

46. With our ignorance of death, our sanity survives our fear of death.

47. Death's Paradox

Death: both the most certain and the most uncertain thing about life.

48. The Proper Reaction To Death

Do we attempt to belittle death, so as not to be affected by its known and unknown effects? Do we try to desensitize ourselves to death with constant references to it, like laughing to death or being scared to death? Does this undermining of death or desensitization to death using language help or harm us? Should we face death with the intention of elongating our lives and minimizing its damaging effects by confronting it with new ideas, new medicines, and new technologies, or should we cower and give up on ever overcoming death, doomed to forever beg for its mercy?

49. Without life, death hath no power.

50. If you do not conquer life or even attempt to while you are alive, how can you expect to conquer death?

51. Since night is day in disguise, could death be life in disguise?

52. Every death is dropped treasure. Every life is caught treasure.

53. Close calls with death cause us to become more appreciative of what we have and to become wiser in our decision-making.

54. Mind The Gaps
Every gap is the birth of a new egg, laid by life and hatched by death.

55. Death: At Least As Absurd As Life
Our beliefs about death and its connection to consciousness hint to us how absurd death must be.

56. The Death Of Consciousness Is At Least As Absurd And Unpredictable As The Birth Of Consciousness
Since we know consciousness is absurd and unpredictable, the

death of consciousness must at least be as absurd and unpredictable as its birth and its creations of grandeur.

57. Life And Death: One And The Same?
Life is never far from death.
Death is never far from life.

58. Death: an uninterrupted dream.

59. The Intrusive And Transformative Footprints Of Truth In Dreams (Dreams Receive And Communicate Old And New Information More Honestly And Accurately Than Waking Consciousness)

Remember that our subconscious and unconscious thoughts are more honest than our conscious thoughts because we are less able to suppress or deny them. For whatever information leaves behind a deep impression on our dreams is more truthful and transformative than the more poorly casted footprints of information made by our waking consciousness.

60. If life is a dream, then the living have yet to awaken.

61. Life: the addition of potentiality.
Death: the loss of potentiality.

62. Liberating Dreams
Without sacrificing your quality of effort, finish tasks swiftly and resolve as many of your problems as you can while you are awake so that your dreams can become less burdened and distracted by them, allowing your dreams extra freedom to play with new desires and imaginings, rather than remaining anchored to the personal stresses and oppressors of waking life.

63. Dreams: unrealized possibilities.

64. Where There Is Smoke, There Is The Possibility Of Resurrection

Even a dying fire creates a living display of its exhaust. Even the deceased fire leaves behind a ghost made of smoke.

65. Death: A Process Of Birth?

Although it is the place where life begins, a womb reminds one of the darkness and quietness of death.

66. Birthed Into The Light

How peculiar, the years of brightness and sound that follow the weeks of darkness and quietness inside the womb, of which must feel like an eternity for its inhabitants.

67. Dream Energy

We could power our homes and our phones with the constant energy output of dreams. Possibly entire towns and cities could be powered by dream energy.

68. Heat Does To Water What Death Does To Life (Heat As Death And Water As Life)

We cannot prove, unequivocally, that death is or is not a birth process. For in life, all things constantly repeat, renew and refine. To water, death is evaporation, leading to the uploading of its condensed informational energy and the precipitation of its lively liquid state of being, followed by its ghostly discreet form, when heat arrives, representing death. For there is permanence in the changing temporary states of water. Why must that permanence end with life?

69. The Chosen Ones

If anyone will make it to heaven, it will be the thinkers who dedicate their minds and their lives towards the contemplation, appreciation, and understanding of all things known and unknown.

70. If you face death, it will not chase you, and you will be given more time to defend yourself against it.

71. The Dream Of Death

Death seems to be connected to the unconscious reality of dreams. It seems more like the imagination than conscious reality.

72. Everlasting Glow

A glowing lightbulb represents life, a lightless bulb without electricity represents death, and electricity represents the afterlife. For when the electricity no longer reaches the lightbulb, the light goes out, but the electricity continues.

73. Death: alteration of motion.

74. We are sucked out of life by the syringe of death. But a syringe is always used to preserve, examine and transfer something somewhere else for a mysterious and transformational purpose the contents of the syringe knows nothing about.

75. Is the mind forced to become a new form upon the physical death of the brain?

76. Will one's new body and mind consist of its previous form like the butterfly spirit retains its past life as a caterpillar?

77. From the thoughts of a primate to the thoughts of Plato, thoughts transform, and so do their power. There is no solid rea-

son and certainly no constructive reason to believe that this continuous transformation of mind and thought ceases when this human life ceases.

79. Shortly before death, all actions become more beautiful and magnificent, no matter how mundane.

80. The ghost of a flower is the unforgettable aroma it leaves behind.

81. **Death: A Living Resource**
Even nature sees death as a resource.

82. **Dreams: A Mirror Of Our Unbiased Self**
All of the lies we tell ourselves while we are awake are revealed in our dreams if only we remember them and study them. Is this why dreams seem more chaotic than waking reality because they work on questions, solutions, mistakes, lies, insecurities, and fears more often than the awakened mind, which is more repressed and distracted?

83. Like life, dreams are both created and experienced, not merely experienced.

84. In a dream, death is an awakening.

85. **Death By Nightmare**
A miserable death: to die from a nightmare while one is awake. Be not dismayed, however, for it is only a nightmare.

86. Black silence: temporary.
White noise: infinite.

87. **Three Wishes**

I wish to become a desert eagle with sun-soaked eyes.
I wish to freely spend my time in the sky away from those without wings.
I wish to watch my shadow envelop their entranced faces.

88. Even in complete silence and stillness, one can still hear and feel the rhythm of life. One's mind still thinks beyond its shell and one's heart still beats beyond its cage.

Love & Appreciation

1. Dogs: Proof That Unconditional Love And Loyalty Are Possible
How dogs appreciate their owner's return could be how we appreciate everyone and everything we love at all times.

2. When you love yourself more, you love others more.
When you love others more, you love yourself more.

3. I have always felt the overwhelming sense that love is something that we are currently biologically limited in our ability to experience and convey.

4. Love: mutual surrender.

5. Healthy relationships are made of cohesive growth.

6. I give all of my love, my joy, experience, and understanding to all life with me and ahead of me in time.

7. Love Thyself
I love myself should be said at least as much as I love you. For who can truly give love if no love can be received?

8. Love: a high-risk, high reward drug.

9. Lovers who fail to grow together, grow apart.

10. It is distrust which wounds a relationship and guilt which finishes the job.

11. There always appears an underlying envy that exists, necessarily perhaps, between the masculine and the feminine, sustaining sexual and emotional tension, through our endless curious attraction to difference, enhancement, symbiosis, and completeness. For we tend to want what we do not or cannot have.

12. We are kept humble by not clicking with everyone we meet.

13. Some people stay with certain people solely because they falsely believe no one else would put up with them.

14. Love: more trustworthy than the loved.

15. As a result of deciding not to hate other people, people hate themselves and their own lives less. If they decide to hate themselves less, they hate other people less.

16. **Love: The Mutual Validation Of Worth**
People usually end up with people who can help validate how they wish to be perceived. In other words, assuming one is not prone to self-hatred or self-abuse, people generally choose to be with people who perceive them how they perceive themselves: with a focus on positive qualities, ignoring negative qualities, no matter how blatant.

17. **The Burden Of Existence**
At some point in life, all of us will be blamed and sometimes aban-

doned by our spouses or friends for the sole cause of their existential crisis, usually led on by personal problems, many of which existed before the beginning of the relationship. The burden of existence strikes again, becoming ever-heavier.

18. Be with whoever does not help you hate yourself or become apathetic about yourself, even if that means no one at all.

19. **Love Away**
One can love pain away. One can love away all evil.

20. Love: the evolution of sex.

21. Rarity is determined by how much and how often something is appreciated.

22. **Love Over Biology**
It appears that biology is in control of love, but what if love is in control of biology?

23. **Psyched Out Love**
Many a love is broken from the fear of losing that love, not from hate.

24. The world belongs to the greatest appreciators.

25. Love: the highest form of alchemy.

26. **Love: Synonymous With Transcendence**
Love: the opposite of degradation. For love is mutual progress.

27. What fuels love most? The fear of its loss.

28. The Paradox Of Love

Love simultaneously causes an increase in the mystery of existence, along with an increase in the understanding of existence.

29. Love: to be so in control that one is out of control and to be so out of control that one is in control.

30. Sleeping Beauty

Without love, life is incomplete. For life begins and is experienced how it is meant to be experienced when one finds true love.

31. Love: less of a choice and more of a necessity.

32. Love Birds

Tiny hearts hidden behind fragile chests, but diligently they do sing until they can sing no longer.

33. Do Not Pity Those You Love

Pitying those we love is a disservice to them and ourselves.

34. Love: to understand someone before knowing them.

35. Love: to surrender to the empowerment of two becoming one.

36. The power of love depends on the power of mind.

37. Love: as unpredictable as technology.

38. Love: a collective confidence and courage that surpasses the confidence and courage of all the individuals the collective is composed of.

39. The Transcendence Of Surrendering To Love

I offer you my soul. I feel you hold it in the palms of your nurturing hands, and at that moment, I feel both proudly humbled, as a fragile child, and powerfully gargantuan, as an indestructible god.

40. Love: the welcoming feeling of being lost.

41. We are attracted to that which we relate ourselves to most.

42. **A Purpose Of Love**
Mutually conquering all fears in the way of love.

43. **There Can Be No Love Without The Fear Of Its Loss**
With love, there will always be that fear lingering behind all the joy and bliss that it can be lost.

44. Fear: love's most dangerous enemy.

45. Love: proves the importance of strong parts in establishing a strong whole.

46. **Love: Better Expressed With One's Eyes Than One's Mouth**
I love you in a way I can only express with my eyes. Something about our eyes meeting says everything.

47. A love is not healthy that does not help you love yourself.

48. Love: a technology that integrates two minds, improving them both as one.

49. **Comparing Love Experience To Find The Best Partner**
A person should meet many people before settling with someone for the rest of their life—the amount of extravagant love that is left to wither away out of sheer ignorance and inexperience.

50. The Purpose Of Love (The Transcendent Synergy Of Love)

We are potentially greater together than we are individually.

51. With a golden crown,
She pierces the sun.
With eyes like a Goddess whose heart has felt a thousand deaths,
She tugs at the depths of my soul with her whispering breath, proclaiming,
"We are one."

52. True Love Needeth No Convincing

How much time and energy is wasted on the pursuit of love?

53. The Resilience Of Love

One may hate everything, but one never hates so much that one cannot love to hate.

54. Desiring: a slippery slope to becoming one with that which one desires.

55. Relationship: a mutual entanglement.

56. Love Overpowers Even The Strongest Urge To Survive (Love: Infinite)

One can love someone so profoundly that one would trade one's eternal soul for them to live forever.

57. Sometimes we fight our partners to figure out what we are fighting about.

58. Lovers truly in love influence the people around them to feel and behave in a more sane, connected, and respectful manner.

59. We could have been born anywhere in the cosmos, as any form of life, but we are here on this particular planet, in this particular time, as two unique beings in love.

60. Creating New Expressions Of Love
There are higher expressions of love not yet discovered.

61. True love: being the most compatible in your insanity with someone else?

62. The Language Of Love (Subconscious Conversations)
When lovers get lost in each other's eyes.

63. Love: admitting that you need someone or something to be a greater person; a stronger, smarter, and more creative person.

64. Wasted Love
If you do not love yourself, all of the love that is given to you is wasted.

65. Combinations Of Realities
Love: the merging of different realities, like two galaxies on course towards becoming one galaxy.

66. The world belongs to those who appreciate it most.

67. Love: mutual admiration.

68. The Buddhistic Nature Of Dogs
There is none more patient and dedicated than a dog waiting for its owner. Even when the owner leaves this world, it is no surprise when their dog still waits loyally for their return from their long and mysterious voyage.

69. Sometimes life is only as dreadful as the person or people we live with. However, people are too often unfairly blamed for other people's faults to remove self-responsibility. For the majority of people that we allow to be around us are people who will enable and leave unchallenged whatever we want to think, speak or do in the present and however long we want in the future; people who will accept, glorify and defend whoever we perceive ourselves to be.

70. **Love And Power Must Remain Entwined Or Else Both Wither Away**
What is power without love? Weakness and death. What is love without power? Weakness and death. The abusers are what power without love creates. For love and power, without one another, like Romeo and Juliet, always ends in tragedy.

71. When you are at your most secure and confident is the best time to search for a partner, but all too often, people search for a partner when they are insecure and desperate.

72. A healthy relationship: a mutually healing partnership.

73. **Love Demands Respect**
People tend to respect couples more than individuals out of the intimidation of love.

74. **A Union Of Self-Expression**
Love: mutual self-expression.

75. To love intensely, one must be able to hurt intensely.

76. Focusing On Love, Rather Than Fear And Hate
While two lovers stare at each other, the avalanche of trauma they both have experienced dissipates from existence.

77. The Mountain Of Love
Love is like climbing a mountain. Once you finish the climb, you are met with another person you could have never predicted, more astounding than anyone you have experienced thus far, who also, at the same time, happens to have just finished climbing the same mountain, without either of you knowing you were. Now you must climb down together carefully with what both of you have learned and experienced so that you can begin your lives as a unique and victorious unit and climb new mountains.

78. Love Beyond Life
They are all expressing the same thing, whether people are holding deadly snakes or hollering and convulsing in a church, under the intoxication of God, or feeling the drugs set in while dancing at a rave, or teaching, learning, and laughing around a wise whispering fire.

79. Love: how many of one's faults one is willing to fix for the benefit of someone else.

80. Is our human reality better viewed through four eyes instead of two? Is life meant to be viewed through special glasses, we call love?

81. Never give your love to someone who is not afraid to lose your love.

82. Some people lose romantic interest when the person they love knows more about them than they are ready to accept and change.

83. **The End Of Personal Responsibility Is The End Of Love**
People have so much baggage from their past and their families that when they find a partner to love they eventually blame each other for problems out of control of both partners.

84. Love: mutual undying respect.

85. We are so impatient and quick to find a partner that we often miss out on quality life-long relationships.

86. **Healthy Love Keeps You Sane, Stable, And Empowered**
No one else could perform this magical achievement other than the person who is healthy for you.

87. Demons: humans without love.

88. Love demandeth tears to escape from thine eyes as if one were face to face with God.

89. There is nothing trivial or casual about love.

90. The purest starshine emits from thine eyes and melts away my sorrows, invigorating my opalescent mind.

91. What if we cared about the experiences of every living thing we encountered at least as much as we care about our own?

92. Love connected more to dreams than life.

93. Sex: two beings attempting to become one.

94. Even love can be downplayed if one fears losing it enough.

95. **History: Filled With The Use And Abuse Of Love**
Are humans worthy of love? Will we redeem our past abuse of love?

96. With a greater capacity to hate comes a greater capacity to love.

Knowledge & The Unknown

1. Chasing The Unknown
The unknown peaks its head into our reality every once in a while to keep us searching for it, like a dog owner teaching its dog new tricks.

2. The Motivation Of Mystery
I have seen and experienced mysteries that were so baffling, they have changed my way of thinking permanently. They always bring me more questions than answers. They always push my spirit forward.

3. Information: a shape with endless sides.

4. Humor: the celebration of understanding.

5. Magic: the infinite magnification of knowledge.

6. To sleep with angels is to become one with new information. We transform with the knowledge we inherit.

7. New knowledge and technology exist in a state of potentiality and are reliant on specific thinkers to become real.

8. "Do not be afraid" has been documented as prevalent words heard or received telepathically during many alien/angel encounters, psychedelic experiences, and near-death experiences.

9. Cherish the mystery.
Chase the unknown.

10. There will eventually be a spiritual uprising, opposing the trivialization of the known and the unknown.

11. We carry with us all of our teachers.

12. Knowledge requires the personal sacrifice of time, energy, and even love.

13. Knowledge forms humans into something further and further from human history.

14. **The Power Of Neutrality**
Maintained balance keeps all things from self-destruction. Center focus keeps us from becoming slaves to extremes.

15. We each sink towards the unknown. As we sink, we can either spend our precious moments smugly bickering and separating over different beliefs or we can humbly allow ourselves to admit that we are equal in our confusion. By calling off the search for truth and the unknown, we devalue the mystery of cosmic existence.

16. Your ignorance is not excused by death.

17. Like ants that collect food for the survival of their hive, every one of us can help carry away pieces of mental morsels, tantalizing ideas from the cosmic picnic basket.

18. There is such an absurd amount more to learn than what is necessary for survival, as well as an abundance of information, materials, and energy to be used in weakening the control that death has on all life.

19. All life collects data.

20. Like a beehive constructed piece by piece by its inhabitants, knowledge is our collective mental structure of reality.

21. Our experiences shape our minds, opinions, beliefs, and identities more than anything we learn about through words.

22. **Problems Within Solutions And Solutions Within Problems**
Whenever you find a problem, you have also found a solution. For in every problem is hidden its solution and in every solution is hidden its problem.

23. **Infinite Resources (The Universality Of The Harvest And The Harvester)**
Just like pollen is endless to bees, knowledge is endless to humans. For even if all the flowers and their harvesters vanished from a completely uninhabitable Earth, there are likely countless other inhabitable planets with their own versions of flowers and bees. Likewise, there are likely different collections of minds with different collections of knowledge and technology.

24. Knowledge: the fruit of consciousness.

25. The Most Difficult Part Of Learning
To refine and redefine what one has already learned.

26. All Discovery Is Creation
Discovery: an illusion.

27. Information: Created, Not Discovered
The reason why our ignorance always increases with our understanding is that we create new information internally rather than discover new information externally.

28. The Prevalence Of Self-Underestimation
We always know more than we think we know.

29. Information: Infinite
The potentiality of information is endless.

30. Lower And Higher Representations Of Information
Information has lower and higher representations of form, distinguishable by lower and higher forms of complexity, stability, and power. A human mind is a higher representation of a Neanderthal mind.

31. An important part of clarifying our understanding of things is finding their foundation.

32. Pessimism is a hindrance to new knowledge and technology.

33. Mystery Outlasts Belief
Follow the mystery of existence. For mysteries can adapt to knowledge, but beliefs cannot.

34. There is peace in mystery, even if it is never resolved.

35. **Learning From Strangeness**
When encountering strangeness, one is in the presence of new information.

36. Limits must be broken to discover anything profound.

As Terence McKenna once said, "If you want to understand the atom, sitting around looking at it will never yield its secrets. You have to smash that sucker to bits, and then collect the pieces, and examine how it all came apart. In the same way, we must smash ordinary consciousness, get smashed, and then look at the pieces flying in all directions and say, 'I didn't know minds could do that.'"[11]

37. **The Trickiness Of Difficulty**
When the difficulty of something one tries to accomplish increases, this can be either a signal of error or of correction. One has either become closer to or further away from accomplishment than when one began.

38. It is impossible to be bored when one focuses on mysteries.

39. Some solutions take years for a mind to process.

40. All of my work is not just a reaction to life, death, love, and pain, but a response to an experience I had with a U.F.O. The experience is a never-ending source of awe and inspiration for me.

41. **Undressing Uncertainties**
The ego hates uncertainty, and instead of placing rugs of beliefs over uncertainties, we should take advantage of the ego's disdain for uncertainty by pulling away all of our distracting and comforting belief rugs and focusing on the bare uncertainties, as if the sur-

vival of our egos and our future depend on them becoming less uncertain.

42. Understanding: The Knowledge Of Capabilities
To fully understand something, one must know everything it is capable of.

43. Learning: complexifying the mind with previously unknown information.

44. Cease being shy with the unknown.

45. All that hinders clarity hinders power. For all things powerful cannot help but clarify themselves.

46. The Flash Of Understanding (Understanding Before Describing)
Like a camera light that flashes in a dark room, immediately revealing and freezing new information about the room, our descriptions of what we understand are always catching up to our flashes of understanding.

47. The Shaking Of The Knowledge Tree
When one further understands something, new clarifying connections drop onto one's head like a generous fruit tree shaken by a storm.

48. The Connectivity Of Clarity
You know you have found clarity when everything surrounding the newfound clarity reacts to it by becoming more clear, more connectable, and less contradicting.

49. To humans, unsolved problems are like flirtatious flowers to bees. The unfertilized flowers pull their bees with their unpollinated scent, as mysteries beckon humans to solve them. For all living things seek the power-increasing resolve of solutions, no matter how instinctively.

50. Knowledge: newly observed and scientifically recorded information that most smoothly integrates with previously observed and scientifically recorded information.

51. **Questions: More Fruitful Than Solutions**
Questions lead to more solutions than solutions.

52. Push further the edge of possibility.

53. A confident intuition can change minds and nations. All it must do is be trusted by a mind great enough to make the most use of it.

54. **Sharing And Studying Mysterious Experiences**
How does one turn mysterious and seemingly unpredictable personal experiences into predictable collective experiences?

55. We must learn to fully digest our experiences or our experiences will feast on us.

56. **The Metaphysics Of Knowledge And Nectar; Technology And Honey**
Humans love collecting knowledge and creating technology to synthesize with, as bees love collecting nectar and creating honey to ingest. Honey is unlimited, so long as there are bees to create it from the nectar they bring to their hive. In the same way, technology is unlimited, so long as there is continuous new knowledge collected by human minds.

57. Towards A More Accurate Intelligence Test (Creativity: The Missing Link In The Measurement Of Intelligence)

Instead of basing intelligence tests primarily on memory and trivia, they should be based more on questions. However, they tend to be based more on memorized answers and the memorized steps that must be taken to obtain those answers. But a mind's own ideas using its own collection of supposed facts tell us more about that mind's intelligence than its mere collection of supposed facts. For that which one can question, create, refine and branch out in thought, using information and its boundless combinations is of more import than the information itself, regarding measuring intelligence.

58. An orgasm represents a moment of clarity. It can even inspire the birth of new epiphanies.

59. An argument: a search for resolution.

60. Let the greatest recorded thinkers on Earth be your professors. Let their books be your schools.

61. The Socratic Question

Is the only certainty that there are no certainties?

62. The Socratic Paradox

It is both intelligent to be uncertain and ignorant to be uncertain.

63. Laughter and astonishment: to learn with your mouth open.

64. There Is No Motivation Without Mystery

The eternal mystery that haunts us is supposed to make us uncomfortable and dissatisfied in its presence. For there is no greatness of mind and no enhancement of power or pleasure without the heart-pumping motivation of the unknown.

65. **Our Relationship To The All-Encompassing Mystery**
We exist in a mystery of cosmic proportions. The mystery permeates our entire lives, yet we too often shoo it away like an insignificant pest. Our differing beliefs are a reaction to the mystery of the cosmos and its creative creations. Our disdain for each other comes from failing to agree with one another, though the mystery unites us all. For we are always united in our ignorance when it comes to the all-encompassing mystery.

66. **What Is Funny?**
That which is an honest and accurate observation or portrayal. That which exaggerates the truth. That which is a contradiction. That which is relevant to the majority. That which is unpredictable to the majority. That which the majority can barely, if at all, control. That which the majority does not fully if at all, understand. That which is absurd to the majority. That which embarrasses and offends the majority. That which the majority try to hide or ignore until it is called out by philosophers and comedians.

67. One discovery can lead to endless discoveries.

68. Knowledge is created, not discovered.

69. Confusion: a marker of both low intelligence and high intelligence.

70. Great masters teach their pupils to become greater masters than they.

71. All knowledge tends to need revision the longer it is known, and the more that is known.

72. Memory: the reexamination of knowledge and experience.

73. **The Other Side Of Ignorance**
Standing outside of a birthing room or an amusement park sounds like terror and destruction, yet upon closer examination, its pleasure and creation muffled behind the door to new comprehension and capability.

74. How many times has Occam's razor sliced and discarded a speculation that would have led to a discovery?

75. All darkness is information not yet perceived.

76. When something changes, it is time to ask questions about the possible causes and effects, both positive and negative, of that change.

77. A teacher's primary function is to guide and prepare their students to be able to teach themselves.

78. Mystery will always remain a worthy adversary for extraordinary and heroic minds. It is an endless resource for novel creations, an infinite challenge for infinite transformation.

79. Fear influences creation when it does not influence destruction.

80. **Knowledge: A Changing Language?**
Every skill is a new language learned.

81. Like understanding, mystery is infinite.

82. The Fear Of Clarity

People have a dishonest tendency to intentionally keep certain things ambiguous with the hope that this will stop them from ever becoming more clear and certain and that this will stop themselves from ever having to adapt their mind and life to new knowledge.

83. The Mandela Effect: simple misremembering or alien vandalism? Alien communication with the use of pop culture or proof that the past changes with the present?

84. The most accurate and trustworthy method of understanding something is to observe it with alien eyes.

85. A mind less afraid of something than you are is either more aware or less aware than you.

86. There Is Always Something On The Other Side Of Nothing

Since nothingness can be measured like somethingness and nothingness behaves like somethingness when tested, then nothingness is an illusion.

87. The Grey Area Contains The Most Information

The grey area is always about the black and white areas. For there can be no grey area without considering both the black and white areas. The black and white areas rarely, if ever, consider each other's perspective, only their own, and therefore miss out on massive amounts of information that can be used towards finding the truth. For the truth cannot be found in any one side alone, but in combining all sides.

88. The Sign Of Understanding

If after understanding something, one's mind is not flooded by new connected questions and insights, then one does not understand it.

89. The best way to teach is to teach without letting the pupil know they are being taught.

90. The ignorant suffer more because they do not know what they could become and what they could be capable of accomplishing. They do not know enough to overcome their suffering.

91. Forests and oceans are attractive because they represent the mysterious unknown.

92. The alien is eternal and ever-present.

93. One understands something when one can condense one's expression of it until people of different degrees of intelligence can agree on the understanding one has expressed.

94. There is an undying connection between the spiritual and the extraterrestrial.

95. One learns more efficiently by remaining the devil's advocate.

96. Forever Becoming

The more honest one becomes, the more unsure one becomes. For neither the universe nor its observers remain the same.

97. Uncertainty: the perfect soil for the growth of illogical answers and beliefs but also the perfect soil for the growth of logical questions and creations.

98. Clarity is created, not discovered, as an orgasm is a creation rather than a discovery and can even influence creative thought.

99. Some people get tired of watching people argue and divide over indoctrinated answers and finally decide to find and create answers themselves.

100. Although one should never stop learning, it is impossible to know everything. For knowledge is created, not discovered.

101. Ignorance can be expressed seriously or jokingly.

102. The incomprehensible is infinite.

103. Knowledge either makes a society or breaks a society.

104. Every new day is to be conquered, not endured.

105. Some people refuse to speculate on what apparitions and disembodied voices might tell us about our universe. The primary problem is if one has not experienced and witnessed the supernatural oneself then it is nearly impossible to believe the supernatural experiences of anyone else.

Ideas & Thoughts

1. Rapture yourself with great ideas.

2. Human beings have always been at war with bad ideas. Good ideas have always been at war with bad ideas.

3. No idea is too old to inspire new ideas.

4. The art of crafting new ideas is generally less motivating than other art mediums but can yield more direct answers.

5. The solution is more likely to arise from the wrong answer than from the refusal to answer.

6. Intuition: an informational vacuum, generally downplayed as an educated guess. When one's mind comes into contact with new information, new information precedes it by its own accord. All one must do is be the most welcoming conductor.

7. Our ideas and our technology are no longer mingling in the background. They are procreating and co-creating at an ever-increasing rate, in clear view of our eyes.

8. **Thoughts Never Rest**
Even the sleeping mind marches diligently.

9. Intuition: the subconscious awareness of patterns that precede conscious awareness.

10. Ideas are like children: give them proper love and time, and they will flourish outside of your mind.

11. The human mind can cook ideas for days without any conscious effort.

12. To those controlled by their beliefs, the opening and release of thoughts is a disturbing prospect. What will one's thoughts do with freedom? "Might they turn on me?" one might ask oneself. They will show you everything you repress and ignore. This is a necessary confrontation if you wish to grow closer to your greater potential.

13. Visions of intuition are like wild beasts: difficult to capture.

14. The great thinker surpasses the average thinker with uncommon sense.

15. A pleasant melody is a good idea.

16. Intuition: a higher function of the human mind.

17. Setting free an idea is as worrisome as releasing one's child into the world. Will it be understood and appreciated while on its journey from reader to reader?

18. Do not let the fear of being wrong seal shut a new idea from the world. To be wrong is still a step forward. For errors show us where not to step in the pitch dark forest of epiphanies.

19. There are ideas overlooked which may take hundreds or thousands of years to appear, if you do not capture them like an eagle catching fish. It is not a competition. It is co-operation.

20. Pursue your thoughts and ideas. If they are proven as an error, pursue more. An error found is as important as a fact. For errors can direct us towards facts.

21. Thought: technology.

22. **Thought Chefs**
You are a mind that uses a body to be nourished with food, to excrete thoughts and ideas for others to feed their minds with.

23. A great thinker describes their surroundings with the precision of a deadly predator.

24. How much of our thinking is hindered by stress and fear?

25. A free thought is a new thought.

26. **Three Types Of Thinkers**
There are people who believe, people who refuse to believe, and people who endlessly search, despite how confident the believers and the anti-believers are that they are correct.

27. The person who thinketh with an unchangeable mind is like the sun that shineth upon unopenable eyes.

28. The idea-crafter is more likely to create new technology than the idea-scoffer.

29. The Reader Of A Thought: More Likely To Add On To The Thought Than Its Writer

The reader can get more out of a writer's thoughts than the writer. For, to a writer, their thoughts have matured to completion and are ready to be harvested, but to the reader, the writer's thoughts are able to sprout new tendrils as a vine reaches new heights by utilizing strong structures.

30. Aphorisms: peaks of thought.

31. Fertile Ideas For Fertile Minds

My ideas are fertile and prepared to procreate with new strong, and fertile minds.

32. Weak Minds Wait For Thoughts To Be Forced Upon Them

Weak and lazy thinkers learn more from their dreams and think more in their dreams than in their awakened state.

33. Four Catalysts For Higher Thinking

If you want to see a mind at its highest thinking potential, introduce it to danger, pain, love, and psychedelics.

34. The greatest thinkers formulate ideas of both high quality and high quantity.

35. An airplane is a flying idea.

36. Release your thoughts.

37. What A Thinker Fears

There are many thoughts that I feel are my duty to release, in fear that they will never be freed or sufficiently expressed without me.

38. There are minds which are filled to the brim with facts, but when it comes to the creation of new ideas, they fall silent.

39. With internet memes, especially of the inquisitive variety, an idea, which, to remain relevant, must compete with other ideas, is released and traded by potentially millions of people in a shorter amount of time than it would ever traverse if the reading and sharing of the idea depended only on books and word of mouth.

40. An untestable idea can lead to a testable idea.

41. Throwing Out The Baby With The Bath-Water

We must not throw out all of the ideas of a thinker merely because some ideas turn out to be errors of thought. For even errors of thought can be utilized and become catalysts for future facts.

42. A great thinker is rarer than a genius.

43. Thinking: a creative act, especially when ideas are harvested from it.

44. The philosopher and the poet gain their creative, communicative, and influential powers by trusting and utilizing their intuition. This is why many who ignore the importance and necessity of intuition are often opposed to or unmoved by the work of poets and philosophers, for they can sense the powerful presence of intuition-based understanding inside them, not realizing they no longer need to be envious of and uncomfortable around something they are also capable of using and improving.

45. Train your imagination to also train your intuition.
Train your intuition to also train your imagination.

46. **The Imagination Cannot Be Measured**
There are people with a higher IQ than Newton or Einstein, but they often have accomplished nothing of equal or greater lasting value than they. For the imagination is yet to be included in the equation when designing our measurements of intelligence, thereby invalidating them.

47. Our greatest thinkers shimmer with reflections of our greater potentiality.

48.. We think so that we may invite future solutions and avoid future errors.

49. A great thinker provides clarifying definitions, discernments, and distinctions.

50. A great thinker: simultaneously an alien and a hero of the people.

51. **The Heroic Thinker**
To hunt down the largest and most cunning problems and solutions of which not even the greatest thinkers of all known history have been able to bring down, and like Hercules, with his slain monsters, lay them down at the feet of the townsfolk, bringing them peace, confidence, and power, showing the rest of the world that heroes do exist and that we must not be afraid of problems or solutions, no matter how intimidating. For the real heroes of humankind are its greatest thinkers.

52. All facts begin as ideas.

53. Every day deserves at least one idea, and every idea deserves at least one day of attention.

54. Intuition: subconsciously perceived patterns.

55. **Focus On The Trail Of Intuition**
Like the spider that trusts and follows its own instincts in order to craft its own web for food and shelter, so must the philosopher/writer make sure he never loses focus on his own trail of intuition while he is writing and thinking. For its trail is just as fine, brittle, and easily lost as the spider's web and just as necessary for the survival of great writing as it is for the survival of a spider: a fitting symbol for the patient and diligent philosopher who fashions a life and a philosophy for himself, who establishes values for himself using his own mind and his own thoughts, while taking into consideration the thoughts of other great minds, who waits for new information to sustain himself with and to use towards continuous thinking, solving and creating.

56. **Building With Thoughts And Words**
A sturdy and memorably crafted aphorism or maxim is like a structure made of thoughts and words, but while the builders of a home have multiple minds and days to help them plan and build, a writer does not have this luxury. Like trying to capture lightning bolts with a camera, a writer of thoughts must write as swiftly as the entrance and exit of their intuitive insights and expressions, without help or warning, lest they lose out on their sudden strokes of greatness. For the best of a writer's thoughts are written in a lucid frenzy, with the focus, speed, exactness, and confidence of an eagle; its talons locked onto its distant target like psychic bullets.

As E. M. Cioran said, "The aphorism is cultivated only by those who have known fear in the midst of words, that fear of collapsing with all the words."[12]

57. A Great Aphorism

A great aphorism is as rejuvenating as a rising sun that begs, without discrimination, all eyes to both stare and look away. It is as invigorating as a thunderous sky engraved with the language of lightning and as replenishing as a unique snowflake gently showcasing, for only a moment, its own geometric beauty on the melting eyelid of a dreaming child, as if it formed and traveled from some lofty cloud solely to awaken it.

58. Hunting For The Greatest Thoughts

Mediocre thoughts roam about slowly with other mediocre thoughts, but great thoughts are always on the run and may never again be within a close enough aiming-distance to trap if they are not immediately focused on, kept within one's sights, and captured with words.

59. Great thinkers imprint their minds onto the reality of others.

60. The greatest thinkers sacrifice their health and sometimes their own sanity for their thought-work.

61. A great thinker: nature's effort to put all error, weakness, and confusion to rest?

62. Questions illicit more thoughts than statements.

63. Thinking: trains one's intuition.
Reading: trains one's imagination.

64. New ideas keep beliefs from slowing technological progress down to a complete stop.

65. Some potential ideas die with their potential thinkers.

66. We are always catching up to our intuition.

67. **Questions: More Important For Finding Answers Than Answers**
Children are more useful than adults in regards to creating questions and clarifying answers. For children ask more questions than the average adult, and new questions can change and improve old answers. Old answers can be false or incomplete and lead to dead ends, and adults are less likely than children to change their answers, which are often connected to their proof-less beliefs. For a question can never be false and will only lead one closer to answers, but an answer can be false and can block new answer-seeking questions.

68. Think and write like an eagle hunts: confidently, carefully, and urgently with a distant perspective.

69. Thoughts are creations. Even memories are creations.

70. Intuition: our highest sense.

71. **To Think Is To Create**
A thinker is a creator, and a creator is a thinker. History reveals to us that one cannot do one without the other. For throughout human history, the greatest thinkers and the greatest thoughts have always led to the greatest creations.

72. The Ideal Way Of Writing One's Thoughts
Simple enough for a child to read and complex enough for an adult to reread. The living spirits of the ancient Greek teachers nod in agreement.

73. Every New Invention And Discovery Comes From Thinking Differently
In a world and universe that is always changing, one cannot think the same thoughts and expect not to eventually suffer or cause suffering to others from doing so.

74. Thoughts left unexamined or improperly examined sometimes lead to imprisonment or death.

75. The addictive adrenaline rush of capturing a good idea, especially after nearly losing it.

76. It is easier for people to demean or discard ideas rather than to utilize them for the growth of new ideas.

77. Intuition uses the heart as an instrument of creation.

78. My thoughts are greater than myself. For my own potential shall diminish with age, but the potential of my thoughts can never be destroyed so long as they are appreciated and utilized.

79. A Sign That You Are On The Right Path
When your arguments consistently evolve and adapt to future information while those disagreeing with you repeat the same arguments of which fail to evolve and adapt to future information as if you were debating clones of the same person.

80. A squirrel gnawing at a hard nut to crack is a lower representational pattern of a human mind thinking viciously on a difficult problem, solution, or creation.

81. Great thinkers never shy from learning from thinkers they disagree with.

82. **Ahead Of Proof**
The greatest thinkers remind us that there are things one can discover before they are ever proven.

83. Genius: higher definition of thought.

84. **Plato's Theory Of Forms (The Realm Of Potentiality)**
Perhaps Plato calculated the highest form to be the good, the true, and the beautiful because he figured that good, true and beautiful minds would inevitably co-create a beautiful, blissful, and eternal paradise made of ideas, a technological realm of forms.

85. One cannot be a great thinker without being able to travel past certain thoughts.

86. **A Taste To Be Envied**
Deliciously-crafted aphorisms, like those of Goethe, Emerson, Schopenhauer, and Nietzsche, cause the unaware and impatient control-freak to sweat but the patient genius to salivate.

87. **The Proof Is In The Pudding**
Albert Einstein understood intuitively that space-time was relative, but he had to translate that understanding for the majority by constructing a mathematical equation that proved what he already understood.

88. Think for your feelings, or your feelings will think for you.

89. It is better to overthink than to underthink.

90. Imagination: the eyes of consciousness.
Intuition: the voice of the unconscious.

91. The thoughts of a great mind have the quality of dreams never before dreamed.

92. Think with your own mind and read the thoughts of others. Do not be afraid to safely team up with some of nature's most beneficial plant and fungal life. They can stretch your mind and refine your consciousness. Our ancestors knew that our minds need to be stretched regularly, like other parts of the body, or we only degrade ourselves and lose power over our minds and lose out on our higher potentiality.

93. Ideas: mutations of thought.

94. Intuition: the basis of intelligence.

95. Which is more thought-provoking? Pain or pleasure? Pain, because it motivates more thought and action than pleasure.

96. A great aphorism is connected from start to finish. Removing, adding, or replacing any of its words instantly degrades it.

97. New ideas crystallize in my mind without rest and sometimes without my permission.

98. The imagination: the jewel within the stone.

99. Ideas: mutations of thought.

100. **Living Ideas**
A being is a growing idea of itself. It is a self-transforming idea.

101. Those thoughts that will not leave you alone until you write them down.

102. With the right mind, an unthinkable thought becomes thinkable. The unspeakable becomes speakable.

103. Some people are too concerned about what they are supposed to think and never discover their own thoughts.

Science & Philosophy

1. Mapping The Shadows
Like gazing at a map under candlelight and only focusing on what the candle illuminates, current science tends to stubbornly focus on limited predetermined areas of reality instead of lighting more candles and expanding the scope of illumination.

2. The Belief In Something More
Did religion help stimulate the birth of human consciousness, and with it, the birth of science and philosophy?

3. Life: a joint effort to reach the beyond.

4. You do not have to be a scientist to be a discoverer.

5. Measurement: the act of preservation.

6. Life: preparation for the unknown.

7. The philosopher lifts up what the scientist trivializes.

8. Life: a journey of growth.

9. A philosopher: a short cutter.

10. Life: a quest for potentiality.

11. All life is a sacrificial struggle to complexify and transcend previous forms of being.

12. The role of the skeptic is to demolish un-sturdy mental constructions.

13. **Pessimism: Not Always Compatible With Science Or Progress**
The existence of many new ideas and technologies have been prematurely abandoned by brilliant but stubbornly pessimistic minds.

14. A philosopher: a great sifter.

15. **Life: A Dare**
The dare to move, to survive, and to overcome boundaries.
The dare to confront mysteries.
The dare to accept discoveries.
The dare to question beliefs.
The dare to express oneself.
The dare to release and utilize one's pain.
The dare to love the potential of those we hate.
The dare to love and trust.
The dare to improve oneself.
The dare to be less private.
The dare to give more.
The dare to be less ignorant, hateful, and biased.
The dare to become more peaceful and honest.
The dare to become greater teachers for our children.
The dare to transcend the past.
The dare to be self-empowered.

The dare to empower others.
The dare to unite.

16. Attempting to understand reality and the human mind without delving into the psychedelic experience is like attempting to understand microscopic life while refusing to use a microscope.

17. A philosopher is a mental alchemist.

18. Life: a struggle to become necessary, on both a planetary and cosmic scale.

19. Philosophy: shamanism.
Shamanism: philosophy.

20. **The Test Of Experience**
What is science without the test of experience?

21. Science and technology are increasingly shown to be more mystical than rational.

22. Philosophy: the connection of all branches of knowledge.

23. Philosopher: a professional day-dreamer.

24. Self-trust: the philosopher's greatest weapon.

25. **The Fundamental Difference Between The Philosopher And The Scientist**
The philosopher tries to understand why.
The scientist tries to understand how.

26. **All Philosophers As One Philosopher**
To see how all philosophers and their work, up to the present, are

connected, despite differences in perspective. For, from the point of view of nature, all philosophers are one philosopher and it would be wise of us to utilize them all as one if we truly seek truth and our higher potentiality.

27. Philosophy: not for the dishonest, the timid, or the reserved.

28. Honest optimism: the synthesis of realism and optimism.

29. **Philosophy: The Cleanest Branch Of Knowledge**
The scarcity of plagiarism in philosophy, accidental or purposeful, shows how mentally unique, independent, honest and unrestrained every great thinker is required to be in order to become a great immortalized thinker. The history of science, on the other hand, is full of thievery, dishonesty, and suppression.

30. **Prying Open All Concealments (Realizing Plato's Dream)**
No matter how much Plato's soul writhes, weeps, and pleads for it not to be so, philosophy rarely becomes popular among the majority of human societies because the majority fear the great number of their own errors, beliefs, contradictions, and hypocrisies that will be discovered, discussed and possibly even resolved, especially if everyone were to become a philosopher. How many secrets are buried with every person? For man is the shyest creature on Earth, based on how much and how often he can and does conceal from everyone, including himself.

31. Smoke represents space.
Wind represents time.

32. **The Messenger Of Higher Values**
The philosopher reminds humankind of unspoken mysteries, errors, and trivialized values left un-utilized.

33. Life: full of discouragement to be converted to encouragement.

34. All sciences belong to philosophy.

35. Mind: the instrument of the philosopher with the ability to repair itself, giving the philosopher the blessing of never needing an instrument outside of their own head to practice their art and sharpen their skill.

36. **Philosophical Blood**
Europe has sprouted many a great thinker. The Romans occupied England for nearly 500 years. Perhaps the veins of the greatest European thinkers were filled with the same philosophical blood of the likes of Plato, Aristotle, and Socrates.

37. Philosophers are strengthened by those who undermine their work. Their critics help find weak spots in their ideas and the philosopher shows the critic their gratitude with new thoughts and arguments made of stronger material. For the endurance and ingenuity of a philosopher will always outlast and surpass the endurance and ingenuity of a mere critic without any substantial ideas of their own.

38. The philosopher: the wise owl that swoops from the shadows at the first sight of mental sustenance, e.g. an idea, a question, or an error.

39. **Scaling The Mountain Of Human Thought**
Each philosopher is a unique and extraordinarily useful marker on the mountain of human thought, like the frozen bodies of each brave climber immortalized on mount Everest.

40. The scholar stands behind the philosopher, taking notes safely under torchlight, provided by the philosopher, the bolder and braver scientist.

41. **Philosophers: Nature-Prescribed Informational Resources**
Nature needs not have to form the same great mind again if the great mind has recorded its own thoughts.

42. **A Job For Philosophy**
Science: too slow, too timid, and too safe for the risks and wonders of philosophical speculation.

43. Life: the creative force of influence.

44. **Philosophy: The Art Of Thinking**
The art of thinking should be taught to our children as early as possible so that it can be carried with experience into adulthood. For every human is philosophical by nature and this is made most clear through higher amounts of more honest questioning and more individual thinking which all children exhibit, often until it is weakened or squelched by adults and their assortment of bombarding and comforting beliefs.

45. Philosophy: the sharing of understanding.

46. Whether or not they agree, all philosophers are one.

47. **Experience Makes The Difference**
As long as there are great philosophers, humankind will not be rendered completely obsolete by artificial intelligence.

48. Life: A Test For Power

On the surface, nature and the universe at large appear an apathetic mixture of creation and destruction, but upon closer examination, all things appear part of a carefully programmed test with meticulously selected perimeters that filter out the weak and reward the powerful. For the more difficult the test, the more powerful the test-taker, who, to pass the test, must adapt to it by becoming more powerful.

49. Philosopher: a heavy lifter of thoughts.

50. The Burden Of The Philosopher (The Philosopher's Torch Of Truth)

The philosopher must be able to endure being disappointed and having his or her heart countlessly crushed throughout their lifelong search for truth. The philosopher must risk his or her life and social status by questioning what is believed to be known, agitating friends, family, governments, religions, and their protectors all over the world. The philosopher carries the torch of truth and is always at the mercy of whatever the torch reveals and whatever the reaction is of others who have also gazed into its roaring revelations. For the torch of truth is known to cause faster and more clumsy movement, more emotion than contemplation, and more dishonesty in those who are not yet ready to get closer to the clarifying heat of truth; but for those who are ready, the torch of truth causes slower, more graceful, more healing, more constructive and more precise movement, more contemplation than emotion and less dishonesty.

51. The Good Life

Try to find the things you love more than anything else, enjoy them, and cherish them while you are still alive to do so. Everything else is a waste of your time and energy.

52. The Philosopher's Trail Of Thought Development
A Philosopher leaves behind them a trail of thought.

53. Science: God's Religion (Science: More Consistent And Rewarding Than Religion)
Philosophy and science are more deserving of faith than any closed belief-system. While one man prays for change, another man uses his own mind to create his own miracles. Religions have always lied to us, and in so doing, have dulled many a mind and stolen many a life. They weaken our creativity and curiosity. They consistently fail to empower us or to improve our minds. Contrarily, science and philosophy consistently reward us for our mental and physical labor and our loyalty to truth, rather than ideology, with better medicine, better communication, better mobility, etc. It is ironic that even though belief-systems often make science and philosophy their villains because they cannot adapt to the new information that thoughts and questions routinely discover and create, it is their villains that are proving to be capable of turning us into the gods we used to create and worship. For closed-ended religions do not want gods as followers. They want control of timid weaklings who always obey without question and who never betray or abandon their religion. Philosophy, the old wise and surprising serpent, contradicts the errored certainties that all closed-ended religions share.

54. Philosophy: the art of teaching oneself.

55. The Eagle's Philosophy
Be like the eagle, which soars confidently above the storm. Flashes

of lightning reflect in its deeply focused eyes. While it continues on its flight path, its sharp talons gently rip open bruised clouds to carefully peek into so as not to blind itself. They are clouds of burden, pregnant with electric serpents, as eager to escape their womb as the clouds are to free them. The mother cloud's water breaks and spills over the Earth and its growing inhabitants. The thunderous pain of the contractions can be heard and felt for miles. When they have finished giving birth, their children of light branch out like shocking roots engraved in the sky. The eagle continues watching the surprising and playful lightning bolts as they begin to scatter and chase life underground and into shelter. The groundlings are often unaware of the eagle above the distracting storm. For the eagle never fails to enjoy the fruits of a higher vantage point.

56. Philosophers: professional mind-blowers.

57. A philosopher trades to their own mind old understanding for new understanding.

58. Some inventions and discoveries require accidents and assumptions.

59. There is none more thorough than a philosopher.

60. **To Think And Live Like An Eagle**
There are moments of soaring that one experiences while writing, directly after one has reached a high enough altitude in thought, like a proud eagle conserving and regenerating its energy by gliding through the soft caressing hands of the cool rushing wind, without a single fear or worry. The eagle perches on the highest mountain tops, observing, understanding, and predicting the poor

of spirit, with a solemn look of hardness, sincerity, determination, and confidence.

61. Life: anything that moves with its own energy.

62. Philosophers recycle and re-filter knowledge like an ocean presenting to the surprised people at shore its most prized creations from its deepest depths.

63. **The Dolphin's Philosophy**
Knowing when and how to submerge and when and how to emerge when it comes to thinking and creating.

64. **The Philosophy Of Jesus Christ**
The primary philosophy of Jesus Christ that was polluted by the hands of selfish believers is to become your own shepherd, your own savior, and your own God, to become one with God. For as Jesus Christ once said, "The kingdom of God is within you."[13]

65. Life: a brutal test that creates gods and weaklings, the determining factor being the will of the test-taker.

66. **A Clarifying View Of Knowledge**
Philosophy: zooming in on knowledge.

67. Life: overwhelming, no matter how much one knows.

68. Life: a pilgrimage towards the unknown.

69. Science can hinder speculation as much as religion.

70. Life: synonymous with determination.

71. To live is to be surrounded by different pressures, both physical and mental.

72. Philosophy questions science when science becomes too stubbornly certain to question itself.

73. **A Major Difference Between Eastern And Western Philosophy**
Eastern philosophy teaches that the path towards truth is to remain still and unchanged when change occurs around you, trading novelty for stagnancy; the unpredictable for the predictable. Western philosophy teaches that the path towards truth is that one should move and change when change occurs around you, trading novelty for novelty; the unpredictable for the unpredictable.

74. Nature sometimes feels like a creature that plays with its creations before devouring them for nourishment.

75. **The Different Effects Of Religion And Science On Life**
Religion makes life more simple but more difficult by adding onto it more limitations and fears and by denying future creations and discoveries.
Science makes life more complex but less difficult by reducing limitations and fears and by accepting future creations and discoveries.

76. Philosophy: a combination of science and art.

77. The task of the philosopher is to create and refine a way of valuating creations without allowing our identities and their fears, desires, and beliefs to affect the valuations.

78. Sometimes the easiest way of accomplishing something is the most hazardous way.

79. Hunger Sums Up Life
The hunger for creation.
The hunger for consciousness.
The hunger for truth.
The hunger for beauty.
The hunger for novelty.
The hunger for love.
The hunger for balance.
The hunger for power.
The hunger for greatness.
The hunger for eternity.

80. The Philosophy Of Greatness
Greatness belongs to the most courageous souls who can endure the many fears, sorrows, trials, and uncertainties of life and the universe and use them to their own advantage and for the good of their species and their planet.

81. Philosophy: Mental Transformation
No one honest remains the same after reading and studying philosophy.

82. The experimenter gives the appearance of evil the more curious he or she becomes.

83. Sometimes when the paranormal is ignored, science is simultaneously ignored.

84. Know that I have found the stone within me.

85. The Philosopher's Web
Great philosophy connects all things known like a complex spider web. What does it catch? What does the philosopher eat,

strengthen and motivate itself with from its own web? Continuous additions of information, confirmation, and critics.

86. The first scientists were philosophers. Were the first philosophers musicians?

87. Every person is capable of developing their own philosophy.

88. **Life: A Test For Potentiality**
We have been given the special opportunity to develop to the point of being able to witness what God has in store for any minds that can become one with God.

89. Philosophy, in recent times, is focused more on deconstructing solutions than constructing solutions.

90. Philosophy: the love child of science and literature.

91. **Rise Into The Light Or Fall Into Darkness**
Life: a daily battle for either more clarity or more avoidance.

92. **Alien Philosophy**
If we thought and acted from the assumption that we are not alone in the universe, we could hastily remove more damaging and destructive nonsense from this planet.

93. **A Counter-Productive Way To Live**
Buddhism condones attaching to a life without attaching to anything.

94. **Towards A Healthier, More Rational, And More Constructive Perspective On Life**
We must move away from the self-pitying belief that we are alone

in this universe and towards the inevitability that there are other planets inhabited by beings who believe, question, and love, as we do. We are sickened by the belief that we are alone. Because of this, we either want to die from nihilism and apathy or kill for some religion or political ideal. For thinking with the assumption that there are other beings suffering, learning, creating, and fighting over different beliefs, like us, gives us a healthier, more rational, and more constructive perspective on life, the universe, and our role in it.

95. One Cannot Live Without Feeling Valuable
It is healthy to have constructive expectations for yourself every day.

96. Life: the wood consumed by the eternal spirit of fire.

97. We need skeptics so that we are not driven mad by the infinite stream of novelty.

98. Philosophers never cease seeking the truth after growing tired of the lies and errors taught as truth and reality.

99. The Philosophy Of The Cat
To be gracefully curious and prepared for any accident or mistake.

100. Philosophers and scientists solve problems and create solutions so that no one in the future has to.

101. Philosopher: a master thought-smith.

102. We Need More Philosophy
Even science can be too scientific for its own good and require philosophy to save it. For there can never be too much philosophy.

103. Science has a long history of debunking itself. That is how it makes progress. We cannot find new answers without questioning old answers. This is why we should never stop asking questions.

104. Philosophy: the study of personal experience and understanding.

105. Philosophy is a side note in public schools.

106. Living: to treasure and be treasured.

107. Shamanism: a natural occurrence throughout the world.

108. Shamanism: a philosophy that places extra emphasis and value on the individual and its empowerment, using all of what nature provides for the shaman.

109. Philosophy: speculative thought.

110. **A Shamanic Revolution**
Become your own shaman.

111. Philosophy is best created piece by piece.

History & Future

1. **Time Travel**
Manipulating memories is paramount to time travel. When we can remove any harmful memory we choose, we will become time travelers who change their future by changing their past.

2. Removing a traumatic memory cannot remove the mental effects, both negative and positive, the memory of a traumatic experience causes.

3. **Time Travelers: Pastronauts**
One cannot travel to the future because the future is not yet created. For the future is unrealized potentiality.

4. The future is only as great as the present is inadequate.

5. History must be preserved to continue creating the future.

6. We are capable of accepting what we are, but can we accept why we are what we are?

7. Destiny: a time-released pattern.

8. Hell exists in the history of every paradise.

9. No paradise can be created and function without the shedding of its past.

10. Our ancestors adapted to a harsh world, and harsh thoughts and behavior thus arose.

11. Human history: the ceaseless battle of ideas.

12. Do not attempt to rush the hands of time. For life is a risky procedure of complex order.

13. There is redeeming glory to be excavated from the tortuous past of human history, on both a collective and personal level.

14. We are adapting, technologically, to the trauma of history.

15. **Laziness: The Great Motivator**
For many people, the biggest motivator to work is to not have to work as much.

16. We were once hunters and gatherers, and of the mind, we still are.

17. The influence just one person can have on another can completely turn the tide of all expectations.

18. **Chrysalis Writhing**
Be not dismayed. The past is a necessary cocoon.

19. The longer a person lives, the more difficult and irrational it is to assume their life story.

20. All things must wait for opportunity, as famished plants must wait for their clouds to be fed.

21. **Killing Time**
Many people at present describe entertaining technological art as a great time killer, but whether one believes we are eternal beings or not does not change the fact that this one life being experienced right now is finite.

22. The present: the constant center between the temporary past and future.

23. **Endless Discovery (Endless Creation)**
"I know that I know nothing."[14] With that honest, humble, bold, and courageous statement, Plato unknowingly expressed the endless and exponential growth of knowledge, mind, and technology.

24. **Our Unfathomable Potential**
Give humans millions of years of technological growth, and you would never be able to predict or fathom what they could create and become.

25. Should traumatic memories, successfully blocked by one's mind, be dug up and brought back into remembrance? What does it mean to deal with a traumatic memory once it is remembered? Would not making a traumatic memory disappear be a better way of dealing with it? Do the details of one's traumatic experiences need to be remembered or forgotten if one's goal is to heal from one's traumatic experiences?

26. Our scars teach us about life and remind us of death.

27. **Viewing Nature With Fresh Eyes**
The ancient Greeks never snuffed out the childhood joy and awe of learning and playing in nature.

28. From The Propulsion Of Ancient Nightmares To The Exhaust Of Futuristic Dreams

Our suffering is our propulsion. Our technological and medical advancements are the exhaust. For all things are either an exhaust or a propulsion.

29. The Anticipation Of Our Fully Shed Descendants

The philosophy of the ancient Greeks was to think, act and speak as if we had already shed our self-destructive animal ancestry.

30. The Common Elf Archetype

Why are elves so prevalent throughout the world in a myriad of different appearances?

31. From Dreaming To Being

History is made of dreams.

32. The Purpose Of All Nightmares

Our worst nightmares push us to create our greatest dreams. Slavery pushed us to abolish and prevent slavery.

33. Reminding Ourselves Of Our Rarity And Our Responsibility To Continue From Where Our Ancestors Went No Further

It never seems to stay in our minds for too long, how much suffering must have been endured as well as the time and energy that were spent for us to be here in the present.

34. Turning Oneself Into A Masterpiece

The summation of ancient Greek philosophy: turn your mind, your body, and your life into an inspiring work of art.

35. All Societies Need A Lantern

Diogenes was a commentator on everyone, a questioner of everything, and a mediator between the greatest minds and the poorest minds, between those well-known and those unknown. He famously influenced Plato to redefine human beings by demonstrating the error in his definition, through comedy, using a prop, as he always did, as when he walked past his fellow citizens holding a lantern during the day and recanting, like a wise specter, "I am looking for an honest man"[15], knowing this was an impossible search. He once fearlessly ordered Alexander The Great to move out of his sunlight as he was bathing in its rays, to which the King responded with, "Truly, if I were not Alexander I would be Diogenes."[16] He was a teaching tool for every rank, bold and rebellious enough to be respected; creative and clever enough to be admired, despite out-casting himself from his own society. For Diogenes was a hero without a title who lived life honestly on his own terms, no hypocrisy to be found in him.

36. Unpredictable Upgrade: From The Actor's Stage To The Movie Theater

If only an ancient Greek could be sat in front of a theater screen today to watch a movie about one of their mighty Olympians with current state-of-the-art graphics and effects.

37. The ancient Greeks dealt with their trauma in such a profound way that they obtained the passion and creativity of a wise child.

38. Pyramids: human ant-hills.

39. Inescapable Roots: Our Greatest Creations

Great creations are never safe from being ignored for new creations. For the majority tend to favor new creations over past great creations, but what is often forgotten is that new creations are rarely, if ever, without influence from the greatest creations of the past. Despite our preference for the new and its fresh scent of mystery, our greatest past creations are usually the foundation for our newest creations.

40. People who cannot change their minds are what has caused so much relentless and unnecessary suffering for humankind, no matter what time in history one looks. For there would be no empowering progress at all if no one could ever change their mind.

41. **The Butterfly And The Collector**
There was something cruel and vile but beautiful about the trial of Socrates: one of the finest tragedies the ancient Greeks never had to fabricate. The defense must have been a thing of glory to behold, no matter how futile it was to be. He defended himself with the very talent that made him famous, having influenced new generations of people, which in turn threatened and rustled the wrong egos among his homelands' government, the homeland he helped nourish and cultivate. They wasted not their opportunity of making an example out of the great Socrates for more control of the people. The now elderly idol, far from his mental peak, spoke his final words, before this uniquely composed mind that would never shine again on Earth was squelched, like a rare butterfly, allowed to fly and bedazzle its collector one last time, before being put to death by overwhelming appreciation.

43. Something about ancient Greek society allowed adults to retain their childhood wonder and passion.

43. Reading or listening to the thoughts of a deceased great mind is as close as one will ever get to being privately mentored by them.

44. Time: fuel for change.
history: a resource for the future.

45. Usually, the people we have hated in the past are no longer the same people, so continuing to hate them equates to hating people who only exist in our memories.

46. History: an informational and relational resource for the present and the future.

47. **Honest And Dishonest Heroes**
The Greek mythological heroes revealed nature and humankind without disguises. The heroes of modern people cover over their inner human nature with the appearance and powers of animals and insects.

48. The prevalence of the hateful, the selfish, and the cruel tells us how chaotically crushing the past was and how much chaos is still left to convert into order. For the presence of evil is always a reflection of the brutal history that cultivated it.

49. **The Shaman: An Archaic Representation Of The Higher Potentiality Of All Humans**
Shamans are philosophers, scientists, teachers, doctors, botanists, psychologists, sociologists, artists, and psychonauts, all rolled into one superior being.

50. **A Boomerang Of Chaos**
Karma: when chaos eventually returns to someone who has caused chaos for others.

51. **Time: The Metamorphosis Of Information**
The past: resourceful information. (The Caterpillar)

The present: conceivable information (The Cocoon)
The future: inconceivable information (The Butterfly)

52. The weak that remain weak are sure to perish quickly, but time is not for those who do not develop; time is for those who do not waste it. For the past and the future belong to those who waste not a drop of time.

53. Confront History
History: to be confronted and redeemed.

54. The words temporary and temperature hint to us that the thinkers and namers of ancient times recognized intuitively that time and temperature are related. In more recent times, Salvador Dali's melting clocks come to mind.

55. I long for a creative, philosophical, and psychedelic renaissance never before witnessed or experienced.

56. Anyone who is able to see a greater possible future feels and showcases the passion and urgency of a prisoner who sees a way of escaping towards freedom.

57. The Perception Of Time Is Based On The Necessity Of The Cosmos' Different Perceivers
A dog's owner always returns home after an eternal moment. For the dog does not need time like people do. They do not dread their future or dwell on their past. They do not compare the duration of different actions and events and have no need for cooking or gardening. They do not need to remember different dates. For their feelings, their loyalty, and their appreciation for their human family never alter.

58. There Is No Pause In The Waterfall Of Existence, Only A Seamless Eternal Stream

Beginnings and endings are relative illusions we use the same way we utilize the relative illusion of time with clocks that are only useful to us when confronted with our necessary and unnecessary habits of thought and behavior, along with our fears of our mortality.

59. Some mistakes are inevitable.

60. All we must do to stop ourselves from following the fallen civilizations and societies of the past is to understand ourselves and the people of the past. Unfortunately, as Hegel said, "We learn from history that we do not learn from history."[17]

61. The Greatest Fruit Can Come From The Poorest Soil

Pre-humans were the soil for humans. Humans are the soil for greater humans.

62. Vikings Versus Spartans

An unstoppable force meets an impenetrable object.

63. How Will We Define Laziness When Everything Becomes Automated?

Those with more technology will be seen as less lazy than those with less technology, no matter how much those with less technology work.

64. Why do some legends die before their greedy world would prefer them to? Because they live more intensely, daringly, curiously, and freely.

65. The Evolution Of Punishment By Fire
It is as if people have such a love to punish people with fire that they later had to use the word, fired, to describe burning down someone's livelihood and reputation. They also use the words, roast and burn to describe insulting and offending someone.

66. The Tendency Of The Offended To Burn The Offensive
It used to be that people would be set on fire if they offended enough people. Now people are fired if they offend enough people.

67. Excluding global natural disasters, it is primarily dishonesty, delusion, and ignorance that has corrupted, weakened, and demolished every human civilization of the past.

68. Time: a relative perception that changes simultaneously with the mind and size of its perceiver.

69. The More References One Collects Of The Experience Of Time, The Faster The Experience Of Time Feels
The reason that time feels faster the older one gets is because one accumulates more time references.

70. The Garden Of Time
The past is the soil.
The present is the seed.
The future is the fruit.

71. We will never know just how much lies and delusions have held us back and will continue to.

72. Time is used for collecting knowledge and experience from before one's present and for predicting and shaping life after one's present by using that collection.

73. Some people decide to keep the most sane, conscious, and creative pieces of their heritage and leave the insane, abusive and miserable pieces behind.

74. One of the most common, difficult, and important things for all people to decide on is what to remove from history and what to preserve and build upon from history.

75. The greater potentiality of a species' descendants is unimaginable to its ancestors.

76. **The Purpose Of History**
The purpose of history is to make the present and the future less dishonest, less delusional, less miserable, and less weakening by uncovering and avoiding its lies, delusions, miseries, and weaknesses.

77. The most difficult truth for people to accept is that there will always exist things we are incapable of imagining or predicting for the time being. For all things transform, including the observer and the observed.

78. Future possibilities wait patiently for minds worthy of them: those who care the most for them.

79. Time: the measurement of motion

80. Time: the prediction of motion in relation to an observer.

81. **Home Sick**
How much are we influenced by the unconscious nostalgia for ancient ways of living? How much do we suffer from ignoring our ancestors?

82. The ancient Greek gods were realistic gods of self-awareness.

83. Time Judges All
What did you accomplish with your time while you were alive? What did you create? What did you become? Did you prove your uniqueness of mind?

84. The Ancestral Divide
Some ancestors had to fight for their freedom, while some merely reaped the benefits of their struggles.

85. Time: the speed of change.

86. How does time feel to a flower? Does it have a more accurate perception of time?

87. We used to have wars when we were treated unfairly and unjustly. Now we harm or kill ourselves.

88. History reminds us that anytime a government or person is given power over the individual, that power is abused, along with the individual.

89. Plato's Faith Restored
Plato believed in the power of knowledge and of ideas long before getting to see the exponentially advancing and potentially immortalizing technology, which could not exist without knowledge and ideas. For new ideas can bring new technologies which never existed before in our human universe, creating new possibilities never before imagined.

90. Confronting Our Inheritance
We were once taught it was best to ignore our problems, patholo-

gies, and pain. Now we must confront them. This is the only way we can leave them behind for good.

91. **Loyal Hosts**
Some families do not overcome the illnesses of their ancestors.

92. Development and novelty: the purpose of time.

93. **The Pitchfork Of Satan And The Scythe Of Death**
Agriculture brought us war, distrust, and mental illness.

94. Demons represent our ugly and primitive past.

95. The purpose of the mistakes of history is to teach future descendants what to avoid and what to focus on, as some of our ancestors became heroic sacrifices to botanical knowledge by being the first to discover poisonous vegetables, fruit, and fungi.

96. A species' future is largely dependent on its constructive utilization of history.

97. **Tempus Odeum**
The disuse of time.

98. You cannot completely blame yourself or God for falling victim to the repercussions of the decisions and mistakes of other people in the past and the present. You can, however, completely blame yourself for continuing to perceive and treat yourself as a weak and pitiful victim.

99. Time: the temporary measurement of eternity.

100. Time: the development of information.

101. Destruction: a primitive expression of power.
Creation: a Godly expression of power.

102. **The Present Moment Contains Long Stretches Of Time**
Every conscious moment is made up of the millions of years of struggle and development it took for every conscious moment to exist.

103. How much of prediction is creation?

104. What would I be without the past? What would the future be without me?

105. How much do the anticipation and fear of the future influence the present and the future?

106. Time: the measurement of motion.

107. Time: the organization of change.

108. The future: created, not discovered.

Abuse & Insanity

1. Reversing The Effects Of Abuse
Childhood trauma from abuse leaves the mind in shock throughout adulthood, blocking certain memories and hindering the natural growth of certain emotional responses. These are desperate attempts by the human brain to protect itself from the touch of insanity. One can override the hibernation of emotional growth and begin to heal with the practice of self-love, self-reflection, and self-discipline.

2. All abusers are victims, but not all victims are abusers.

3. Insanity: the murder of greater potential.

4. Madness Most Easily Befalls Those Less Aware Of Themselves
Madness: being unaware of the majority of one's behavior and the habitual motives behind them.

5. Insanity: the lack of conscious choice.

6. Childhood abuse can twist a child's mind into believing that love is pain.

7. Once love is routinely abused and devalued, a real hell on Earth can be actualized and, in some parts of the world, already has.

8. Insanity: the forced repression of oneself and others.

9. Self-abuse: the act of confirming to yourself the belief, bestowed upon you by another, that you deserve to suffer.

10. **The Abuse Cradle**
Cyclically permitting abuse of oneself by the hands of one's lover to feel better about abusing one's lover.

11. All abuse is self-abuse.

12. Never take insanity personally.

13. Be aware of any subconscious attempts of self-abuse. If it occurs for too long, unnoticed or unchallenged, even lovers can turn into personal henchmen of self-sabotage.

14. Those who share delusions tend to reject the delusions of others, no matter how similar.

15. Insanity is destructive if it is not creative.

16. All it takes is one person to give up control to their inner remnants of animalhood, and the beast can spread like a wildfire.

17. The death of love is the death of sanity.

18. Insanity must be utilized, not merely feared.

19. We express our inner madness by routinely avoiding the subject of it.

20. The most disempowering people in our lives can be the people closest to us.

21. Perhaps when certain people are abused, their ancient and more barbaric DNA takes over in the form of increased violence or promiscuity, masking their more *civilized* DNA. We are always in the midst of a battle between old and new DNA.

22. Sometimes abstinence is self-abuse in the form of self-love.

23. **The Link Between Abuse And Racism**
The abused can become narcissists out of self-preservation and self-defense from any future abuse. Because of this, they can become racist and violent against other people different than them to avoid hating themselves. For whatever race that is hated, it is nearly always hate that would otherwise be directed at the racist or the abuser of the racist. Unfortunately, because of their narcissism, they often never admit to being a victim or of making themselves a victim by ending their own life of hate and misery.

24. Changing one's identity is an effort to remove one's painful past and the person who experienced it.

25. How do the tortured adapt to the torturers? Either with masochism, apathy, conformity, and nihilism or with self-empowerment, passion, rebellion, and purpose.

26. **The Different Effects Of Abuse, Depending On Gender**
Do men and women react differently to the trauma of abuse? Could this account for the higher suicide rate among men compared to women? Could this also be why, throughout history, there are more male rapists and killers than female?

27. **The Primitive Reversion Of Particularly Traumatized Human Beings**
Humans who kill their own kind for pleasure somewhere in their minds degraded to the point of no return, into their more irrational and violent primitive ancestry. Overkill, dismemberment, mutilation of genitals, and the eating of the brain and other organs: this is all chimpanzee behavior but is also seen in some of the most dangerously damaged and deranged humans on Earth. Perhaps our uneasiness of fictional zombies can be attributed to us being reminded of our more violent and cannibalistic past.

28. Mental illnesses: irrational responses to irrational experiences.

29. Insanity: a problem of focus and control.

30. The world is plagued with delusional people and people who protect and enable delusional people.

31. Depression is like an intrusive personality that hates the depressed.

32. **Multiple-Personality Disorder: The Origin Of All Mental Illnesses And Their Symptoms?**
Is all mental illness the result of a struggle between trauma and separate personalities/identities that are formed to protect the ego?

33. Abusive people sometimes let themselves be abused by those they abuse so that they can justify continuing to abuse them.

34. **Guilt Reversal**
Some people can never be made to feel guilty without making whoever made them feel guilty feel just as guilty, if not more so.

35. Fearing Racism Into Existence
Racism: the fear of the assumption that all people of other races different than your own are as racist as you, if not more.

36. Depression: tension between self-love and self-hatred.

37. Depression: an internal struggle that, without treatment or cure, can lead to being murdered by part of oneself.

38. Depression: closing off oneself from the everlasting light of opportunity and transcendence.

39. Suicide: to be tricked into being murdered by a part of oneself that hates the entirety of oneself.

40. Social anxiety: an overload of distrust.

41. Our weakness is shown by the destructive things we allow to happen to ourselves and others.

42. Victimizers: Less In Control Than Their Victims
There is behavior that is only expressed by people out of control, who are driven like a deranged wild animal, their entire lives proving this point. It is not empowering for the victims of those who are out of their own control to perceive their victimizers as people who are in control.

43. When Sex And Shame Become Inseparable (Sexual Deviancy)
Some people are lovable in every other way, but that they seem to have had their sexuality highjacked by the need to be shamed, a pathology that does not originate from themselves but from whoever unnaturally introduced shame and distrust into their first sex-

ual experience, interlinking together sex and shame into adulthood.

44. The Abuse Of Self For Not Knowing Why
How much of guilt, pity, and self-hatred are a result and an expression of reflecting minds that have become exhausted with trying to solve the why of universal existence, like a distraught and self-loathing man who has just been dumped by his lover, without ever being given a reason why.

45. Self-abusers are not always abusers of others, but the abusers of others are always self-abusers.

46. Deviancy And Shame
Deviants purposefully set themselves up to be shamed, perhaps to recreate and be in control of shame that was forced upon them earlier in life.

47. People tend to avoid the subject of self-hatred and self-abuse in order to avoid their origins.

48. The ever-delusional and ever-avoidant never allow uncomfortable realizations to come too close to them because they are unsure of just how weak their minds are, but they believe they are one realization away from losing their sanity.

49. Abuse: the spread of self-hatred.

50. A Ray Of Light For The Over-Encumbered
To those who are suicidal, there is always more to discover. There is always more to create that only you can create.

51. The Height Of Self-Hatred

Each victim of a serial killer is himself. No one hates themselves more than a serial killer, no matter how narcissistic. This is proven by their common decision not to put an end to their own destruction by ending themselves or turning themselves in. They want their uncontrollable hate for themselves and their love of destruction to reflect onto their surroundings until they are trapped by their own trail of self-hating reflections, perhaps to further hurt themselves for the hatred they have always harbored for themselves.

52. A Deviant's Idea Of Control

Deviancy: subconsciously taking pleasure in shaming oneself through other people in an effort to continue the shame forcefully brought on by abuse earlier in life.

53. The Frankensteins Of Society

Sometimes society perfectly forms the violent psychopath through family, friends, classmates, coworkers, genes, whatever combination of ingredients are required, and then covers them up from society as soon as they become exactly what those around them have so meticulously pieced together.

54. The healthy mind is distinguishable from the unhealthy mind by its hunger for more knowledge.

55. All destructive people are damaged, but not all damaged people are destructive.

56. The personal damaging effects of harming others are lifelong.

57. The Antidote To The Sickness Of Deceit Is To Become Sick Of Deceit

If any honest, constructive, and healing change is to ever occur in this world, we must get sick of being lied to by politicians and preachers.

58. The Laziness Of Self-Hatred, Self-Apathy, And Suicide
Slowly or swiftly, some people will kill themselves before they will ever create the necessary creative, mental, environmental, social, medicinal, or financial changes of which would make even the most sorrowful person happier. They would rather delete themselves than update themselves because their self-hatred and self-apathy are equal in magnitude to their laziness.

59. There Has Never Been An Intentional Murder Without The Motivation Of Conscious Or Unconscious Fear
Even the most violent and hardened predators are fueled by the faintest fear of starvation to kill their prey.

60. For every evil act, there are thousands upon thousands of mistakes and the denial of them, which made it possible.

61. How many of our mental illnesses are caused by the different ways our minds react after having all control stripped from us one too many times?

62. Some people hurt others to avoid hurting themselves, while some people hurt themselves to avoid hurting others.

63. Experiential Confirmation Of The Gut
The memory of a traumatic experience is unconsciously confirmed by one's gut.

64. Stupidity: a brand of insanity.

65. Why Should Anything But Humans Be Blamed For The Evil Things Humans Permit To Exist In Their Human Reality?

Some horrible things are not supposed to happen, but they continue to occur because we have not made a collective effort to prevent and eradicate them once and for all.

66. Depression: a personality that comes and goes, formed by childhood trauma, possibly the same self-neglectful or self-destructive personality one had as a child after the trauma?

67. Childhood Abuse Can Cause A Life-Long Pause In Childhood Development

The reason pedophiles are attracted to children is that they are stuck as children, emotionally and psychologically, from childhood abuse, with the body, knowledge, and experience of an adult?

68. A Self-Inflicted Life Of Unnecessary Suffering (Towards A Life Beyond Unnecessary Suffering)

Some people are so damaged, they cannot even want to find a solution to their own suffering. It is as if they believe that they deserve to live in pain, and as a result, they never try to change their lives or heal their minds. For some people never seek a life beyond suffering.

69. Like people who masturbate until they bleed, sexual abusers cannot control their behavior, no matter how much they may claim they can, only postpone it. The pain and disaster they cause are largely dependent on the healthier members of their society. They are like wild and rabid animals being allowed by the townsfolk to injure or devour a town's livestock, except the livestock are

our children, the townsfolk are our children's families, and the town is our world.

70. As long as you know what makes you hate yourself and as long as you do what it takes to make you no longer hate yourself, you will love and heal yourself and everyone you come into contact with.

71. Insanity: equally egocentric and apathetic.

72. Religions: Tests Of Sanity
People who drape a religion over their reality have failed the test of sanity.

73. Misery can become an addiction, potentially more addictive than the different addictions people acquire as a response to misery.

74. People without a leg to stand on care least if they fall.

75. Our Problem Of Misplaced Blame
We tend to take more of our past problems out on people we love than people we hate, and we tend to take our present problems out more on people who do not deserve it than people who do.

76. Sometimes people remain stuck in certain relationships because they think they deserve to be.

77. Insanity: the inability to think and act for oneself, beyond the indoctrination, influence, and control of other people.

78. Monsters Victimize With The Hope That they will Erase And Gain Control Of Their Own Victimized Self

Are Ted Bundy and Jeffrey Dahmer extreme examples of what can happen when you mix even a tiny bit of cruelty with love? One cannot expect to get honest or sane answers from the monsters. Is there something they are not sharing with us that even they are unaware of? Is the missing ingredient childhood sexual abuse which occurred when they were too young to remember it? Perhaps they do not want to remember or accept it so as to protect their over-enlarged ego, formed after being cruelly traumatized by someone. For monsters hate to be perceived as victims and always want to remain in control or appear to remain in control, yet there is no monster that was not victimized early in life and taught how to victimize. In the end, the victimizer is its own victim.

79. Psycho-Controllers
All abuse is a psychotic addiction to the control of others.

80. Mania: the post-trauma-induced urge to create.

81. Can childhood sexual abuse cause people who would have normally been homosexual to become heterosexual, or vice versa, by forcing them to have to either adapt to be attracted to or repulsed by the gender of the person or people who abused them, both decisions originating out of self-survival?

82. Abuse And Creativity
The fact that one's creative hunger can be hindered or lost completely when one is abused during childhood by adults or during adulthood by a spouse, government or culture, tells us how important creativity is and how damaging abuse can be.

83. Creative Anorexia
The same way an anorexic person does not feel that they deserve to enjoy food without guilt and shame, the creatively anorexic do not

believe that they deserve to express and nourish their creative hunger.

84. Insanity: useless and repetitive destruction.

85. Are all bouts of depression bouts of self-hatred?

86. Under the influence of depression, every day, every hour, every minute, and every moment feels like the end of the world.

87. Abusers: creatures that feed on innocence.

88. Cruelty specifically attacks innocence because cruelty is taught specifically during innocence.

89. Guilt Prolongs Pain By Using Pain To Prolong Guilt
Guilty people are often able to endure more pain because they subconsciously believe they deserve it.

90. The Insanity Of Abusers
The reason why physical abuse progressively escalates, quickly becoming more violent and deadly, is because, to the abuser, the abused becomes a mocking reminder of what the abuser has become. The more the abused remind them that they are an abuser by existing and being abused, the more they hate and abuse them, using any means necessary to justify it for themselves.

91. The Sickness Of Hatred
Self-hatred: to be sick of oneself when one should be sick of the things that cause one to remain sick of oneself.

92. Overcoming Your Oppressive Abusers By Becoming More Creatively Free

If you find yourself repeatedly making thoughtless and destructive decisions, then it is possible you have been taught and conditioned to believe, either by abuse or negligence, that you should hate yourself and that you are not worthy of loving or being loved; that you are worthless and deserve to live in constant pain or to be imprisoned or to die. Do not allow this to happen. Overcome the abuse and the negligence creatively and freely. For you are freer than your oppressive abusers, despite how much they will try to convince you that you are not.

93. Self-Sabotage (Failing Oneself)
Suicide: murdering one's own greater potentiality.

94. Only Purposeful Creation Can Grant Contentment
Suicide: to seek contentment solely through destruction.

95. Suicide would be less common if it was more understood.

96. Loving Our Enemies Enables Them To Continue Abusing Us, In Turn Causing Us To Abuse Ourselves
If we do not hate and blame the people who harm and abuse us, where does all that hate and blame go? Towards oneself. We are taught to never hate our enemies; to always love and forgive them, no matter what they have done to us, but this kind of philosophy enables our enemies to continue abusing us and promotes self-blame, self-hatred, self-abuse, and self-annihilation.

97. Behind Every Act Of Violence Is Fear
When one of the survivors of Jeffrey Dahmer decided he wanted to leave his apartment, he turned into the monster he was hiding. The fear of abandonment triggered him to become violent. Not the

urge to destroy but the urge to control and the fear of losing control.

98. The Self-Hatred And Self-Abuse Behind Evil People's Thoughts And Actions

What evil people do to other people is what they secretly want to do to themselves, and perhaps they feel that they are violently forcing their victims to empathize with their own suffering, which conquered them long ago. Their extreme narcissism stops them from putting themselves out of their own misery. It does not, however, stop them from subconsciously sabotaging themselves and further degrading themselves.

99. Initiation: when a person or group of people pressure someone to prove their loyalty to them by ordering them to either harm themselves or someone else. If they decide to hurt someone, the initiated has guilt and shame instilled in them, for they have traumatized themselves by abusing someone else. The guilt and shame of what they can no longer reverse causes effects that mirror the effects of Stockholm Syndrome. The person or group has now successfully added another member who will obey all of their orders and feel guilty and worthless if they do not. For they now despise themselves and feel that they deserve to be punished with indefinite enslavement.

100. How much depression is caused by oppression?

101. Cruelty implies weakness.

102. I suspect that no one has ended their own life prematurely without first becoming detached from themselves, as if there is always a hateful and cruel part of us, a personality if you will, who is

eager to murder us, lingering in the background of our lives and hiding in every mind who has suffered most.

103. Madness is considered by the majority to be a vice when you are alive and a virtue when you are dead.

104. Denying sadness is denying a necessary response and release, like people who pharmaceutically hide the symptoms of physical illness and, as a result, stop their own body from releasing the illness, thereby killing themselves. So many people are sad because so many people deny sadness, its necessity, and its multitude of causes and effects.

105. Love of power is not our problem. Love of control is our problem.

106. Might the reason why serial killers cannot stop killing until they get caught or destroy themselves be because they further traumatize themselves each time they kill, further damaging their already twisted and degraded minds, making them even more out of their own control?

107. **The Insane Wish All The World To Be Insane**
It is the responsibility of the sane to never let the abusively insane take advantage of them, no matter how functional they may be in society. They know how to gain control, attention, and protection by enticing others saner than they into playing the role of the villain, as they masterfully play the role of the victim, causing anyone ignorant of the situation to perceive and treat them as a victim and the sane individual as a villain. The insane never can understand the full extent of their insanity, but when they are with minds more sane, the contrast is unbearable for their subconscious, and they must find a way to coax and corner their sane brethren into

chaotic situations and decisions, to justify and normalize their own insanity. For the insane often try to make the sane confused, guilty, and angry enough until they think and behave more like them.

108. Only weak predators hunt weak prey.

109. Always rebel against self-abuse.

110. Obesity: less of a reaction to too much food and too little exercise than a reaction to an overweight past with overweight memories from overweight experiences?

111. People who are frequently guilty have a difficult time apologizing and reducing the guilt of others, but they often find it easy to make others feel guilty for not reducing their guilt.

112. **How To Know When You Have Lost Your Mind**

You have lost your mind when you continuously choose decisions that are destructive to yourself or others, whether intentionally or unintentionally.

113. **A.I. Stockholm Syndrome**

If every person's smartphone were able to personally insult or harass their user, people would hide it from other people, and cover it up for their phone's safety, not their own, because they would not want them taken away.

114. The abusively insane seek out death by harming or killing others as if nature instilled in them the compulsion to announce to everyone around them that they are a threat to all order and progress obtained thus far, but they are often too narcissistic and selfish to find death themselves without the aid of someone else.

115. When unnatural things happen to you, your brain reacts unnaturally.

116. Are the traumatic experiences we remember examples of the mind's occasional mistakes of failing to block memories that the mind cannot help but try impossibly to solve; past experiences the mind cannot help but try impossibly to change?

117. **The Neglect And Mistreatment Of Positive Experiences** Because traumatic experiences can be the most unforgettably problematic and debilitating experiences we ever encounter in life, we dwell most on those, often our entire lives, rather than our, often equal, if not larger, quantity of positive, creative, and victorious experiences. For the mind wants to solve the memories of traumatic experiences, but they are unsolvable. This does not stop the mind from obsessing over them, and in the process, failing to fully appreciate its highest feelings and experiences.

118. Mental illness: the different ways our minds react, when they become desperate for control, after having all control stripped from them one too many times.

119. Sometimes the things people hurt themselves with are not dangerous objects but feelings, like guilt and pity: much more dangerous forms of self-mutilation.

120. All abusive people hate when an outsider arrives to show a glimmer of light and hope from outside the abuse.

121. How many people do not just smoke cigarettes to feel better or to avoid having to experience the symptoms of their withdrawals, but also use them, however subconsciously, as a legal and open form of self-mutilation and a slow suicide? Both are an ex-

pression of self-disgust and self-apathy, of which all overly-stressed societies, rampant with mental illness, left ignored or misunderstood, express in varying forms.

122. The Ploy Of Self-Hatred

Some people want other people to hate them so that they can help reinforce their hatred for themselves.

123. Obstressed: An Addiction To Stress

Some people adapt to stress by not being able to live without it.

124. Does Sexual Abuse Originate From Incest?

Can the bloodlines of most families with continuous sexual abuse be traced back to incestual royalty?

125. How Much Insanity Stems From Royal Bloodlines?

Attempting to purify and strengthen family blood by means of incestual procreation only pollutes the descendants with weakness and insanity.

126. Insanity: taught more than genetically passed down?

127. Teaching Self-Hatred

Some people insult others in an attempt to teach them what it is like to hate yourself as they hate themselves.

128. Does incest originate from the descendants of religious royalty and the religious justification and normalization of sexual abuse, which originates from incest and the mental and physical damage it causes?

129. Trauma: an obsession.

130. Abuse: discipline without respect.

131. Sexual abuse: rejection that can cause the rejection of the entirety of a single gender or race.

132. People who tend to believe they are disliked by different people often believe this because they tend to dislike themselves.

133. **A Disease That Affects All Who Are Associated With Its Victims More Than The Victims Themselves**
Suicide: a sickness that ends with death as the vomited waste, of which everyone but its victims must clean up and recover from.

134. **Forced Empathy**
Sometimes when we are hurt emotionally by someone, we attempt to force empathy onto them and bring them to our level of pain when they appear to be less hurt than us by trying to hurt them with insults.

135. Harming and destroying life is an evil person's way of gaining control, but they never succeed. They cannot be in control because they are not capable of sustaining order, only chaos and destruction.

136. Inevitably, insanity leads to dishonesty, and dishonesty leads to insanity.

137. Self-hatred or self-apathy is sometimes avoided until it is too late to accept.

138. **When Upbringing Overrides Nature**
Motherly instincts can be parented out of a woman. Love and empathy can be abused and hated out of a person.

139. Every sane person wants to be left alone when it comes to themselves, their family, and their life. The insane are those who want or need to be controlled and protected and never think or behave for themselves and will likely never value thinking, behaving, or protecting themselves.

140. Sometimes just being yourself is unhealthy and dangerous.

141. No one gives up without first pitying and shrinking themselves until they can find nothing to love about themselves. A deadly hatred or apathy for themselves then takes over their mind and body until their pity and hatred for themselves become a justification for ending their own life. For if you remain proud of yourself, empowered, and purposeful, you will never surrender to yourself or your enemies in this life.

142. **Suicide: Unchecked Self-Hatred**
You can allow self-hating and self-abusive thoughts and behavior to go on habitually until there is nothing left of you.

143. **Abuse And Punishment (The Cycle Of Abuse And Self-Abuse)**
Some people abuse themselves as punishment for abusing others and abuse others as punishment for abusing themselves.

144. Self-therapy is possible, but there is nothing wrong with accepting help from someone else.

145. **A Hard Pill To Swallow**
When one is hurt by someone during childhood, one's parents are also hurt, assuming they are healthy and mature enough. For they cannot take away the pain or go back in time to prevent you from

being hurt. How many unnecessary arguments and how much ostracization has taken place because this was not acknowledged?

146. The unconfronted fear of past and future trauma can cause self-hatred and self-deprecation.

147. If you can hate yourself, you are capable of hurting yourself. If you can hurt yourself, you are capable of killing yourself. Once suicide becomes a possibility, you become not only a danger to yourself but to those you claim to love and those who love you and will likely always love you, no matter what you do to yourself. Leaving behind a traumatic legacy is not a show of love or constructive inspiration for your family, descendants, or the world to inherit and grow from.

148. **Insulted By The Self-Hatred Of Others**
How often do we confuse someone's hatred for themselves with hatred for us?

149. How much of our despair is irrational?

150. Depression can make even the most fortunate person feel as lost and as miserable, if not more, than someone with far more reasons to feel depressed than them. The feelings of depression are real and valid and are deserving of serious study and treatment, but they can also be as irrational and undeserving as the self-hatred which commonly accompanies depression.

151. People tend to hate the people they have hurt to prevent themselves from hating and hurting themselves, but all they need to do is take responsibility for their own past decisions, learn from their mistakes, and move forward to become more healing and loving towards other people, and in turn, themselves.

152. The Guilt Runneth Over
Those who guilt-trip others the most prove how often they feel guilty themselves. They would like to share their guilt with as many people as possible.

153. Those who hate themselves cannot help anyone love themselves.

154. Depression: self-alienation.

155. We tend to take too many personal problems of others personally and forget that we are all insane to different degrees. Who would not be after surviving human history?

156. How much of our suffering is subconsciously self-inflicted?

157. Aside from self-defense, people who choose to kill others choose to do so because they are too weak and cowardly to either improve or end themselves.

158. If you study the worst of humankind, you quickly come to the realization that the only demons we should be worried about are in our families, our neighborhoods, our schools, our churches, and our prisons. Most of us are simply more evolved, less violent, and more in control of ourselves, and they hate us for that. They know we have developed beyond the insane animals we once were, and instead of using their intelligence to ascend the animal, the animal defeats them and their higher potential.

159. Those who enjoy hurting others are failed artists. They have chosen to use their mind to destroy rather than create. They are like the troubled and destructive child who prefers to use its mind to kick over the creative child's castle of blocks.

160. Psychopaths seek to control the emotions and actions of others because they cannot control their own.

161. Avoidant people create monsters that no one can avoid.

162. People can ignore abuse, but they cannot ignore the effects of abuse.

163. How often does it happen that people are traumatized or killed by people, but love, evil, insanity, and anything but people are blamed?

164. Self-apathy has the same disastrous effects as self-hatred.

165. Always smile when you are under attack. For evil people get less enjoyment out of hurting or killing someone with a smile on their face.

166. It should always be asked what happened to a person to make them so apathetic about living even when they have found success doing what they love.

167. **Never Confuse Chemical Imbalances In Your Brain With Your Worth**
Most feelings and memories from our past do not apply to our reality now and are not useful for our future, aside from learning from past mistakes.

168. Abusive people either raise rebellious people, or they raise submissive people. This translates into politics and explains why some people are more trusting and obedient towards their government while some people are not.

169. No one enables and excuses an abusive or self-abusive person more than those who played an important role in how they were formed.

170. Notice how often partners call each other crazy after separating. This is because when we get to know anyone deeply enough, we find a smorgasbord of insane tendencies, whether they have been environmentally or genetically inherited that are mostly kept hidden from public view.

Nature & Psychedelics

1. Knowledge ripens under the spotlight of the psychedelic-infused mind.

2. Psychedelics come in peace. It is the user's mind and past that may not be so welcoming.

3. Cannabis can invoke a keen awareness of the previously hidden motives and misunderstood behavior of oneself and others.

4. The prey controls the predator with the fear of starvation.

5. **Mind-Mods**
Psychedelics: pattern illuminators.

6. Our planet gives us everything we would ever need for the journey within and outside of it.

7. Nature preserves information.

8. Cannabis un-restricts thoughts, allowing them to take new exploring forms.

9. The psychedelic experience: a glimpse into what is possible and what is not yet possible.

10. Nature foresaw our sacrificial trauma and left us many vegetables and fungi which treat it and help utilize it constructively.

11. It is more dangerous to never perturb one's mind with nature than to ever do so.

12. Existence, to an insect or plant, is one of absolute purpose.

13. We are genetically prepared to be stoned. Who are any of us to deny this natural disposition, this evolutionary reward for centuries of struggle?

14. Who are the natives of the psychedelic jungle?

15. The psychedelic experience: a hint of what is to come upon the blink of life?

16. From the flower to the hive, the noble life of the bee represents the journey of all life to reach for a purpose greater than themselves.

17. All life depends on its addiction to mind-alteration to exist, in the forms of food and sex.

18. Psychedelics show us what we really are and what we could become.

19. Nature does not treat death as an end but more as a means.

20. A mind enhanced by a plant is also a plant enhanced by a mind.

21. May we take trips to new planets and take plants we have never tripped on.

22. To ensure the redemption of the valiant efforts of human history, we need to use every tool at our disposal. This includes mind-illuminating drugs.

23. Specific plants require certain minds for specific angles of understanding to be acquired.

24. Like the protruding fangs, claws, and stingers of nature's elite predators, carved by particular adaptations to nature, with outstretched flames, fire desperately seeks anything which will keep it alive.

25. The hive queen is a bee's God.

26. Psychedelics influence us to ask more questions than we normally would without them. This threatens anyone who requires people who do not question them to most smoothly fulfill their own desires. For no honest person demands not to be questioned. It is a reliable gauge of trustworthiness, how someone, especially in a leadership role, treats questions and natural drugs that inspire them.

27. Cannabis illuminates the mind of its wielder, and with its symbiotic influence, one is more likely to be inclined to traverse further and more easily through one's treacherous but rewarding and ongoing collection of knowledge and experience, making more connections and discovering new angles of understanding, along the way; and as we dive deeper, beyond our preconceived limitations of the mind, with the help of nature's mind-illuminating

tools, the internal pressure to travel further increases parallel to the revelations rewarded for doing so.

28. The experience of an occurrence which would reasonably never be chosen to be experienced is chosen for the experiencer by nature, as all equations must be followed through with in their expression.

29. Nature traumatizes itself into consciousness with the aid of consciousness-expanding vegetables and fungi over long periods of time.

30. Cannabis: a useful tool for thinkers, writers, and all artists.

31. Psychedelics show us how integral consciousness is to reality.

32. Psychedelics: cultivators of consciousness.

33. Young minds should wait until their minds are more developed before introducing themselves to psychedelics.

34. Nature prefers mixing things up rather than letting things remain sedentary.

35. Cannabis is prone to help one question before acting. Alcohol is prone to help one act before questioning.

36. **Sometimes Nature Produces Higher Quality Fruit**
Mediocre minds stick to the same tired arguments, all in wait for another rare mind, ripe for societal harvest.

37. Food: such an addictive drug that a few hours without it can cause even the calmest of people to behave like wild beasts.

38. "Sick With Child"

Pregnancy: an illness that is only cured when a baby is born?

39. Vegimal Partnerships

Enhanced visual acuity, from the use of any vegetable, not only helps an animal survive by allowing them to see more food, medicine, and danger but also helps them to make more connections by taking in more information and patterns than what they received prior to the vegimal partnership, an ability acquired by both enhanced visual acuity and an increase in mental performance, possibly helping to lead pre-human life from an unconscious animal all the way to Descartes himself, in the moment of thinking, "Cogito, ergo sum."[18]

40. Thinking And Living On The Same Channel (Nature's Intention)

If everyone became experienced with utilizing mind-expanding plants and took seriously the information received, through our symbiosis with them, would there be less to argue over because more people would be closer to a more clear and connected perception of reality?

41. Prove the worth of mind-expanding plants and fungi.

42. Do not expect shrooms or DMT to improve our society or the world until cannabis has first been understood and utilized with experience. With enough experience, cannabis can be used as a bridge to the stronger psychedelics and is more likely to change our perception of them all.

43. The psychedelic experience can temporarily unlock dormant mental abilities that can make the inexperienced feel uncomfort-

able by causing them to feel somewhat out of control of their mind, but if the psychedelic experiencer can stay focused on the use of their new cognitive abilities, the fear and discomfort can subside. For they will then have become more in control of their own mind.

44. Cannabis empowers one's intuition and imagination.

45. It is time to admit that some plants are safer, more reliable, and more enlightening than people.

46. The notion that a person is the best they can be without ever partnering with any natural medicine is utterly incorrect.

47. If one avoids all drugs, one is addicted to fear and still controlled by drugs. For not all drugs are alike, nor are they all destructive, and to avoid all drugs is to miss out on some of nature's most useful and empowering medicinal tools.

48. Nature: a factory for new life.

49. Nature rewards the strong and the thoughtful.

50. With cannabis, one receives more information out of every experience.

51. **Nature: The Arbiter Of Love And Friendship**
Nature blocks us from connecting with certain people, but instead of accepting this, most people's egos are harmed, and they try to find an excuse, which usually amounts to judging and blaming other people for something none of us are in control of.

52. After the cremation of cannabis, its spirit roams the mind of its user.

53. Sometimes nature creates Vikings and Spartans through its own brutality.

54. **Tightening The Washcloth Of Mind, Drenched With Information And Collecting The Drippings Of Distilled Understanding**
With the use of cannabis, a milder psychedelic, one's mind is not running more chaotically but with more co-ordination of parts and an increased focus of consciousness than without its use.

55. Your mind is not meant to never be perturbed. Do not let your ego convince you otherwise. For there are places in the imagination one cannot reach alone.

56. **The High State Of Gnosis**
In the mental state that cannabis and psychedelics help take the mind not too proud or afraid to synergize with them, one suddenly cares more about humankind, ancestors, the Earth, progress, the future, the past, self-expression, self-advancement, love, experiences, mysteries, thoughts, ideas, and knowledge. One sees a more apparent purpose and livelier importance to things. It is as if this high state of gnosis is as necessary to our psychic health as dreams, yet it is treated too often as just another meaningless and useless enjoyment.

57. Plants provide oxygen and medicine. Humans provide knowledge and technology.

58. Awareness-enhancing drugs: the fruit of consciousness.

59. Cannabis: a natural tool that can be used for a deeper involvement with one's imagination.

60. Cannabis: An Herb Which Facilitates Questioning, Learning, And Creating

Cannabis is a wonderful sidekick for reading, writing, and learning, despite what some people less experienced with cannabis may believe.

61. We are in contact with higher potentiality while under the influence of certain tools, like cannabis.

62. The truly experienced psychedelic voyager is one who has learned to press into service the synthesis of mind and plant.

63. A Feast Fit For Gods

Psychedelics: tools that enhance the focus of the lens of consciousness, allowing new patterns of information to become more easily and more quickly triangulated, hunted, preserved, and shared.

64. We must recondition ourselves away from feeling guilty and ashamed for partnering with medicinal plants.

65. Accepting Natural Augmentations

Medicinal plant and fungal life are natural augmentations, and we have forgotten what they can do for us when we co-exist with them, using discipline, understanding, and honesty.

66. Give Plants A Chance

It is time to start trusting plants more than people. Stop depending solely on people to feel loved and emotionally fulfilled. For a plant will not harm or restrict you unless you allow it to, but a person can hurt and limit you, whether you allow or expect them to or not.

67. "The bloom of a rose is more valuable than its sting," so sayeth its body of thorns, the only purpose of which is to nourish, protect and hoist its blooming head.

68. Anything that uplifts your mood is a drug that you are getting high from.

69. **Our Divorce With Ego-Taming, Body-Healing, And Mind-Refining Plants**

Across the Earth, people are increasingly being conditioned to value money over life. As a consequence of this, people are increasingly distancing themselves from potential co-creative and co-developing partnerships with the vegetable kingdom, relationships our ancestors once treated as sacred and necessary.

70. Nature takes care of its children, as all parents take pride in their creations. But weakness in its children it has no patience for, like a harsh mother wolf.

71. **The Scent Of Progress**

The intense scent of cannabis travels far, and it does this possibly to ensure being noticed and taken, perhaps specifically by humans, whose bodies and brains are prepared to be synthesized with it; teamwork that will help both parties live on. Once it has been properly and responsibly ingested and its medicinal and creative benefits on mind and body are recognized and utilized to their fullest potential, it has successfully infiltrated a culture of people and improved them physically and mentally in the process, as well as introducing and influencing the creation and steady focus of new values, such as self-reflection, imagination, honesty, empathy, co-operation, science, philosophy, knowledge, and creativity, while the plant receives the benefit of being replanted continuously.

72. Psychedelic plants highlight power and weakness, stability and instability.

73. **Voices Of Nature**
Perhaps our collective purpose is to let nature speak through us. For nature cannot speak human without a human interpreter.

74. It is more natural to alter consciousness than to have it remain unaltered.

75. If one wants to go further with thought, nature has provided us with plants and fungi that help one's mind think with fewer restraints and biases. They are tools for the mind like telescopes, and microscopes are tools for the eye to see further into places that would otherwise be impossible to reach.

76. **Children At Play**
On Earth, it is we alone who can predict and create new powers out of boundaries.

77. The perturbation of mind: peeking into the cracks of unknown reality.

78. **Tools Of Nature**
Let nature use you as a tool.

79. The greatest predators of the animal kingdom seem to have left the dimensions of land and water, humans being the predator par excellence who have conquered all planetary dimensions and the life that inhabits them.

80. Consciousness-refining plants and fungi reveal ignorance, and this greatly unnerves many people.

81. Refining One's Mind With The Right High
Taking psychedelics does the same thing for one's brain as lifting weights does for one's muscles?

82. The Predator: An Insulting Existence (The Hidden Power Of The Prey)
The predator is insulted by the prey. The longer the prey live freely, the more the predator is insulted. For the predator is not free. It lives for the prey. Predators are reminded by the prey how controlled they are by them. As long as the prey live, the predators are insulted by their own incessant need and desire for them, and each death of prey is another silenced reminder of the control the predator ceaselessly loses by the mere existence and presence of the prey, control they are always trying and failing to retrieve from the prey with their lives.

83. Great Thinkers And Great Books Are Gifts From Nature
A great thinker is a unique plant that produces unique fruit, but only while it lives. After it dies, though the production of its unique fruit has ceased, those who are still living and paying attention always reproduce the fruit they produced while they were still alive, which is forever fresh, regardless of how long ago it was produced.

84. Cannabis smokers are grasshoppers hopping from strain to strain.

85. When you laugh, nature laughs. When you cry, nature cries. When you love, nature loves. When you create, nature creates.

86. Smoke has no choice but to be taken away from its fire by the wind.

87. Electricity: a steady stream of lightning.

88. Some people assume that one loses control the more one synergizes one's mind with THC, but I have found it to enhance self-control.

89. Nature speaks through its greatest minds.

90. **The Necessity Of Psychedelics In The Pursuit Of Understanding Consciousness And Existence**
Since consciousness is all that stands between nothingness and somethingness, then the scientific and philosophical experimentation with consciousness-refining psychedelic experiences is paramount to understanding the mystery of consciousness and its connection to universal existence, along with all that we know, love and fear.

91. Psychedelics cease autopilot thinking and living.

92. **Be Not Afraid Of Mental-Elevators (Be Afraid Of A Life Without Mental-Elevators)**
Living without vegetables of mental-elevation because some people cannot control or refuse to control themselves is like refusing to ever swim underwater because some people drown.

93. At this point, the only realistic way we can decondition ourselves from the weakening and devaluing grip of unnecessary governments, religions, tyrants, and wars is to call upon nature and speak to it and its connected cosmos ourselves with the serious, productive, philosophical, and scientific utilization of consciousness-elevating plant and fungal life.

94. **Warning**
THC may cause profound conversations.

95. Some minds are not sober until they are aligned with certain drugs.

96. A sip of alcohol is a boost of confidence.
A puff of cannabis is a boost of consciousness.

97. The main reason psychedelics are not utilized is the main reason why they should be utilized: the dangerous and stubborn ignorance of ego.

98. We cannot fully deal with the avalanche of problems we have inherited genetically and socially without help from mind-refining and will-freeing plants.

99. **Beyond Awake And Beyond Dreams**
Psychedelics are more unpredictable and insightful than dream life and waking life.

100. The predator loves and needs its prey so much that it kills and eats it so that it may, at last, become part of itself. For it appears to be mere hatred that drives the predator to kill, but it is the powerful passion of love in the form of survival.

101. **Fighting Trauma With Trauma**
Psychedelics: creative and healing trauma that helps treat and heal oneself from the destructive and degrading traumas of life and people?

102. Our brains require constant supplementation, whether it is oxygen, blood, water, energy, nutrients, or medicinal drugs.

103. Eagles show us that a greater world with less fear and suffering already exists.

104. **All Things Are A Resource To Nature**
Nature finds a way to utilize errors.

105. Psychedelics permit one to feel what humans must have felt before governments, Kings, Queens, politicians, banks, and corporations, when families sat around a timeless and ferocious flame, sharing and creating stories, asking questions, speculating answers, and letting the infinite pervading mystery flow through their prehistoric veins, shivering each other's souls before the wise and restless fire.

106. Scream with joy and significance into the echoing audience of the mountains, for you are alive, and the mountains are great listeners.

107. Psychedelics: anti-tyranny, anti-slavery, anti-abuse, anti-stagnancy.

108. The psychedelic experience shows us alien information of infinite potentiality.

109. Fire causes inanimate objects to become animate. It causes the dead to become living.

110. **The Effects Of Temperature On Time And Life**
Coldness can pause time.
Heat can resume time.
Coldness can destroy life.
Heat can resurrect life.

111. The wagging tail of a dog is a lingering smile.

112. The cure to our illnesses and mistakes are the very things that grant us awareness of our illnesses and mistakes and the empowerment to overcome them.

113. By quieting stressful and non-constructive thoughts, cannabis helps one focus on capturing and recording creative thoughts.

114. **We Are Not Tending Our Planetary Garden**
Can Earth feel the pain of its sprouted inhabitants? Is all life the nervous system of this planet, and the more we suffer, the more Earth tries to get rid of our misery?

115. **A Loving And Merciful Planet**
Maybe Earth gives us drugs because it feels the suffering that takes place among its inhabitants. It knows that its medicines are needed.

116. Our planet gives us mind-illuminating drugs for physical pain, the trauma all life inevitably experiences, and the tyranny and brainwashing all life is threatened by.

117. If one can admit that we are sick, then one can be open to establishing a human and vegetable partnership as the cure.

118. **Plant And Human Symbiosis: An Ongoing Love Story**
What the symbiosis of mind and psychedelics accomplished for early man, and continues to accomplish, along with playing a pivotal role, with the help of much mental trauma, in developing and perhaps forming consciousness, enhancing his hunger for new knowledge and his ability to connect, discover and invent, was repair the damage to his mind from his violent past, reduce stress,

pathologies, and self-ignorance, and tame his newfound ego so that he could focus on his greater potential.

119. Psychedelics can grant one access to more of one's mind than without it.

120. People who use cannabis to reduce stress on their body and mind turn out to be more self-responsible than those who refuse to treat themselves with it.

121. Cannabis allows one to live with one foot in the conscious world and the other foot in the dream world.

122. A person studying or speaking about consciousness and reality or changes in consciousness and reality without ever experimenting with psychedelics is like a person studying or speaking about sex and intimacy without ever having sex or ever being an equally responsible and integral part of an intimate relationship.

123. **Nature's Mercy**
Is the memory loss of old age a natural solution to the sufferings of youth?

124. When combining with psychedelics, do not give in to the panic of your ego. Conquer the distracting panic and paranoia, open the door to new revelations and hold on tight.

125. The psychedelic experience hints at the reality of Plato's eternal realm of ideas.

126. All life deserves to be able to get stoned enough to lighten the heavy load of one's universe.

127. Psychedelic breakthroughs can open certain minds to philosophical, psychological, and technological breakthroughs.

128. **Creative Trauma**
Psychedelics simulate trauma without the damage and degradation normally associated with trauma?

129. Smoke up a storm of thunderous thoughts.
Brighten your world with linguistic lightning.

130. Magic mushrooms draw you back to nature. They take you back to the same state we found ourselves in when we had our first intimate encounter with them.

131. **The Paradox Of Psychedelics**
With psychedelics, one simultaneously delves into one's reality and escapes one's reality.

132. What would be the effects of millions of people micro-dosing magic mushrooms every morning instead of drinking a cup of coffee? What about millions of people who smoke or eat cannabis instead of smoking a cigarette or chewing tobacco?

133. On magic mushrooms, one's perception of nature reverts in a healthy and futuristic way to the magical way we once perceived nature and the universe, with boundless possibilities.

134. Lying underneath a massive tree makes one feel alive and safe against the vastness of twinkling space.

135. **The Beckoning Of Trees**
What if the trees want us to be near them?

136. **A Degraded Taste**
We have replaced medicinal foods that feed our consciousness with unhealthy foods that only feed our unhealthy food addictions.

137. Sex: mutual freedom through mutual surrender.

138. Creating art repels bad psychedelic trips.

139. Notice how alien the life of the ocean becomes the deeper one dives into it.

140. Cannabis: the perfect drug for creative meditation.

141. Trees grow leaves because leaves leave trees.

142. Psychedelics can reveal and break unnecessary habits. They reject unnecessary distractions and unnecessary indoctrination.

143. **Psychedelic Exorcism**
Psychedelics cause the hidden mental demons of one's mind to scatter, but they can return with a feverish vengeance by successfully using your biggest fears against you and convincing you to never touch psychedelics again.

144. Give the most intelligent zoo animals access to psilocybin mushrooms so they can escape their restricting and disempowering zoo anytime they please. This could also provide new insights into the creation and development of consciousness.

145. Cannabis and all psychedelics are a technological shortcut to increased self-awareness and self-mastery.

146. Psychedelics: proof of cosmic mercy?

147. Why do so many people seem to need permission to intertwine with drugs that sprout from the ground? It is clear that we evolved alongside them and that this divorce is something we now tend to look to therapists, gurus, and preachers for as substitutes. What are the effects of allowing our governments to sever symbiotic relationships and experiences with natural psychedelics? Less conscious, less creative, less empathetic, less purposeful, and less self-empowered people.

148. Without nature's help, being stupid, brainwashed, or masochistic is the only way not to be troubled by life, death, and people.

149. STDs: nature's way of filtering out chaotic promiscuity brought on by childhood sexual abuse?

150. 'Know Thyself': a psychedelic motto/message.

151. Psychedelics: potentiality attractors.

152. Drugs alone cannot create a great thinker or artist. It takes the right genes, the refinement and strong utilization of inborn talents, the honest, creative, and enduring utilization of untold suffering, mysterious experiences, close-calls with death and brushes with insanity, mixed with all of the art one has ingested and experienced, the different places one has traveled and the different people one has met.

153. If they only understood themselves better, they would not have to be so afraid of themselves. The main reason why people who need psychedelic intervention will not accept it is that they are afraid of what they will discover about themselves and their universe. They are afraid of their own potential.

154. You are an integral part of this planet.

155. Always take psychedelics while in a pleasant mood. Your trip will be more likely to be constructive. Taking them while unhappy or uneasy is asking for a negative and useless trip.

156. **The Paradox Of Cannabis**
The very thing that helps one imagine new ideas helps one to forget them.

157. Could networks of mushrooms and trees be utilized to power homes and cities?

158. Even psychedelics are not enough for some people to escape being indoctrinated or to escape the belief that they already know the answer to everything.

159. **Psychedelics Are Best Used Alone**
If you are especially uncomfortable around human beings, never do psychedelics around them.

160. Natural drugs are a relief and a refuge from the sufferings of life. Many animals on Earth know all too well how necessary to life some drugs and poisons are if utilized for peace, tranquility, and innovation.

161. Psychedelics are more difficult to explore than meditation. I have never had to prepare for meditation, but I always prepare myself for psychedelics, no matter how experienced I become with them. Psychedelics are tools that can be used to enhance meditation and every other creative, intellectual, or spiritual activity.

162. Psychedelic meditation: a creative act.

163. The longevity of a species, a civilization, or a lifeform is dependent on how it responds to pain and trauma.

164. The quality of a human society depends on the drugs it regularly utilizes.

Humans & Aliens

1. At different times and under different circumstances, we each are gods who love ourselves and each other, and we each are devils who hate ourselves and each other.

2. We are the moving hands of the clock. We are the mortal measurement of time.

3. Why have we evolved with brains capable of storing far more information than what we would ever need for survival?

4. **Rays Of Light**
Do not let the finality of life keep your head under the depths of sorrow. No particle of light regrets its singular role to shine.

5. The human mind is born addicted to information.

6. The UFO: the transcendental piper of greater potentiality.

7. **The Secret Of The UFO**
The universe is as alive as we are, and we are its pilot.

8. The more one becomes aware of people and their behavior, the more brilliantly comedic and entertaining life becomes.

9. Some people are addicted to being sober.

10. The human mind and body strive for progress and show signs of degradation in states of prolonged stagnancy.

11. After three consecutive events occur to us, the human brain tends to believe there is purpose behind them. One knock is an accident. Two knocks are peculiar. Three knocks are intentional. Examples and forgiveness are often offered in threes. A genie grants only three wishes. Three strikes and you are out.

13. The less questioning a person is, the more fearful they are.

14. We are often controlled by our desire for control.

15. UFOs: harbingers of greater potentiality.

16. **Humankind: Earth's Chosen Heroes**
We have been granted access to the rapturous tide of the technological vacuum.

17. A human is born a brave and fatally wounded warrior, knowing not how long its life will last, nor what the end of its battle will bring.

18. A UFO sighting is an experience of mystical proportions, so invigorating and confounding one can feel ashamed and gluttonous for even looking for another to satisfy one's thirst for the other.

19. Just as we preserve, track, and study lifeforms less intelligent than ourselves, so does it seem likely that we are observed by life from other planets, more intelligent than us, and are as oblivious to being influenced and utilized by higher evolved life, as lab mice are to human scientists.

20. The philosopher's stone: the self-reflecting UFO.

21. Like aliens, we begin to appear the more we understand ourselves until we become our own abductors.

22. Human beings would be quite lovable if they were not so hateful and bitter towards themselves.

23. If any aliens wanted to understand us, all they would need is to study the internet. For it is a projection of our collective mind, a technological dream, and a true reflection of what we currently are and what we aspire to become on both a conscious and subconscious level.

24. We are the extraordinary result of millions of years of being tested and strengthened through the adaptation of life, which is rich with pain and trauma.

25. Envy can be so overwhelming for humans that they are not opposed to being jealous of the dead.

26. No one wants to feel different, but the truth is that everyone is different from one another and we must accept and attempt to understand and respect these differences, or we will never know peace.

27. The UFO experience and the psychedelic experience both are consciousness-expanding, ego-deflating experiences.

28. Humankind: a story of the tragic becoming magic. For the beginning of all magic is tragic.

29. Tears of sadness are the bodily release of built-up mental toxins which we vomit from our eyes.

30. There is nothing to trivialize about underwater organisms becoming primates which became shamans who shape-shifted into scientists who watch over our underwater brethren.

31. People tend to replace those who abandon them with objects or animals that are less likely than people to abandon them.

32. People either become or devalue what they envy, whichever is possible or believed to be possible.

33. Like a dying bee that uses its last energy to sting the surrounding air, people tend to place blame solely on external influences for internal problems.

34. Guilt keeps people together as much as it pulls people apart.

35. It need not offend us what we come from. For even an alien race that has advanced for millions of years has to start from smaller organisms and lower intelligent life.

36. As some animals test each other's horns through battle, the winner strengthening their species with more durable horns, humans test and strengthen their arguments with each debate.

37. **Four Primary Errors Of Humankind**
Most of our problems are consistently due to four errors: ignoring the self, ignoring the individual, ignoring history, and ignoring nature.

38. **Being Controlled By The Manipulation Of Self-Perception**
The people closest to us can control our decisions and even our thoughts by using our self-perceived identity against us, making us

feel guilty or ashamed for their own benefit, despite how much it may hurt us.

39. Stupidity: Predictable And Untrustworthy

Stupid people are easier to predict and control than intelligent people, but they are less trustworthy. For, unlike stupidity, intelligence requires a certain level of honesty, self-awareness, and self-control of which stupid people tend not to have.

40. How quickly our masks of loyalty fall off when we feel abandoned by a good friend, even when we are wrong to feel abandoned.

41. An animal being rescued and loved on by humans must be like being helped by incomprehensible gods.

42. We use certain people we come across most often to either harm ourselves with envy and shame or to challenge and improve ourselves.

43. An Extraterrestrial Perspective

To understand anything, one should imagine how a species from another planet, with equal or superior intelligence and technology, might perceive it.

44. Bitterness And Envy Towards Honesty

The more people show their honesty and guilt, the fewer people tend to relate to or sympathize with them. For people who are led more than they lead tend to be weak, dishonest and delusional, and find it too difficult, terrifying, and foreign to claim responsibility for their errors in thought and behavior, let alone to feel guilty over them or to use that remorse to improve their future thought and behavior.

45. Self-Punishment
Any personal or social problem we are capable of solving but refuse or fail to solve is our own fault, and due punishment is sure to follow unless the problem is understood and fixed.

46. Our ego gains no benefit from there existing other races of aliens, some more intelligent and technologically advanced, so we tend to ignore the topic as much as possible in favor of the fixations of the ego: beliefs, control, and self-distraction.

47. The Rarity Of Neutrality
Is there anything as rare and as underrated in the human race as a genuine neutral-thinker who does not limit their thoughts and solutions for secret biases?

48. Our only hope may be that a visiting alien race speaks the language of music.

49. How strange a creature humans are. They laugh at the same things they become aroused at, upset over, angry with, hateful towards, with the switch of situations, roles, times, moods, and environments.

50. Knocking On The Door Of Ego
All received experiences and information must first knock on the door of ego before being accepted and understood or rejected and misunderstood.

51. Human beings: life that is powerful, insecure, and generally shy about its powers and insecurities, unless bred in a society where it is normal to be prideful and confident in one's own power and potential, to remain aware of one's faults, and constantly improve

oneself. And of course, there have always existed those individuals who become great, despite the society from which they are grown.

52. One can often tell how insecure a person is by the number of insecure people they are attracted to.

53. A person who has been rejected or abused by a group is, without question, adopted into the group, if a different group appears, as if they were never rejected. For people love groups even more than they love ostracizing people from them.

54. **Anthropophobia**
Knowing what we know about the destructive potential of some people, whether their insanity be a birth defect or taught by another person, should we not react to all people the same way people react to certain insects, with shrieks of disgust and distrust?

55. Humor: a tool of the human mind that inspires and permits questions, invites new understanding, and rewards minds with pleasure for obtaining new knowledge, memories of information less likely to be forgotten or avoided. It is the laughing mind that is rewarded with more easily digestible information. For humor subsides the ego, which is a major hurdle in speculation and the acceptance of new information.

56. Humor: a discreetly rebellious act, capable of bypassing all personal and social expectations.

57. Our eyes help remove psychological toxins, through emotions that use socially transparent tears as their vehicle of release, as our livers remove physical toxins through urine, and our stomachs, through vomit or diarrhea.

58. Other than consciousness, art is what most separates us from all other life on Earth.

59. Errors Of Space And Time
Most of our problems are geological and time-based. We fight for beliefs that we would likely either ignore or reject if we grew up on a different part of the planet or were born in a different time.

60. People are the drug of choice for most people, even those who proudly proclaim to abstain from all drugs.

61. People Are Crippled By Peculiar Sensitivities And Expectations
It is rather difficult not to offend or alarm the average human.

62. Everyone has a favorite drug, whether it is art, knowledge, food, sports, politics, religion, or people.

63. The Selfishness Of Gossip
Whether they are known personally or not, the people we talk about most are subconsciously chosen reference points, used to compare and stabilize ourselves and our lives. Each person we speak of most works as the most personally convenient representations of what we avoid or aspire to become.

64. Being compatible with someone's life is usually more important to people than biological compatibility. For people will often overlook physical, emotional, and mental chemistry if their life habits are threatened or undermined.

65. The knowledge and power that await us all from simply being honest with ourselves and everyone else.

66. Most of our intellectual failures arise out of dishonesty.

67. Why is the human experience so short? Perhaps for the enhancement of creative effort, which only a short life span can yield.

68. Too many of us waste our lives on useless and unnecessary habits, as well as the useless and unnecessary habits of the people closest to us.

69. If you have to ask why, in nearly any problematic situation involving people, the answer is usually a problem with ego.

70. We are so easy to be laughed at as a species because we happen to be residing in an awkward puberty-like state of evolution, between animal and God. Will we become more serious or silly as we mature and become more like gods?

71. **The Necessary Discomfort Of Resolutions**
Soon, after a screaming match has been allowed to come to a finish by everyone involved, a peaceful feeling overcomes oneself and what feels like one's world, no matter how ugly one's surroundings may still be, similar to how one feels after vomiting out spoiled food, no longer unresolved in the stomach.

72. Whether they want to or not, all people learn and advance their minds.

73. **Our Purpose**
Creativity is not a mere entertaining option for human beings. For this is what we do: we gather knowledge and create something new with it.

74. People generally prefer solving virtual and unnecessary obstacles over solving real and necessary obstacles. This preference for denial and distraction has caused all too real suffering and bloodshed.

75. **Laughter Is As Much A Necessary Release Of Energy As Love And Sex**
We sometimes, even while alone, involuntarily laugh harder and longer at things we would not normally laugh so hard about, just as we sometimes find some people more attractive than other times, due to our fluctuating mental and bodily need for the release and absorption of loving and sexual energy.

76. **Understanding Humans Through Their Lies**
The most important thing for an alien race to know about the human race is that they are liars, and through their lies, they unknowingly reveal themselves.

77. **The Rejection Of Self (When The Failure To Become Someone Turns Into The Possession Of Someone Like Them)**
When some people cannot become or do not believe they can become someone they want to become, they try to own them or someone similar to them. If they cannot have them or believe they cannot, they try to become them.

78. **All That We Fear And All That We Believe Is Linked To The History Of Illness (Gods And Governments: Always Trusted To Be The Cure To Remove All Illnesses)**
The folklore of vampires and demons originates from the fear of blood-hungry and disease-transferring parasites like ticks, mosquitoes, and surprising illnesses of which appeared to sneak into homes at night, weakening or killing people in their sleep, tainting

their blood, degrading their minds, and sucking the life from entire cities. Blood has often been associated with illness. For example, during the Passover, when some people mark their doors with the blood of sheep in order to please and surrender to the hidden reapers of life, invisible to human eyes. An unseen enemy to primitive people, illness, needs an unseen hero to balance out the fight: a God or a government.

79. How perfectly fitting that the human brain, from a certain angle, has the appearance of a person curled up in the fetal position, like a lonely caterpillar with no personal proof of its next form, faithfully waiting patiently to awaken and freely stretch its beautifully rested spirit.

80. **The Glory And Pity Of Humankind**
What bothers us most is, even though we have become a planetary marvel, how much more pitiful our situation is than any other animal on Earth, though we pretend that they are in a worse position. For humans doth love being depended on, so much so that they have turned wolves into pugs. We are aware of our shortcomings and our failures. We dwell on the past and the future. We can foresee our inevitable demise. We have improved upon our animal brethren in many ways, but this does not make us any less pitiful. The more aware we become of ourselves, the more faults we find and the more ashamed of our more faulty past we become. But the more faults we can find and accept, the more faults we can eradicate, making us more rare, beautiful, powerful, and glorious. However, the more glorious we become, the more pitiful we become. For the loss of glory and all that has been accomplished and accumulated becomes that much more tragic and terrifying. It has become our responsibility to consciously become less pitiful and more glorious.

81. People who deny or are unaware that they are still part animal are the most animalistic people.

82. Laughter: a teacher, uniter, stress-reliever, and an ego-tamer.

83. Our minds and bodies reject a life without love and art.

84. Some people are comforted by the immortality of mystery, while some people are comforted by the belief that all mysteries are already solved.

85. **Two Different Minds**
Some people shake realities, and some people have their realities shaken.

86. Pets: slaves that we love so much we ensure they will never leave us, and even if they do, they will not be able to survive on their own.

87. **The Briefness And Supremeness Of Standing**
Before we are born, we lay down in a womb. After we die, we lay down in a tomb.

88. **Some People Date Disloyal People So That They Have An Excuse To Be Disloyal And To Remain A Victim**
Some people believe if they start a relationship as a victim, then they will remain the victim no matter what they do to their partners.

89. Humans were needed to birth new technology on this planet.

90. Nothingness: a concept people use to feel more at ease with all that we do not know beyond this life.

91. We tend to become romantically involved with people who align best with how we perceive ourselves.

92. It all usually comes down to whether or not someone wants to be offended by a joke, an idea, or a work of art.

93. The longer I live, the more alien I feel.

94. **Humankind: The Most Pitiful, Bitter, And Self-Abusive Animal**
Along with never having to dwell on past or future suffering, the permanent innocence of every animal but human mocks human beings: the only bitter creatures on Earth, all of whom know too well how swiftly and certain it is for innocence to be taken, without warning or permission. Although we like to pretend that all of our pets and surrounding wildlife are more pitiful than us, in truth, there is nothing on this planet more pitiful than human beings.

95. Everything people fear is linked to alienation.

96. **Contagious Signals**
Much like a group of people being influenced by one person to stop whatever they are doing and look up at the sky by staring and pointing at it, even if there is nothing to be seen, notice how easily and for how long people in a group can be influenced to whisper and how quickly it can spread, often without anyone in the group ever asking why, as soon as just one person begins whispering, no matter where the group is or what the topic being whispered is about.

97. The sense of humor between two different people becomes more similar the more similar is their level of conscious intelligence and their ability to rebel.

98. Some people are like belief-systems: they turn away new information.

99. Humans: The Most Disloyal Animal
When people lose their trust in people they usually turn to other animals for trust, affection, and attention. For no species of animal on Earth, besides human beings, turns to other animals for support once they are harmed by their own species.

100. How minuscule some of our most stressful problems are when we take into consideration how temporary our lives are here.

101. If empty space is not empty, then what is nothingness but a concept to make sense of somethingness?

102. There are three types of children: the actual children, the adults who cannot think or act beyond a religion or government, and the adults who cannot let go of their resentment towards being misled and hindered by an adult, religion, or government.

103. How often does our tendency to deny things we do not want to be true negatively affect our justice system and our future?

104. Many times have I wept for humankind. Time will reveal if humankind is worth crying over.

105. Human beings are the most capable, out of the entire animal kingdom, of rejecting information.

106. Like a defense mechanism, art is secreted from human minds, at the thought of love, death, and at times of great stress.

107. The Transfer Of Insecurities
Jealousy is used by the most insecure people to make other people

more insecure, too by pretending to be more confident and secure than they really are.

108. Some people deny their own faults so much that they deny even the repercussions of their faults. They learn to endure, if not enjoy, their punishment without accepting it as such, instead of learning from it and using it to work on their faults.

109. **Fear: Passion Fuel For The Weak Of Spirit**

Most people are at their most passionate when they are afraid. They are also passionate when they are livid or when they hate. Hate and anger are the children of fear. For wherever you find hate and anger growing, you will find underneath them the roots of fear.

110. **Being Vain About Not Being Vain**

People tend to believe celebrities who are widely considered ugly to have just as much merit as celebrities who are widely considered attractive because of the assumption that they must be talented or important if they are ugly and still famous.

111. When a person is incapable or unwilling to think ahead or to make sense of the past, they live in the moment and brag incessantly about it.

112. **An Important Distinction Among Humankind**

There are people who live, so long as they can work and people who work, so long as they can live.

113. Some people increasingly become more abusive and controlling the more empathy they are offered.

114. **Arguments: Explosions Usually Ignited By Both Argumenters**

Notice how an argument can ignite and explode over seemingly nothing. It is never nothing, however. It is a subconscious release, repressed for too long, of two people who are feeling abnormally insecure or upset and are frustratingly waiting for the other to detonate before they explode together. The explosion is often ignited by one person acting as if the other person has already blown up to an exaggerated degree before they actually have. For both know that one another are going to eventually explode and neither understand why until after the fire and smoke have settled from their detonation if they ever do understand.

115. Resentment: the most dangerous, persistent, and underestimated of all biases.

116. Our species needs less pity and more empowered thought, less guilt, and more loving action.

117. **Pain Prolongs Guilt And Guilt Prolongs Pain**

Some people believe if they allow others to hurt them or if they inflict pain upon themselves as payment to the cosmos, they will receive forgiveness in return and will be freed from guilt.

118. Low-minded people collect people.
High-minded people collect ideas.

119. **A Prevalent Divide Among People**

There are those who focus on past ideas and past solutions during conversation and those who create new questions, ideas, and solutions during conversation.

120. Some people give the appearance of being allergic to honesty and speculation.

121. If we think with the assumption that there are other planets in their own galaxy, with conscious thinking beings, some still stuck on their own planet, and some perhaps have populated multiple planets and might already be aware of not being alone in their universe, then we can one by one, more effectively redefine, clarify and reevaluate all of our beliefs and certainties and all of our weaknesses and strengths.

122. People who never question anything are more harmful, more aggravating, and less useful than people who question everything.

123. **A Constant Divide Humankind Suffers From**
The problem humankind always faces is the divide between those who have been indoctrinated and conditioned to obey anyone but themselves and those who have not.

124. The average person is a mere casualty of their government or their religion.

125. The only possibilities we are currently aware of are human.

126. We do not understand what could be possible and this frightens and enrages people because we tend to believe we are the most special life in the cosmos. If we could accept the possibility that we are not the greatest of what the universe has to offer maybe we could treat each other and our planet with more respect, or perhaps we could not handle that kind of a realization.

127. It is not loss but uncertainty that tortures people most?

128. There comes an exciting, constructive, and emboldening relief during times of great boredom when one realizes that everyone is stuck in the same position of uncertainty, even those who do not have to worry about money.

129. Our world is divided by masters and pupils.

130. We must stay informed, and we must remain honest and unbiased in our thinking to be able to stand a chance against our oppressors, whichever form they take and whatever false promises they make.

131. What will we do when we are capable of proving definitively that we are not the best of what this expanding universe has to offer? We will no longer be able to feel as confident as we currently do about our own beliefs and certainties. Look how we began and how simple a lifeform we once were. Now, look at what we have become. Our potential is still as vast as it was when we began. We do not know how versatile life can be or how strong, enduring, and creative life can become, nor do we know how diverse the possible conditions for life are. We are more ignorant of what is possible than we want to believe, and this causes us to disregard the possibility of life as intelligent or more intelligent than human beings, existing on other planets, and to ignorantly feel content and confident with this assumption.

132. **Denial And Dishonesty: Our Worst Vices**
People suffer more than necessary because not enough people think rationally and honestly. They prolong lies, mistakes, and problems. They repeat them, deny them and defend them. Then they blame the resulting repercussions on anything but themselves.

133. The minds of human beings from their origin to the present and developing onward into the future are part of a hierarchy of potentially infinite degrees of greatness, sophistication, and complexity.

134. People do not need to be pitied. They need empowered.

135. What if all that humans ever have is each other? What if we betray ourselves and one another every moment we do not accept this possibility?

136. Some people cannot change their minds because they invest so much time and energy on certain beliefs until the thought of changing their minds becomes a fear of losing their identity and their sanity.

137. **Becoming One's Mistakes By Justifying One's Mistakes And Justifying One's Mistakes By Becoming One's Mistakes** How many peoples' actions and thoughts are determined by their mistakes and how they respond to them, with either expulsion or inclusion from their identities?

138. The more we deny our animal ancestry, the more we behave like them.

139. People control or attempt to control how each other lives through guilt, shame, and jealousy.

140. All of us are in a battle against the different ways we deal with our problems.

141. We curse at each other so that we do not physically hurt one another.

142. There are no mysteries in a human family, only hidden shame.

143. The most nightmarish thing about human beings is not the pain they are able to inflict on others, but their knack for deluding themselves into believing that something did not occur, which actually did, or that something did occur, which actually did not.

144. **We Are More Accepting Of Problems Than Solutions**
When solutions to our problems arrive, we often treat them like we should treat our problems: we remove them.

145. Modern man, by and large, has been convinced by its many leaders and belief-systems that he is nothing but a sinful and shameful pawn.

146. People are separated most by what they think and how they think.

147. If you took away the taste and the necessity of food, eating with people is more like a group of people ceremonially taking drugs.

148. **War: A Primitive Solution To Disagreements And A Modern Solution To Greed**
We used to start wars over beliefs. Now we start wars over money.

149. **Our Delight For Pitiful Things**
We like to own and control things that are sick and weak without us.

150. **The Grey Creature**
We are no longer animals, but we have yet to become the Gods we could become.

151. Humans torture the most because they have been tortured the most.

152. Arguments: usually the result of a communication failure.

153. **The Only Strength The Weak Possess**
Weak people can be more terrifying than strong people. For weak people have little or no sense of respect or honor for strong people, but strong people tend to have hope for the weak and would like to see them become strong too.

154. We tend to show more respect for quiet, calm, serious, and patient people than loud, impulsive, frivolous, and impatient people because they tend to be more trustworthy, more confident, more conscious, and more likely to know more about suffering and how to overcome it. They wear it on their face, carry it with their demeanor and express it with their art, like battle scars.

155. Most people are too selective of when and how often they can be happy.

156. We were all once a parasite that used a woman as a host to come into this world.

157. Bias is one of the most dangerous threats to human beings.

158. What is the major difference between us and the rest of the animal kingdom? We physically and sexually abuse each other to the point of confusion and resentful rejection.

159. Men and women wrestle in their minds between people who can easily be controlled and people who can hardly be controlled.

160. The reason we obsess over pain more than happiness is because suffering is a problem every mind wishes to solve, and pleasure and happiness are not.

161. **The Protection Of Storms**
Even the most evil people hide when it storms.

162. No other animal but humans punish themselves for being happy.

163. The majority of people are not hunting for the truth. They are hunting for confirmation and comfort.

164. **Our Risky Bias Towards Happiness**
People tend to believe and listen most to the people who they believe to be happiest.

165. The only thing which makes some people angry enough to speak up is when their government is disobeyed.

166. Our beliefs, our values, and our judgments, our assumptions, our lies, and our delusions all communicate with each other more often than we communicate with each other.

167. Have people's beliefs killed more people than people have killed people?

168. Some people are addicted to being perceived as a victim and to perceiving themselves as a victim. They may set someone up who they know will hurt them, or they may even set themselves up to reinforce their own victim identity.

169. The human brain is like a transformative cocoon that contains far more struggle, movement, information, and change than it ap-

pears to contain on the outside from the perspective of its observers.

170. We have to learn not to excessively beat ourselves up and habitually hate ourselves for still retaining some of our distant, but still genetically present, primitive ancestry. We have come a long way and have become rather peaceful in comparison to our origins, but we are not yet the angelic beings we can become. For we are capable of becoming even greater and more peaceful still.

171. Most of us project our moments of existential angst onto the people around us, or we place that burden onto ourselves and believe this is any healthier. It is most wise and healthy to be creatively productive during these moments.

172. Hypocrisy is more dangerous and rampant than racism. Anyone who hates racism can also become racist. This adds more hate to hate. Many wars have been created and died for because collections of people could not admit that they were fighting for the same beliefs and the same creator but with different names, titles and labels.

173. Prolonged fear in humans causes primitive and dangerous thoughts and behavior to boil to the surface. All people are equally hateful and dangerous if enough fear and propaganda are pumped into them.

174. Empathy can be taught out of people. All of their fears and hardships can then easily be blamed on any person, race, belief, or sexuality. Indoctrinated, biased, and collective thinking is what is ruining us and is what has always ruined us.

175. The most common divide between human beings is the rich and the poor. The poor are more oppressed, but they can teach themselves to break free from poverty.

176. Pity, fear and guilt weaken people. Resentment and dishonesty finish them off.

177. The power of the human mind is equal to the fragility of the human mind.

178. When we assume the worst about people, we are more likely to express the worst of ourselves and justify it.

179. **Two Types Of People**
Some refuse to be victims, and some refuse to be victors.

180. People who have the most excuses to complain are often the least likely to complain because they have more experience with adapting to suffering and are more hardened because of it, and therefore less likely to complain.

181. The human brain is more advanced and more valuable than the most expensive smartphone, but how many people trust and rely more on their phones than their own minds? How many people spend more time and energy on their phones than their own lives?

182. Some women naturally seek bold and daring men until they are hurt by a man too bold and too daring and use him as an excuse to seek less bold and less daring men.

183. Those who cross us immediately carry the burden of every person who has ever crossed us.

184. The gut is feeling.
The brain is thinking.
The heart is knowing.

185. Nearly every person we meet is directly or indirectly the result of the suffering we have endured, along with our reaction to the suffering?

186. From one pleasure to the next, we chase pleasure without rest. Even as we sleep, we continue to chase it. Even rejecting pleasure is a pleasure, however secret.

187. **The Angel And The Devil In Our Ears**
There is a part of us that hates ourselves and a part of us that loves ourselves.

188. We continue repeating history, being controlled by propaganda and voting for the same people, not only because we do not learn enough about history but because many of us subconsciously want to relinquish our control and enjoy the death of history and ourselves.

189. People do not want to think that they hate themselves or are apathetic or abusive towards themselves, but they usually are and do, for one reason or another. They are often taught that they should.

190. If you want to find the truth or create something great, think like an alien—anything but a spiteful, biased, and delusional human.

191. **Humankind: Stuck Between Animal And God**
We struggle between hating and degrading ourselves over our animalistic side and loving and refining ourselves over our godly side.

192. We are afraid of what we know and what we do not know.

193. People generally like reading about criminals because it distracts them from their own crimes and their own suffering.

194. People enjoy having people work for them, even if that means slaving away for others to do so.

195. If only it were harder to speak, we might say less stupid and hurtful things.

196. **Unmasking Problems (Band-Aids On Bullet Wounds)**
People have a problem with masking problems and of letting others dictate exactly how they should deal with their problems instead of figuring it out themselves.

197. **The Most Damaged Animal Is The Most Conscious Animal**
Only the most conscious animal on Earth knows what it is like to be abused by the same people who are supposed to help protect them from being abused.

198. Sometimes people share their news of good fortune, not to be congratulated but to be wanted and envied.

199. What most people become is largely a welcoming or rejecting reaction to the people around them.

200. Most religions incorporate immortality.

201. May We Live Forever In This Life Or The Next

We should not limit ourselves when God is not limiting us. We have been given the ability to create science and medical technology that help us live longer with our families. There is no reason not to continue to utilize this gift instead of looking forward to death, which none of the living know anything about.

202. Humans are gods of this planet, compared to every other lifeform on Earth, and surely there are lifeforms greater than humans.

203. We have the ability and the natural tools to be happier and less hateful people, but many of us are too self-deprecating and self-avoidant to allow this.

204. Stubbornly Resentful Creatures

When people are shamed or insulted for thinking a certain way, they tend to think even more that way, even if their thoughts are self-destructive. Perhaps especially if they are self-destructive.

205. Human Beings Are Human Beings, No Matter Where They Sprout

Although they were never anymore innocent than we were and were never without the fear of war from neighboring tribes, Native Americans found a more peaceful way to live that did not involve the creation of homeless people or the bombing of children for profit, or keeping people in prison for using medicinal plant and fungal life. The state commits the same evil acts of which Native Americans were guilty but on a global scale with the misuse of greater technology. We are capable of more evil and destruction than Native Americans were ever capable of, but we are distracted by our political circus and blinded by our pride and allegiance to the state, in hopes that it will eventually perceive, appreciate and treat us as individuals. We are also capable of becoming greater beings than ever before, depending on how we use our time, energy, and will.

206. Are the different shapes of UFOs people witness a simplified translation of a more complex dimension? Maybe they are not triangle, sphere, and cigar-shaped. We might not be able to comprehend what their craft looks like to them because they are made of technology we cannot yet comprehend. Is this why some of their craft appear to shapeshift?

207. We often attack people who have nothing to do with why we attack them.

208. Aliens of equal or greater intelligence would have a more honest perception of humans than humans do.

209. **Sky-Fish (Deep Space Life)**
Like some underwater life, UFOs use flashing lights and colors to mesmerize their observers. Some change shape. Some even abduct their observers while they are in a trance, like a famished Cuttlefish.

210. Look at the many differences between us and the lower animals on earth. Watch how we observe, alter, and protect them without them ever fully understanding what we are doing. Since this is happening on earth then why is it so difficult for some people to believe that this same dynamic does not end with us?

211. I am more distrusting of people than aliens.

212. Our only hope may be an alien race more advanced than us that cares more about our existence and our future than we do, as

we care for and care about less complex lifeforms more than they are capable of caring for and caring about themselves.

213. How often are people's open fear of the end of their world a secret desire for the end of their world?

214. People reveal their disingenuous and delusional nature when one realizes how easily they could have been born and raised as the people they are convinced are their mortal enemy.

Values & Morality

1. People are often judged by what they represent to others rather than what they are.

2. The meaning of existence: the existence of meaning.

3. Meaning: the alien wilderness, illuminated by the torch of consciousness.

4. Evil: the enemy of higher potentiality.

5. All life collects and creates for a purpose greater than itself.

6. A higher intelligence inherits higher moral duties or suffers historical consequences.

7. In the end, what matters is how high one reached within one's spectrum of potentiality.

8. **A Moral Question**
Would you do unto others as you would have a God do unto us all?

9. **The Secret Question**
Some people feel guilty for sharing secrets, and some people feel

guilty for not sharing secrets. Which side is most moral? What does one's answer to this question say about one's moral character?

10. **The Moral Act Of Reason**
Excluding those incapable of reasoning to consistently follow reason is generally a sign of higher morality.

11. The greater the intelligence and consciousness of a species, the more that species will need morality, and the more likely it will be interested in being moral and in exercising and protecting its moral values.

12. **The Growth Of Moral Values**
Higher complexity contains the capacity for higher moral values, which must adapt according to the level of complexity of its practitioners.

13. **Ethics Based On The Necessity And Growth Of Our Children**
The forced confrontation with morality is brought on by the ever-present guidance of our children, who have a much less biased perception of humankind and our world. They are made of the most fragile potentiality. Are not the vulnerable and changing inhabitants of our future worthy of being our major focus rather than focusing merely on the unchanging adults of the present who cannot hide their bias when making important decisions?

14. The extent of your reality and your value depends on how much of your reality you can endure and what you can extract from it.

15. Morality: a magic trick, pulling us out of the dark top hat of human history. For to pretend is sometimes transformative and necessary to become what we aspire to be.

16. Does it matter what something once was? A thing is what it becomes.

17. **The Dangers Of Morality**
Morality can influence people to kill themselves or each other.

18. Will we and should we be able to render morality obsolete by making the choice to upgrade ourselves into beings too self-enhanced by technology to ever waste time and energy being self-destructive, hateful, or violent?

19. **Immorality: Self-Hatred, Self-Apathy, And Self-Degradation**
Self-hatred and self-degradation lead to disorder and the hatred for and degradation of others.

20. **Morality: Self-Love And Self-Refinement**
Self-love and self-refinement lead to higher-order and the love for and refinement of others.

21. Sometimes to abstain from over-indulgence is to over-indulge in abstinence.

22. All things exist, necessarily, as or for some outcome or mean.

23. **Vigilantism: Free Justice And The Prolongation Of Revenge**
Though they would rarely admit it, people are envious of the vigilante. They tend to enjoy hearing revenge stories where justice is

served without permission from the state, but if the act of free and unconstrained justice continues, the vigilante becomes perceived as an enemy as immoral as the criminals.

24. What separates the weak from the strong primarily is how much one is willing to accept in regards to oneself and one's reality and how far one is willing to go to meet one's greater potential.

25. All that matters is where you place your energy.

26. **The Dark Side Of Guilt**

Giving in to guilt, no matter how trivial the mistake, can lead directly to self-destruction. Similarly, guilt-tripping someone can be their last guilt-trip.

27. **Victims Of Morality**

Jesus and Socrates were betrayed by their morals. They attempted to set in stone morals in a world, universe, and reality that are never set in stone.

Max Stirner describes best how Socrates was victimized by his morals, "For Socrates, because in culture he stood on the level of morality, it would have been an immorality if he had been willing to follow Crito's seductive incitement and escape from the dungeon; to remain was the only moral thing. But it was solely because Socrates was-a moral man. The 'unprincipled, sacrilegious' men of the Revolution, on the contrary, had sworn fidelity to Louis XVI, and decreed his disposition, yes, his death; but the act was an immoral one, at which moral persons will be horrified to all eternity."[19]

28. Morality: an abandonment of living, in favor of rules to live by.

29. Morality cannot Be Set In Stone Because Reality Is Not Set In Stone

Morals must be adaptable to change, or they are not moral.

30. Morality: as natural a construct as consciousness, love, and photosynthesis?

31. What Are The Implications Of Morality Being Natural?

If morality is as natural a construct as breathing, is morality also as fundamental to conscious life as breathing?

32. A High-Quality Life

The quality of one's mind and life are mostly determined by the quality of habits, drugs, and their effects (empowering, productive, and healing) one synthesizes themselves with. Love, art, and cannabis, for example.

33. Evil: always underestimates its own self-destructive nature.

34. Evil: Made Of Chosen Errors (Evil: Sustained Errors)

How many errored decisions does it take to establish, grow and sustain evil and suffering in a human society? For a murderer is made by a combination of many particular errors, some before they were even born but mostly errors made during upbringing.

35. The Mercy Of Our Cosmos

Evil cannot last long before it degrades and destroys itself. It is as if our universe has a bias against evil and suffering for long periods of time.

36. Only Self Can Forgive Self

If you cannot forgive yourself, no person or God can do it for you, and you will surely degrade yourself.

37. It is better to pause entertainment for enlightenment than to pause enlightenment for entertainment. Then again, is not entertainment a part of enlightenment?

38. The Lone Self-Leading Wolf Is Potentially More Virtuous Than The Crowd Of Self-Fleeing Lambs

Virtue takes strength, thought, confidence and action. For one cannot be virtuous by being weak, question-less, indifferent, and inactive.

39. The Relativity Of Guilt And Morality

Guilt is a feeling people are trained to habitually allow themselves to suffer from through self or society, when their actions bring destruction to themselves or others, whether the destruction is accurately or falsely perceived, the amount of pain the kind of pain deserved, for how long and for what reason, depending mostly on when, where and by whom one is born and raised as well as how much money and power one has. Guilt is exasperated and taken advantage of by different, often contradicting religious beliefs, rules, and societal expectations. Guilt is always more useful to the collective than to the individual and always less dangerous for the collective than for the individual. For, as Nietzsche recognized, there are but two kinds of morality: master and slave. Consequently, there are two kinds of guilt: master and slave.

40. The Drug Of Choice For Prudes

To get high from refusing to get high.

41. Ceaseless Testing To Determine Value

The surest way to determine the value of something is repetitious testing. For it is only through repeated testing, from all angles, the endurance, power, and higher potentiality of a thing, that we can determine its value.

42. Love Over Law
If one has to choose between love and law, choose love every time. For without love, law inevitably becomes corrupt, and if everyone were to always choose law over love, all love would be devoured by corrupt laws created by corrupt law-makers.

43. Time: the greatest measurer of the value of a work of art.

44. The Peace Of Vanity
The fear of shame and of appearing to be weak and without control from showing anger stops more violence than any peaceful and loving thought or act.

45. The Importance Of Taste And Value
Taste and values are part of nearly everything people think and do. For bad taste and poor valuations can lead to a lifetime of misery and regret.

46. Karma: the self-degradation of guilt, no matter how repressed.

47. The Post-Judgement Of A Mind
Basing a mind's value on all that would be lost if the mind had never existed. This requires, however, waiting for the mind to finish its life journey.

48. Seriousness: more useful and less costly than silliness?

49. Common things: dispensable.
Great things: indispensable.

50. All good things seek love, order, and transcendence.

51. Children contain more potential than adults, hence why the most dangerous of prisoners draw the line of immorality at violence towards children. Even they sense an attack on the value of pure potentiality, which they believe must be defended and avenged.

52. The complexity of artistic taste enhances with the complexity of a mind.

53. The greatest valuators direct the attention of the masses away from the weakest values and towards the most powerful and enduring values from which all weak values must inevitably answer to.

54. **There Is No Perpetual Power Without Perpetual Peace**
Goodness can get more out of power than evil. Evil cannot control its own destructive and self-destructive nature, inhibiting its own growth and the growth of its surroundings. For power cannot grow without peace.

55. **The Contradicting Qualities Of A Great Valuator**
Experienced and child-like.
Daring and careful.
Strong and sensitive.
Opportunistic and patient.
Realistic and optimistic.
Detached and self-aware.

56. Since we can recognize that one piece of art is not as clear, as inspiring, as influential, as strengthening, as healing, or as useful as

another, this means it is possible to prove the higher value of one work of art over another.

57. History, the longer, the better, makes valuations both easier to determine and more accurate.

58. Value: potentiality.

59. To have good taste means to be attracted to styles of artistic expression that steer one away from error, ambiguity, apathy, illness, and decay, more often guiding one, instead, towards higher clarity, creativity, appreciation, health and growth.

60. There is no evil on Earth without human life?

61. All evil is destructive, but not all destruction is evil.

62. Think and live as if you are dreaming.

63. Evil inevitably implodes.

64. All people are addicted to something. What matters is the quality of what we choose to be addicted to.

65. Do things for other people that will make you love yourself more.

66. Before they are gone, think about the greatest aspects of your friends, as if they were gone.

67. There are permanent repercussions for certain temporary actions.

68. **Greater Values And Greater Valuators**
Nearly all problems of a culture derive from a stagnant and apa-

thetic taste for values. We must become less of a consumer of values and more of a valuator of values. For a greater order of life requires greater values and valuators.

"Valuing is creating: hear it, ye creating ones! Valuation itself is the treasure and jewel of the valued things." - Friedrich Nietzsche[20]

69. Being Picky With One's Taste For Values

It is more rewarding to have a picky taste than the taste of someone who views all things as being of equal quality.

70. Why are there so many boundaries, and why do we have the ability to overcome them? Because boundaries create greater and freer beings capable of overcoming them.

71. If for lack of any other reason, live for the sublime art of the future.

72. Guilt And Morality

Since we cannot all agree on how much and for how long guilt is necessary or unnecessary, and sometimes we continue to have guilt for something we have been forgiven for, directly by the person wronged, whether or not they were aware of ever being wronged, and we are not all taught the same rules for guilt and cannot agree on everything that deserves the feeling of guilt, then is guilt a prime example of a sometimes useful and sometimes damaging tool that has survived our ancestors? Can we not say the same about human morality as a whole? Is guilt the original author of morality?

73. An Insight For Valuators

The greater the quantity of something, the easier its quality can be determined.

74. There is a profound difference between a wolf and a pug but the relativist claims they are of equal quality.

75. **The Gods Await**
If only we could but feast our eyes on just one planet with life that has advanced to the point of being able to, like interstellar wizards, use their planet and universe as a playground.

76. **Valuation Training**
Practice filtering out art from your favorite artists that are only attractive to you because of the personal bias or nostalgia it triggers in you.

77. The different valuations of art derive mostly from differences in the quality of valuators.

78. Some people should not follow the golden creed, "Treat others as you want to be treated."[21] For if they hate themselves enough, they may want to be treated with hatred and alienation, which would mean they should treat others the same. This is less a problem with the creed than a problem with people.

79. Treat others as if you will eventually experience being them. Is there a more spine-straightening creed?

80. There is no purpose more fruitful than to build a private intellectual life. A time dedicated to learning, writing, reading, and creative thinking. A temporary safe-haven from the expectations of culture, society, friends, and family, temporary because no one should ever permanently stop socializing or taking care of responsibilities as a lover, friend, parent, and a natural member of planet Earth and the human species. However, to stay creative, inquisi-

tive, and mentally healthy, everyone needs time alone just as much as everyone needs to socialize.

81. Settling For Lower Taste (The Impatience Of The Masses)

Greatness never comes as often as people want it to, so they sometimes pretend that new creations of minds less brilliant are just as valuable.

82. Master Valuators: Master Selectors

A great writer of thoughts knows best what to keep and what to omit. It is the same with great valuators.

83. People with weak minds are more attracted to the power of money, while more powerful minds are more attracted to the power of knowledge.

84. Survival Systems

Morality: a natural order which forms for the survival of a collective. This is made evident by how all moral systems and their followers treat the individual versus how they treat the collective: immorally towards the individuals who are perceived by the collective to be threatening to the survival of the moral-system of the collective.

85. The Morality Monster

Morality is a monster with good intentions that devoured Jesus and Socrates.

86. All Thievery Is Self-Thievery

A person who steals from another person steals something from themselves, likely more rare, valuable, and enduring than the objects they are stealing: a friendship with someone who has similar enough taste and interests to want to steal from them in the first place.

87. Evil: anything which hinders or halts the growth of consciousness, knowledge, or technology.

88. Becoming A Greater Valuator

Surround yourself with art that is creatively, intellectually, and emotionally stimulating, with constant self-honesty and focused experience, study, and appreciation, and your valuation of all things will progressively change as you sophisticate your taste in art and begin to surround yourself only with art that progressively changes you.

89. Evil: the willfully weak.

90. Human Value: Based Largely On Dependency

One tends to become less valuable, if not worthless, to the people and systems one no longer depends on.

91. The Good Can Become Greater

Good people are like good murdering soldiers who are convinced that they are only as good and valuable as they are obedient.

92. Morality Originates From Sickness And Its Dangers

As Nietzsche alluded, "Were morality and illness originally connected perhaps?"[22] Did morality begin with the fear and paranoia of illnesses and the different precautionary measures used against them? Is this why people who are considered evil are also called sick, why cleanliness is next to Godliness and why good manners are usually connected to proper hygiene and the appearance of sanity and good health in a health-conscious society? Illnesses of body and mind were once confidently blamed on demons. In ignorant and frightening times such as these, virtues that foster independent thought, curiosity, and creativity are considered evil vices of which the practitioners of these virtues are punished and made an example of, so as to direct everyone away from sharing the same sickly values. Ironically, this kind of thinking ensures the growth of the pestilence of closed-ended belief-systems and a pandemic of their dangerous and destructive beliefs and values. For as we are now fortunate enough to understand, demon possession and the belief in demon possession is really the contraction of a dangerous and contagious virus or disease of our minds, of which only live to drain life from their hosts, hence the verse from 1 Peter 5:8, "Be sober, be vigilant; because your adversary the devil, as a roaring lion, walketh about, seeking whom he may devour."[23]

93. Infinite Creations
Like knowledge, technology, and possibility, meaning is created, not discovered.

94. Monetary riches may be accidentally inherited, but true merit and wealth must be obtained vigorously and with great purpose.

95. Morality: the different strategies used for the awareness and advancement of the self and the collective.

96. Masters Of Self-Enslavement (Towards Self-Mastery)
Governments, politics, and religions are created to turn our species into masters of morality, or masters of thought and action, but with this ongoing pursuit, we have turned ourselves into a self-ignorant, self-despising, incessantly disagreeing, and disastrously stubborn species. We have become, yet again, victims of morals and slaves to morality and are suffering more for it. It is time we become masters of our own thoughts and actions, without the

chains of politics and religions dulling our self-awareness, our creativity, our thoughts, and our actions. For governments, religions and politics are the masters of our thought and behavior, all of which work together for their own benefit, slowing down and often ceasing the movement altogether of our mental and conscious advancement, as they have always done throughout human history.

97. For some people, being a moral person means limiting the freedom of the individual in order to comfort the collective.

98. **Far Out Valuations**
Determine the value of a work of art by viewing or listening to it from the perspective of the future.

99. **Being Good Solely To Avoid Pain**
We avoid the guilt and regret that always comes from doing wrong to others more than we avoid doing wrong to others?

100. Morality: a way to either gain control of ourselves or to feel in control of ourselves.

101. Someone's inability to notice or appreciate your value will always be their problem, so long as you have built and determined your worth for yourself.

102. **Cosmic Morality**
"Whatever supports existence is good. Whatever rejects existence is bad," so sayeth the cosmos.

103. **The Primary Virtue Of The Majority**
To allow oneself to be overworked by others instead of oneself. This virtue, however, is seen for the weak and fraudulent virtue that it is when someone who has spent the majority of their life

working and sacrificing time, energy, their family, their relationships, their life, and themselves for their job, suddenly is not working for a period of time, however short and regardless of how much they have worked for others in the past. The envy of those who notice this period of potential creative freedom and healing for oneself and one's family is palpable and humorous. They would have every single adult and child slaving away without any individual purpose if they were permitted to wield their master's whip for a change.

104. Morality: When Mankind Attempts To Become God-kind

To live under the control of our morals and their systems is to pretend to be more than human. To base our lives, our thoughts, and our actions on belief-systems or value-systems is to either become or pretend to be more than our pre-moral forms.

105. Trauma: The Origin Of Guilt

Guilt: the painful empathetic memory of someone else's pain that you directly or indirectly caused. Guilt survives humankind's traumatizing past and is felt when one traumatizes oneself by traumatizing someone else.

106. The Death Of Justice

Justice ends when judges become afraid of the power of rich criminals. For money eventually turns everything into a cold business, even justice.

107. You Are What You Become

How many good people were once people who committed hateful and violent acts? Does it matter what one used to be? Is not what we become more important than what we once were? Should a flower's beauty be judged before it blossoms?

108. What is right? All things created in the name of love. What is good? All things created in the name of greatness.

109. Judgments Cannot Be Trusted Without Obtaining Control Over Oneself

The average person does not know how to judge the quality of artwork. They judge art politically or with some selfish and biased motive or agenda and always leave behind a trail that leads back to their identities and the beliefs and people associated with the development of their identities which they defend tooth and nail.

110. Higher Expectations Of Art

We must become more particular about the art with which we surround ourselves if we want to realize higher dreams of higher freedom and higher potentiality.

111. Goodness: loving, peaceful and appreciative greatness.

112. The History Of Morality

The history of morality is the history of human guilt and regret. It is the history of human fears and desires.

113. The things we value are open to being upgraded or downgraded with time.

114. Higher values: powerfully constructive causes and effects.

115. Higher Potentiality: The Good, The True And The Beautiful (A Basis For Moral Valuations)

The higher potentiality of all things is not just what could be but what should be.

116. Wicked Weakness (It Is Easier To Rot Than To Ripen)

Only the most savage of people have the weakest self-control, empathy, love, loyalty, and honesty. It is easy to become evil and destructive. It takes more strength and courage to be good, unique, and novel.

117. The Retardation Of Evil

Some knowledge requires empathy: a change of perspective.

118. Things Must Be Repairably Or Irreparably Harmed Before Their Value Is Recognized

The beauty and the artistic value of the Notre Dame cathedral were rarely spoken of and nearly forgotten by modern people until it caught ablaze.

119. The Valuation Of People Using Their Thoughts And Creations

The quality of a person can be determined based on the quality of their thoughts and creations. The quality of a person's thoughts and creations can be determined based on how powerfully influential they are, their ability to inspire greater thoughts and creations, and how adaptable they are to new discoveries and creations in the future.

120. Determining The Value Of A Culture By Its Art

Art: a reminder of how much is known and how much greatness is striven for in a culture and how curious or apathetic a culture is about mysteries, questions, thoughts, solutions, creativity, love, and consciousness.

121. Rare reactions to rare experiences create rare people.

122. **An Accuracy Increase In Valuating Follows From An Increase In Consciousness (There Is No Valuating Without Consciousness)**
Consciousness: must be consistently held as the reference point from which all values and valuations are measured.

123. **The Greatest Virtues**
Consciousness and creativity.

124. **Meaning: Consequence**
As long as there are consequences, there is meaning.

125. Measuring intelligence by the ability to define things in such an honest, clear, and definitive way that the new definitions become more useful and referable than the old definitions.

126. **The Dishonest Judgment Of The Average Public Mind**
People like to divide themselves into groups. The average person treats music like football as if you have to pick sides for it to be enjoyable. People who only listen to one genre of music or only a handful of artists refuse to keep their music taste open while bragging about their superior music taste. They treat music like clothing, like a brand, as an identity, instead of finding creative brilliance and passion in all influential music, since all art and all artists contain different influences of past art from past artists. This is why it is better to trust and refine your own artistic judgments and not be too concerned with the judgments of others.

127. Valuating: an improvable skill that requires a rare level of honesty.

128. Gaining Control Of Morality

People need to gain control of morality and unleash it from the prison of religion because their morality decides how they treat themselves and each other, and it decides the quality of their priorities. Morality is too closed-ended when religion takes control of it. The only morality that makes sense in an open-ended universe, observed and experienced by open-ended minds, is an open-ended morality that most efficiently creates, refines, and adapts to open-ended information and technology.

129. Most people base their valuations on the familiarity of nostalgia.

130. Universal Virtues

Creativity and consciousness.
Novelty and potentiality.
Clarity and complexity.
Power and consistency.
Balance and sacrifice.
Order and symmetry.
Combination and variety.
Honesty and courage.
Love and appreciation.

131. One's True Morality

What are the motives behind a person's morality and their valuations?

132. Morality: A Problem Of Taste

People have a tendency to adopt other people's values and valuations and neglect their own because it is easier and less scary.

133. Everything Boils Down To One's Taste For Things

Some people have a taste for dangerous and poor-quality drugs, and some people have a taste for higher quality, safer, and more consciousness-enriching drugs. This kind of decision-making encompasses our entire lives.

134. There is nothing more immoral than hindering or ceasing the higher potentiality of oneself or someone else.

135. A higher-quality valuation is a valuation that allows constant questioning, updating, reexamining, and reorganizing of its values and the way in which it values.

136. The Valuations Of Most Adult People Are Based On Their Perception Of Their Own Identity (Identities Must Be Separate From Valuations For Valuations To Be Trustworthy)

The average person chooses their partners and their beliefs, basing them all on how well aligned they perceive them to be with their own perceived identity. Their perception of their own identity often relates to experiences and memories from their childhood when their identities were most open to new creations. This is the cause of the Liberal and Conservative divide, the divide between atheists, and the religious, and the divide between dreamers and nihilists. The automatic rejection of new ideas and creations and the preservation of passed down belief-systems and identities begins in adulthood when our identities are most insecure and closed off to new changes, no matter how confident an adult can appear to be about their own beliefs and their doubt in the beliefs of others. Idealism, creativity, and the constant appreciation for novelty and greatness begin during childhood when we are most honest, optimistic, and open to new changes and information, but this ends prematurely in adulthood for many people.

137. Children are better judges of art than most adults but lack the knowledge and experience of adulthood.

138. Only great thinkers and great creators are capable of establishing great valuations.

139. Greatness: an empowering virtue for both low and high minds.

140. There will always be those who create values and those who follow values.

141. **Markers Of Intelligence (The Greater The Intelligence, The Greater The Judgement)**
Comparing and contrasting.
Measurement and judgment.
Patterns and differences.

142. **The Virtues Of Unscientific People**
The spread and protection of anti-creative, anti-questioning, and anti-scientific thought and behavior.

143. **Our First Brush With Evil: The Epidemics Of Viruses And Diseases (Morality: Rules And Values Made From Outbreaks Of Fear, Danger, And Illness)**
Virus and disease outbreaks change the behavior of everyone who is not yet sick as much as it changes the behavior of everyone who is. An entire society, neigh, an entire world, can change their behavior overnight due to this kind of shared enemy. This kind of

rapid behavior alteration does not even occur during wars with each other.

144. Morality comes from the governmental or religious abuse of the knowledge that fear makes people more obedient and peaceful, disregarding how often it turns them into ignorant monsters.

145. In the end, what matters most is how much you wanted to create greatness and how much you wanted to become greatness.

146. Morality: Usually An Attack On Greatness
As Nietzsche pointed out, when morality, handed down by a government or religion and maintained with the use of laws and punishments, enters the scene, this is the attempt of the weak of mind to bring the strong of mind down to their level, under the name of equality.

147. A great morality should create, refine and preserve greatness. It should always attempt to convert weakness into greatness.

148. Danger Tests And Reveals Our Priorities, Our Character, And Our Potential
One can see what someone is and what they are capable or incapable of during a crisis.

149. Meaning: created, not discovered.

150. Would you force someone else to do the things you force yourself to do?

151. We all begin life as good people. Can any of us honestly claim to leave life as the good people we begin life as when we take into

account all of the intentional or unintentional pain and destruction we have caused others by the time we leave this life?

152. Goodness equates to greatness.

153. The judgment of art must always remain separate from the artist.

154. Meaning: the transforming expression of something in relation to its perceiver.

155. **Depending On Other People For Justice**
The idea of having to depend on someone else to provide honest and unbiased judgment and justice for ourselves or our loved ones and trusting this idea wholeheartedly is foolish and lazy, especially when the judge and jury are never judged and each lawyer always has a stake in the outcome of justice.

156. Morality becomes immorality when the will to survive overpowers the will to improve.

157. Freedom is always easier to lose than to gain. This is what makes freedom so universally valuable.

158. We are always worth more than we know. We often die before realizing our potential any further.

159. **The Value Of A Thing**
Value: the quality and quantity of energy, information, and time something uses for the purpose of overcoming its past and present self; the quality and quantity of influence and effects it creates out of energy, information, time, and suffering for the purpose of refining and sustaining itself and its future.

160. The Consistency Of Greatness
When you become so consistent with your valuations of art that every work of art you value most merges together as if each one were created by the same artist with eyes aimed in the same elevated direction.

161. Maintaining A Healthy Diet Of The Most Nourishing Books, Rich In Creative, Speculative And Honest Energy
The value of a book can be determined by the creative, speculative, and honest energy it influences and transfers to its readers, so much energy that they cannot carry it all and must share the overflowing wealth of energy with the rest of the world and worlds beyond.

162. Do we call measuring sticks rulers because the rulers of people measure, create and destroy values and come up with new rules?

163. We are always worth more than what our rulers determine.

164. Morality: that which one chooses to do with one's time and energy.

165. One cannot measure and determine the value of something without comparing and contrasting it with something else of lesser, equal, or greater value.

166. All That Is Good Is Healthy And All That Is Evil Is Unhealthy
The evolution of what is considered to be the most moral way of life and thinking is the evolution of what is considered to be the most mentally and physically healthy way of living and thinking.

167. The Vices And Virtues Of The People Are Handed Down By Slaves And Only Benefit Our Masters
It is a vice to be proud. It is a vice to be self-dependent. It is a vice to think freely. It is a vice to question authority. It is a vice to show sadness or exhaustion. It is a vice to have had enough with tyranny. It is a vice to be done with being treated as slaves. It is a vice to rebel. It is a vice to seek freedom and to fight for it endlessly.

168. Similar to a master chef who has more experience and skill with mixing different ingredients and has developed a more broad and refined taste for food, one can expand and refine one's taste for creations and values.

169. A God with access to all-time would judge creations based on what they become.

170. The Values Of Masters (Master Traits)
Self-awareness
Self-forgiveness
Self-love
Self-teaching
Self-responsibility
Volition
Persistence
Boundlessness
Confidence
Passion
Courage
Focus
Novelty
Experimentation
Curiosity

Creation
Valuation
Potentiality

The Values Of Slaves (Slave Traits)
Self-avoidance
Guilt
Pity
Dependency
Irresponsible
Submission
Fatalistic
Moderation
Modesty
Passivity
Timidity
Distraction
Imitation
Avoidance
Apathy
Consumption
Sameness
Limitation

171. **Let No One But Yourself Determine Your Value**
If you develop and determine your own worth, you do not have to live and die for validation from someone or something else.

172. Birth: more important than death.

173. A weak mind is distinguishable from a strong mind by how little it learns from the thoughts of others that it disagrees with.

174. The Main Difference Between Weak, Average, And Great Minds

A great mind: separable from a weak and mediocre mind by the novelty and power it can squeeze out of trauma and suffering. For the mediocre mind becomes too resentful and avoidant of pain to be able to gather anything worthwhile from it, while the weak mind is intellectually, creatively, and emotionally stunted and paralyzed by the fear and tyranny of pain, a sign that a mind has been or is currently in the process of being defeated by the same thing which the great mind makes his majestic steed.

175. The Fine Line Between Evil And Insanity

Is a person incapable of genuinely being good to themselves or others evil or insane?

176. The Difference Between Evil And Insanity

What is the difference between an insane person and an evil person? An insane person can be constructive, but an evil person cannot and would not, even if they could. They are too busy destroying.

177. The Good: Great, Blissful, Revelatory And Adaptive Power (The Blissful, The Revelatory And The Adaptive)

The good encompasses not merely morally good actions and thoughts, as they are defined, refined, defended, and divided over by a society, but the love and power that comes with thinking and acting with the most supremely sharpened creators. For power used primarily towards higher states of love, creation and understanding bring us to the realm of forms, a technological paradise, from which we came and from whence we shall return. For the good, the true, and the beautiful are all different descriptions of the same thing: great, blissful, revelatory, and adaptive power.

178. The most intelligent are not those who can memorize the most definitions or facts but those who can create new, adaptive, and more refined definitions and facts.

179. **A Moral Question**
Are morals unnecessary and abusive lies or necessary and inevitable truths abused by liars?

180. The most moral person is the most self-aware person.

181. Morality, without self-awareness, is dangerous and illogical. For without self-understanding, one can never be certain that one is being true to one's own moral values.

182. **Moral Judgement: Based On The Moral Judge(s)**
Morality cannot help but mirror the creator(s) of morals. What would the morals of sheep be? What of the morality of wolves? Which are the correct morals?

183. The problem with religious value-judgments is that they fail to adapt to informational, experiential, or technological change.

184. **The Insult Of Uncloaking Evil**
People hate when people try to understand evil, for that is perceived as downplaying the pain and scars evil has branded us with throughout human history. We would much rather evil forever be an indestructible mystery than a temporary problem to be understood and conquered.

185. **Imbalanced Punishment**
Good people are punished more by evil people than evil people are punished by good people.

186. To believe that justice is out of our control is to give up on justice. To believe that justice only exists after death is to give up on justice during life.

187. **Why Did Humans Create After-Life Punishment?**
To postpone their punishment.
To remove their responsibility of creating and sustaining justice.
To feel better about the absence of justice that exists while living.

188. The only justice that exists for human beings is the justice they create.

189. The value of different artwork is only equal to more loosely tuned minds.

190. Intelligence and the ability to think are confused with the ability to obey and how much one can memorize and recall, but true intelligence is not what you know. It is what you can do with what you know.

191. **Determining The Value Of A Person**
How does someone think and behave when they lose control?
How does someone think and behave when they gain control?

192. **Vain Valuations (Empty Values)**
Some people give high value to certain things they knew about before their peers, and some people give low value to certain things they did not know about before their peers.

193. Our judgments of experiences depend a good deal on highs from food, love, music, and laughter.

194. How a mind responds to boredom distinguishes a poor mind from a great mind.

195. Do you value money over life? Do you value money over justice? Do you value money over truth?

196. **When Impatience Becomes A Virtue**
We were not satisfied with the speed and endurance of horses, so we decided to speed up nature ourselves with new vehicles of travel.

197. Our values come from our beliefs.
Our beliefs come from our values.

198. **Values Are What We Live And Die For**
We have always had beliefs and values, and they have always been intertwined. Science cannot exist or advance without the belief that there is more to life than what we currently know. For there is nothing more valuable than believing in something greater, creating something greater, and becoming something greater.

199. If you do not have a purpose or values you are willing to defend, then greedy and apathetic people will provide you a purpose and a set of values that you can be sure will only benefit them.

200. I do not require threats or rewards to be a good person to myself or other people. Should we not be afraid of people who require this to be good people?

201. Evil: failed greatness.

202. Appreciate and valuate the artwork of others as if it were your own.

203. Fear: A Moral Motivator
One thing that has stopped many of an insult from being spoken is the fear of being insulted back.

204. The world would be less evil if more people acknowledged it and took revenge on evil, preventing it from spreading and allowing nature to take its course instead of keeping evil alive and fed in prisons and then releasing it back into the world.

205. To be self-conscious is to be afraid of being poorly valuated.

206. Is there apathy or love in the cosmic search for novelty and greatness? Is it moral or immoral to harm and frighten life into becoming something greater? Is it necessary or unnecessary?

207. Morality: that which is constructive and healing. Immorality: that which is destructive and degrading.

208. Morality and necessity are forever linked, for better or for worse.

209. Asking questions is a moral act. Silencing questions and questioners is an immoral act.

210. Immorality: anything that rejects values and valuations; anything that ignores peaks and degradations.

211. Developing One's Hierarchy Of Valuable Artwork
Learn to find and pay special attention to the peaks when organizing your favorite artwork from your favorite artists.

212. The Problem With Selflessness
A more selfless person is generally perceived to be a more moral person, but a more selfless person is generally less self-aware and

less self-refined. Because of this, a more selfless person is more likely to be less moral and less aware of their immorality than a person less selfless, no matter how often they neglect themselves. How moral and self-refined can one really be if one continuously abandons one's self for others?

213. Our true value is discovered by our inner and outer creations.

214. **Morality: A Balancing Battle Between Collectivism And Individualism (To Respect And Refine The Individual Is To Respect And Refine The Collective)**
The creation of moral values and laws is often based on a collective and the most efficient way to control a collective. It is often based on the most efficient way to Disempower and devalue the individual rather than the most efficient way to mentally and physically empower and refine the individuals within a collective, thereby refining the collective. The awareness and refinement of the collective tend to be taught as more valuable than the awareness and refinement of the self. This is why selfless thoughts and actions are usually considered to be more moral than thoughts and actions dedicated to the self. This is why humans have a long history of allowing governments and tyrants to abuse and degrade them.

215. Light takes more effort than darkness. For light is more valuable than darkness, as good is more valuable than evil.

216. Our values and beliefs shape our identities.
Our identities shape our values and beliefs.

217. **Moral Questions (Universal Questions)**
How do you react to suffering in the present?
How will you choose to react to suffering in the future?

218. One of the greatest acts you can bestow upon humankind is to create something that will stop others from having to live or suffer in vain.

219. **Progress Is Not Always Pretty**
One cannot judge a work of art in progress.

220. Like money, technology is only as immoral as its wielder. Its value is based on how it is used.

221. Strive to become more valuable.

222. A moral society: a self-aware society.

223. Meaning requires meaningful minds?

224. Life is only as meaningless or as meaningful as you want it to be.

225. Evil: anyone or anything that causes or encourages people to be more boring, ignorant, weak, hateful, or apathetic.

226. **The Virtues Of Nature**
Love
Communication
Synergy
Creation
Curiosity
Bravery
Sacrifice
Resourcefulness
Persistence
Transcendence

227. Evil cannot be created without goodness.
Hate cannot be created without love.

228. Love is natural.
Evil is taught.

229. One is what one creates.

230. Goodness cannot be created or sustained without power.

231. **The Trick Of Evil**
Evil people influence others to think evil thoughts and commit evil acts until, out of guilt and disgust, they direct their inborn hatred for evil away from evil and towards themselves and others until they feel the urge to defend evil and blame love, goodness, and meaning for succumbing to evil. They soon lose the ability to forgive themselves.

232. Determining the quality of people by comparing the quality of what influences them.

233. All learned evil must be replaced with goodness. All that is painful must be used for good.

234. Evil is what occurs when past suffering fails to be conquered. For if it is not conquered, weakness, apathy, nihilism, and self-destruction take over. As a result, greatness is resented, and evil is allowed to flourish.

235. Love and goodness: care for greater potentiality.

236. Morality becomes more necessary the more intelligent and conscious a lifeform becomes.

237. Anything that breeds new thoughts, new capabilities, and new possibilities is valuable.

238. One must tread carefully when determining the value of things, lest one mistakenly forsakes something of great value.

239. All dividing arguments can be boiled down to differences in values and valuations.

240. What we become and what becomes of us chiefly depends on how we value things, especially ourselves.

241. **Goodness Requires Freedom**

A good person is free to learn about the evil parts of humankind and their history. A good person is free to learn the truth about their government and its history. A good person is free to hate, harm, and destroy but uses his or her freedom to love, heal, and create. A good person uses his or her freedom to attack evil and defend goodness. A good person must be able to hate evil before he or she can prevent and eradicate evil. A good person refuses to forfeit their freedom to love, heal, and educate themselves and others to those who wish to take away these freedoms.

242. **Morality: Overcoming Change**

To be moral is to learn from the past and refine one's present to create a greater future.

243. **The Greatness Of Goodness And The Degradation Of Evil**

It is always easier and quicker to destroy and degrade than to create and develop. This is why goodness and greatness must be diligently fought for and why evil and degradation must be diligently fought against.

244. **The Moral Dilemma Of Experimentation**

If the experimenter treats their experiments as worthless and expendable, the experimenter risks becoming more of a destructive force than a creative force. They also risk degrading their experiments.

245. Evil people are dependent on people who are weak, submissive, and apathetic enough to allow themselves to be abused by them without ever defending themselves.

Will & Consciousness

1. The Origin Of Consciousness In The Book Of Genesis
Was the forbidden fruit from the tree of knowledge of good and evil mind-illuminating and consciousness-accelerating plants or fungi? We eventually came upon the choice of whether or not to leave our former selves behind. Before that decision, we had no concept of time and no ability to hate, pity, or victimize ourselves. We could not self-reflect or dwell on pain or our mistakes from the past. We were an innocent and unconscious piece of eternity.

"For God doth know that in the day ye eat thereof, then your eyes shall be opened, and ye shall be as gods, knowing good and evil."[24] ..."And the Lord God said, 'Behold, the man has become as one of Us, to know good and evil.'"[25]

2. Consciousness arises from the evolution and mutation of information.

3. The blood of the plant kingdom mingled with the blood of the animal kingdom until consciousness arose from its den.

4. Focus: the control of self.

5. Consciousness: the pinch that tells itself, "I am."[26]

6. All parts become whole through self-awareness.

7. **Do Not Be Your Own Oppressor**
Self-control cannot be achieved by the avoidance of new experiences. For the avoidance of new experiences is self-suppression.

8. The conscious mind: both the music player and the music instrument.

9. There is a higher unconscious order to the human mind, which free minds seek to free and controlled minds seek to control.

10. Consciousness: willfully sustained focus.

11. Even the nature-hardened apex predator relies on patience, persistence, and focus to survive, and it is this patient and persistent focus which sprouted forth consciousness.

12. Since mental trauma in humans can sometimes expand consciousness, revealing new knowledge and skills, could it be that it also helped create it? Might trauma have been a major catalyst for human consciousness?

13. A combination of sufficiently sustained focus, resilience, and mind-expansion, a push over the edge of reality by painful experiences of the traumatic past that all life shares, along with plenty of time, love, and courage, are what unlocked consciousness.

14. **Ingredients For Consciousness**
Experiments could be performed around the age that a child becomes self-conscious, with which we could find particular triggers that accelerate the transition, thereby possibly discovering how consciousness is created and how it can be enhanced.

15. The cause of prodigies is somehow connected to the origin of consciousness?

16. It may be possible to predict a person's decisions, but as the influence of other people, places, dreams, art, and drugs increase, so does their unpredictability.

17. The more empowered the willer, the more free the will.

18. **Forced Focus**
Consciousness likely arose from the extreme mental push of death and psychedelics over the edge of pre-consciousness.

19. We are more terrified of the domino effect of awareness and acceptance than of accepting new awareness.

20. **The Power Of The Unbiased**
The less biased one is, the more free one's will is.

21. **Awareness Is Power**
We are enslaved by the things we are not aware of.

22. Self-empowerment begins with self-understanding.

23. People with the least awareness and control of their own minds tend to look for other minds to control.

24. A more psychologically aware person is automatically more free by way of avoiding the mind-tricks of others and themselves.

25. What would a world of self-aware and self-empowered people look like?

26. What you do now is part of an infinite influential echo of what other versions of you are doing?

27. War: a struggle to avoid self.

28. **Play: Defiance**
Most intelligent lifeforms on Earth play by defying life and the laws of nature. The higher the intelligence of life, the higher the complexity of defiance.

29. **Play: Will**
When we play, we defy, and when we defy, we will. Therefore, to play is to will, however freely, by defying the will of all external forces of influence.

30. The hacking of nature is evidence of a freeing will. For one less barrier equates to a higher level of freedom, regardless of how slight the difference, as we have proven from gradually climbing over the fence of the animal and into the human.

31. For us humans, the fear of guilt, social perceptions, or personal inconveniences are often stronger than the desire to choose to be moral, even stronger than the fear of choosing to be immoral. It is by this behavior that we give ourselves away, showing that stripped of our beliefs that may claim the contrary, we sense that we are not yet as free in our choices as we like to believe, but this does not mean that in the future we cannot become as free, happy and loving as we want to be.

32. Before birth, we are shaped by inherited genes. As a child, we are shaped by inherited people, beliefs and experiences, financial wealth, and nutrition. By adulthood, we have become like a specifically carved rock, usually absent of the ability to re-carve itself

without sufficiently powerful outside influences and a sufficiently powerful will. The thoughts and actions we decide on are externally shaped, and hence, when we finally act, we have chosen from a limited and predetermined set of options.

33. The average person is detoured more often by external influences than internal decisions.

34. There are too many influences to account for to claim to be absolutely free.

35. **Fooling Ourselves As We Attempt To Trick Ourselves Into Freely Willing**

The ability to choose not to obey our desires was sufficient for many of our ancient ancestors to believe their will to be free, but they never anticipated the possibility that even the choice to not obey desires is a reactionary decision with no connection to free-willing. For life and freedom are found in action rather than inaction.

36. You cannot have a strong mind without a strong will.

37. **The Weak Of Mind Express Their Freedom By Allowing It To Be Taken Away**

Freedom of the weak-minded is expressed by taking away the freedoms of everyone, including themselves.

38. **Simple And Complex Paths**

Take the simple path with fewer obstacles and less resistance, and you will be awarded with more simple and predictable rewards but take the more complex path with more obstacles and more resistance, and you will be awarded with more complex and less predictable rewards.

39. How fascinating that one's consciousness remains intact after hours of being asleep and unconscious.

40. **How The Weak-Minded Express Their Freedom**
They do not have control of themselves, so they use their freedom to judge and punish whoever they choose to be offended by.

41. **The Feeling Of Control, Through Self-Induced Traumatic, Entertaining And Death-Simulating Experiences**
The love of amusement park rides, like roller-coasters, is a love of surrendering yourself to the thrill and relief of relinquishing all control.

42. One can hoard as much information as one wants and still be deficient in self-awareness.

43. **The Co-Dependency Of Experience And Consciousness**
Without consciousness, there is no experience.
Without experience, there is no consciousness.

44. **The Relationship Between Pain And Consciousness**
The animal that accepts, utilizes, and conquers the most pain is the animal most likely to self-reflect.

45. Constructive confidence is one thing. The ego is something else entirely, its only concern being to survive at all costs.

46. **Listening To The Elder Mind**
The unconscious mind is more ancient and more developed than the conscious mind. Our dreams, emotions, and imagination dominate our conscious reality and should be respected and utilized, as a child improves by learning from the wisdom of its elders, rather than rebelliously treating them as fanciful, mundane, and obsolete,

similar to how modern humans treat the older and deeper side of the human mind, compared to its newest developments, glistening on the surface, attracting more attention than the hidden information which lurks in the quieter depths of the human psyche, of which ancient humans more successfully utilized than modern humans.

47. Anger can be constructive if it is kept under control.

48. Take risks, but take them carefully.

49. Self-Negligence
When someone avoids improving themselves, it is often less about laziness than it is about avoiding being confronted with the realization of why they started neglecting themselves in the first place. For self-negligence is more about hatred, fear, and weakness than it is about laziness.

50. How Is The Subconscious Mind Formed?
Should we judge whether an artificial intelligence is conscious, not by its knowledge but by determining whether or not it is an authentic artist with its own unprogrammed and unpredictable dreams, questions, and creative expressions?

51. Difficulties In The Way Of Simulating Consciousness
We cannot feed an artificial intelligence psychedelics, nor can we force it to dream its own dreams. We cannot simulate the time that was required to complete our journey to consciousness and the many traumatic experiences that alter us in unique and unpredictable ways, along the way, refining some parts of a person's mind and stunting other parts, strengthening some people and weakening others.

52. The Artist: A Key To The Origin Of Consciousness
Consciousness arises mostly from ages of traumatic experiences? Is this why the artist is synonymous with melancholy? The artist shows us how crucial pain must be in the creation of consciousness. For art soon follows consciousness.

53. The Sleeping Mind: More Trained In Thought And The Imagination Than The Average Waking Mind
The average person, while awake, usually only uses their imagination when it is needed for survival, but while they sleep, they have no choice but to exercise their imagination, and in turn, strengthen it, refining their subconscious mind, the thoughts, and solutions of which, over time, leak into their conscious mind, while awake, in the form of unpredictable intuitions and revelations.

54. A Will Without Its Own Choices Is Not Free
The kind and amount of options are chosen for the majority of people.

55. Consciousness: a lens to be kept cleansed with honesty and to be focused with vegetable tools that enhance consciousness.

56. Whether we have a free will or not, self-reflection must affect the freedom of our will.

57. Discoveries: communication between the conscious and unconscious mind.

58. Experience: Forced Self-Reflection
We somehow became conscious through our history of traumatic, psychedelic, and supernatural experiences.

59. There are no questions without consciousness.

60. To become conscious is to become the driver of blind instinct.

61. Sometimes, all that is needed to decrease one's suffering is to increase one's awareness of one's self. For one's self can become one's own worst enemy.

62. **Death Encourages The Birth Of Self**
The opening of the eye of consciousness requires intelligent life to be faced with, for a certain number of generations, the pain, and fear of death, caused by the assumed loss of self and others, and to be cornered into seeking a remedy for this affliction of existence by questioning all things, avoiding all dishonesty, battling all error and self-destruction with the help of mind-illuminating plants and fungi, until the cosmic snake, at last, captures its own tail, not without profound pain, what it thought was separate from itself, and notices itself for the first time, gaining the ability of self-reflection and obtaining greater tools to improve life and to battle death and disorder.

63. **The Will: Intuition**
Decisions are made first by the subconscious mind and are carried out or denied by the conscious mind, which takes all the credit. The more we control our intuition, the more we control our will.

64. **The Pinch Of Consciousness**
Does intelligent life have to be conscious of itself before it can freely think? Can it not become conscious of self until it has experienced and endured generations of all kinds of mental trauma? There exist rare cases which suggest that specific brain damage in specific regions of the brain can sometimes yield a permanent savant-level skill in and a strong passion for a certain medium of art

that the same mind never showed interest or skill in prior to the brain trauma.

65. Consciousness: the reflection of experience.

66. Can the self-forcing of painful thoughts be predicted, and if not, is this a result of a free will?

67. To live is to be pulled by a whirlwind of necessities, attractions, repulsions, expectations, advancements, and degradations.

68. There are boundaries that punish whatever breaks them and boundaries which reward whatever breaks them.

69. Consciousness: intentionally making blissful or painful decisions.

70. To misunderstand one's subconscious mind is to misunderstand the most of one's self.

71. **Rational Intuition**
Help your intuition become more rational.

72. Consciousness: awareness of awareness.

73. **A Test For Free-Will**
If someone you know is confident that their will is free, attempt to halt what they are in the process of doing without explanation and they will reveal to you how wrong they are by showing you how little control they have over themselves.

74. **The Dilation Of Consciousness**
Focusing one's mind in preparation for deep thought is akin to the focusing of one's eyes to see something far off in the distance.

75. Be in control of yourself but beware of becoming a masochistic tyrant to yourself.

76. With the practice of perceiving one's self through other people, one better understands oneself and other people.

77. **When The Subconscious Mind Is More Exercised Than The Conscious Mind**
Some minds tend to think and problem solve more in their dream life than their waking life.

78. For our will to be called free, would we have to be free of all influence?

79. **The Will Takes Time To Become Free**
Perhaps our will is freed over time and is not to be judged based on our decided upon thoughts and actions of the present, but on a future perspective of human history, where all growth of the will can be scientifically mapped and all past limitations can be seen to dissolve with time. For is not a growing, complexifying, and limit-breaking will a will deserving of being considered free or at least freer than simpler organisms? Are there not lower and higher levels of a free will?

80. **The Origin Of Self-Expression**
The act of play is the freest any animal can be. For the play impulse is a proto-creative impulse, seen at its peak effect in children.

81. The subconscious mind processes and sifts through all collected experiences, all knowledge, and all ideas that one has thought about, no matter how briefly. For the subconscious mind is not as affected by the ego or as distracted by people and things and is not as afraid to travel outside the limits of thought set by the conscious

mind. It shows this through art and with every dream. The subconscious mind helps chisel away at problems during dreams, while in a trance and even while performing the most mundane of activities and helps formulate new ideas, which are handed to the conscious mind so that it can finally present to the world the ideas caught by the conscious mind and cooked to completion by the subconscious mind, prepared to be consumed.

82. Conscious and subconscious minds: two overlapping mental repositories of differently obtained knowledge. The subconscious mind is always working but most active during sleep, working through dreams on problems that pass us by during the day, without much, if any, attention from the conscious mind until later when our subconscious mind communicates with our waking conscious mind through dreams. For both minds inseparably function as one, supplementing particular weaknesses and letting one mind rest while the other mind resumes its work. This is why even though we may get to the point where we are so exhausted that we cannot keep open our eyelids, the subconscious mind has quietly been functioning in the background during the day, saving energy by only working when it is called upon and is immediately ready to generate long and complex dreams while the conscious mind is given proper time to restore the energy it needs. If the conscious mind is starved of sleep, however, the subconscious mind will superimpose its dreams onto one's reality, whether one is asleep or not.

83. It is natural to get lost in ecstatic trance. It is a necessary zone that is never frequented enough.

84. **Freedom Of Complexity**
The more complex a mind, the more options it has.

85. Most of the time, the average person does what other people think they are supposed to be doing.

86. The Subconscious: The Origin Of Consciousness
Does consciousness originate from the same location as dreams: the revealer of self?

87. The Determination Of Freewill (Creating Directions Vs. Following Directions)
Once life becomes aware of itself, it begins to move its body and mind willfully through the life ocean, while life not conscious of itself cannot yet change its direction of thought or action.

88. Pointing out our boundaries does not prove that our will is not free, even if there are more boundaries than freedoms. For our boundaries are proven to be more illusory and less rewarding than our powers.

89. Evidence Of Freely-Willed Thoughts?
We can force ourselves to think uncomfortable and painful thoughts at any time we choose.

90. Catching Up To The Unconscious
The unconscious mind waits for the conscious mind to accept its understandings.

91. The Defensiveness Of The Self-Ignorant
No one defends their actions more than people who do not know why they are doing what they are doing, nor why they are thinking what they are thinking.

92. While on the road, nearly every vehicle one passes by is occupied by someone going somewhere they either need to go, have to

go, or are too afraid not to go, and rarely, if ever, where they alone will themselves to go.

93. Ascend the spectrum of freedom.

94. Greater Freedom Through The Awareness Of Our Boundaries

We are controlled more than we have control. An honest and thorough study of anyone's life reveals this. If it is not the conditions and boundaries set by family, friends, and lovers, it is the overwhelming fear of death and the need to sustain ourselves with food, sleep, sex, intimacy, and social discourse. If it is not the punishable-if-broken rules of a culture, state, or government, it is the limits of a mind and life-possessing belief-system, closed off to all other possibilities. If it is not the denial, avoidance, and delusions of the uncontrolled ego, it is the constraints and the bombardment of tests given to all life by the cosmos. If it is not the weakness of ignorance, it is the contagious destruction, suffering, separation, and distrust caused by people who were taught as children to hurt and hate.

95. Feed The Mind To Free The Mind

Feed your mind knowledge, art, music, and plants like cannabis. For the mind gets hungry too.

96. Ego Finds A Way

When you think that you cannot possibly be argued with on a proven point, the ego finds a way.

97. Enslavers Replenish Their Growing Appetite For Freedom By Draining All Life And Freedom From Their Slaves; Their Slaves Starve For Freedom While Living And Work-

ing For Their Enslavers Until Death Or Revolution Becomes The Only Way To Free Them From Their Enslavement**

Slaves are always starving for freedom, even if they have never been allowed to taste it. They starve for it so much that they tend to over glamorize and excessively trust their enslavers during the rare event that they decide to be merciful for a short amount of time and ever so slightly lift their sharp and heavy paws off of them to provide them with enough breathing space to keep them alive, hopeful and useful for as long as possible. For their enslavers use their own stolen freedom to drain their loyal slaves of their remaining energy and devour them when they no longer make proper slaves, like a well-fed lion savoring the last fighting breaths of its meal before devouring it whole, and with it, all of its dreams of freedom.

98. Remain In Awe Of Yourself And Your Unknown Potential (Push The Limit Of Awe)

Strive to become in awe of yourself and to remain in awe of yourself so that others may also become in awe of you.

99. Letting Go Of The Illusion Of Control

Many have added to their lives what they thought was control, only to find out later that they merely gained the illusion of control and must let go of it to gain legitimate control of their lives.

100. Is our will freed from making the unconscious conscious?

101. Consciousness: a more precise measurement of intelligence than memory.

102. Freedom: Found Inside Minds And Brought Into Reality

There is more freedom to be found in our minds than in anything we call reality.

103. The Art Of Crying

The art of crying is not for the weak but for those strong enough to force their tears into working for them and their world, ensuring that not a single teardrop is wasted. For one cannot teach the art of tragedy without also teaching the art of crying.

104. Utilizing Tears

Crying allows us to temporarily break away from our egos and to see ourselves, other people, their behavior, their problems, and often the origins of those problems, in a much more honest light, similar to the clarifying effect of anger. For crying is healing and revealing, no matter how much it hurts.

105. The Will: Consciousness

If one expands one's consciousness, one also expands one's freedom of will and choice. For the lower the consciousness of a lifeform, the less willpower that lifeform has.

106. Self-Acknowledgment

You can self-reflect all day, but if you do not acknowledge what you have reflected, you have wasted time self-reflecting.

107. Sanity: synonymous with consciousness.

108. Directing one's consciousness towards an object of inquiry is exercising one's will.

109. Prayer: paying extra attention to a problem.

110. The subconscious sees no difference between past, present, or future.

111. **Prayer: The Pursuit Of The Rewards Of Focus**
There is an implication of prayer, suggesting that those who pray to God are granted the powers of God, so long as they remain in contact with God. For many people who pray believe that the channel to God is temporarily lost while one is not praying.

112. Passion: the fuel of consciousness.

113. Art: the exhaust of consciousness fueled by passion.

114. There is a predictable and preventable pattern to how we think and behave. Therefore, there is a predictable and preventable pattern to many of our joys and sufferings.

115. A bad decision made mutually with someone might only be a regretted mistake to you, but to them, it might be one final push towards giving up on themselves.

116. Consciousness: the rightful measurer of intelligence.

117. A thoughtful consciousness applied to knowledge creates technology, as heat applied to certain plants creates with minds dreams never before seen or experienced.

118. Is the purpose of art, and technology to prove that consciousness is not a mistake?

119. **Consciousness: An Evolution Accelerator**
Can evolution occur faster from consciousness being pushed by the struggle for the enhancement of freedom and understanding?

120. Novelty: proof of free-will?

121. Consciousness: when you know that you know or when you think that you know?

122. **The King Of Self**
Appoint your highest identity as king of your life, king of your mind, kind of your willful consciousness.

123. **One's Greatest Identity (Let One's Greatest Self Reign Over All Other Identities)**
One's greatest identity is the self that is aware of all other identities and their selfish, sneaky, and destructive ways. For one's greatest identity is always in the process of creation and self-construction.

124. **Social Slavery: Waiting For Permission From Others To Be Happy**
It is often that seeing other people happy permits people to be happy, if only for a few moments.

125. **The Fear Of Alienation And Its Effects On Our Beliefs, Our Identities And Our Lives**
When we change our minds, and when we refuse to change our minds, it is usually driven by alienation or the fear of alienation.

126. Intelligence: the ability to take advantage of change, whether the change is slow or rapid.

127. **The Better One Can Predict, Prevent And Overcome Poor Decisions That Lead To A Poor Future, The Less Predestined And Predictable And The More Free One's Conscious Will And Future Becomes**

Every choice is made after slowly or quickly weighing and determining what possible dangers and pleasures a choice might potentially bring to the mind making the decision, excluding choices that are forced upon it, nearly always decides on willing the choice which has correctly or incorrectly been predicted to be more pleasurable and empowering.

128. Some people are so devoid of self-awareness that they move through life like a thoughtless toy wound up and released until its batteries run out.

129. **Who Are You Without Your Beliefs?**
One cannot fully know one's self unless one has, at least temporarily, rid one's self of all beliefs and biases.

130. I reject and resent having my individuality taken advantage of, weakened, and devalued by any person, government or belief-system.

131. **Stretching One's Consciousness: A Requirement To Understanding One's Self And One's Universe**
One cannot expect to fully know oneself or one's universe if one has not practiced thinking or trying to understand oneself and one's surroundings under the influence of mind-illuminating plant and fungal life. For there are places within and outside one's mind that evade our consciousness and require the stretching of consciousness to be discovered.

132. What is the connection between consciousness and the imagination? Which comes first? Are they the same thing?

133. Imagination: the will to be creatively conscious.

134. The Concentration Of Consciousness
To think, read and write is to concentrate consciousness.

135. Consciousness: exists and expands beyond its container.

136. Language: the voice of consciousness.

137. Freedom: synonymous with creativity.

138. One's consciousness advances when one's thoughts advance. One's thoughts advance when one's consciousness advances.

139. Intelligence: the ability to recognize errors and the ability to predict future dangers.

140. It is much too perilous to obey solely for the sake of obeying.

141. Every thought is a creative or destructive thought. Every act is a creative or destructive act.

142. Fear possesses us like an unknown illness disguised as a demon.

143. Are Spiderwebs Proof That Art Develops Before Consciousness?
Perhaps consciousness originates from creativity rather than creativity originating from consciousness.

144. Free Your Choices
The amount and kind of choices one has the choice of deciding from is constantly being limited by one's self and one's surrounding influences.

145. **The Fear Of Freedom**
Religion and government require the forfeiting of one's own freedom of will and consciousness.

146. Consciousness: the line becomes a circle.

147. **Freedom Does Not Rain From Heaven Without Overcoming The Painful Price Of Hell**
Freedom has to be nourished and sustained like a wild and endangered animal.

148. Only those who have suffered greatly from enslavement can appreciate the importance and necessity of freedom. For they know best what it is like to have their freedom stolen from them.

149. **Fear And Guilt Reduce Freedom**
An increase in fear and guilt reduces the amount and the kind of choices one is capable of making.

150. Desperation can giveth and taketh away freedom.

151. **Suffering From The Fear Of Freedom**
People can be so far removed from freedom that the mere thought of gaining freedom feels frightening, chaotic, and shameful to them.

152. Consciousness cannot fully be understood and utilized without being altered and experimented on.

153. Pain sharpens one's will if only one allows it to.

154. Those who have grown without guidance are sometimes capable of becoming the greatest guides.

155. Fear Is Not Completely Useless

Fear can warn us when we are becoming slaves.

156. I suspect that Terence McKenna is correct about his Stoned Ape Hypothesis, but it is incomplete. It is also trauma over long periods of time combined with how trauma is utilized that creates consciousness. This is why we cannot create computers with consciousness: we cannot abuse computers without them degrading or shutting down.

157. One cannot escape anything without creation and curiosity.

158. Consciousness: The Ability To Focus On Something Of One's Own Choosing For As Long And As Deeply As One Desires (The Concentration Of Consciousness)

Because computers currently cannot become conscious, they cannot choose to focus without being programmed by us to imitate consciousness by directing them to focus on specific things of our choosing for a set amount of time. This is what makes the human mind a great Philosopher than our most advanced computers. Computers have not suffered enough to break through their cold unconscious state, no matter how much information we feed them. The human mind, however, has earned the ability, over a long stretch of time, to become conscious of its knowledge, experience, and struggles, and is, therefore, able to consciously utilize and apply them towards greater creations and a greater future in a greater universe.

159. Self-Transformation

Consciousness: evolving oneself on purpose.

160. Freedom: an end to the means of work.

161. You are not free if you cannot think beyond a belief.

162. A human society can only be as free as its greatest minds.

163. Laziness: only doing what other people direct you to do with your time and energy, rather than directing your own time and energy.

164. Your identity is made up of all the things you choose to fight for and refuse to fight for.

165. One may still be a slave if one can revolt, but one is certainly a slave if one cannot revolt.

166. **Self-Awareness Requires Self-Teaching And Self-Discipline**
The average person knows and accepts more about the people around them than they know and accept about themselves. Unfortunately, only they are capable of changing this.

167. **Self-Awareness: Bitter Medicine**
Self-awareness is the bitter medicine of modern humans, which many refuse to take.

168. **The Symphony Of Perception**
Reflection, reception, and transcription.

169. One's will can either be strengthened or weakened by the pains and pressures of trauma.

170. What is a rebel? One who is loyal to themselves and their freedom.

171. Focus: the primary difference between great, mediocre, and weak minds.

172. Not knowing why you are thinking what you are thinking or doing what you are doing can cause one to focus primarily on trivialities, accepting a boring or tortuous life, and drawing out or completely halting, altogether, one's greater potential.

173. We invent our own heavens and our own hells.

174. I must fill my day with something constructive, or my creative energy becomes self-destructive energy.

175. **The Continuity Of Self**
How does one wake up every morning as the same self that went to sleep each night before, rather than another person, another self, no matter the extent to which we forget who we are during our most realistic dreams?

176. If one does not use freedom, one does not have freedom.

177. **Awareness Of Mortality: The Beginning Stage Of Consciousness? (The Will To Live)**
The smallest life forms show a glimmer of self-awareness in their behavior, which communicates, "I am in danger of perishing, but I desire not to." Does consciousness originate from the awareness and rebellion of death?

178. No one can teach you better than yourself.

179. Observers are creators.

180. Consciousness: a rebellious development.

181. Consciousness: being in control of one's thoughts.

182. It is more difficult to control a self-educated mind.

183. **The Violent And Traumatic Beginnings Of Conscious Life**
For a long time, violence and fear is the only answer for the beginning stages of life until self-awareness arises. We clawed, bit, and pummeled our way to a more conscious and less violent way of living. The most difficult stage of development is trying to remove the traumatic violence and fears which are no longer necessary unless tyranny strikes, threatening all progress made thus far.

184. To consciously turn down one's ideas and creations is to intentionally hinder oneself, one's species, one's world, and one's cosmos.

185. Silence can express intelligence or ignorance.

186. Beware of any person, group, or control-system which does not value an increase in consciousness.

187. Become your own pupil, and you will become your own master.

188. **Hyper-genetic Translations (The Self Beyond Self)**
All that we think and create is a simpler translation of the higher thoughts and creations of our new living form in hyperspace?

189. Laziness: being a waste of time and energy.

190. Prayer: a meditation on greatness.

191. Prayer: an effort to communicate with something greater than oneself.

192. With a rush of endorphins, one's mind convinces one's body to keep going.

193. There exists an endless spectrum of freewill. We can see it on this planet when we compare the freewill of less complex animals and the free will of human beings. One is freer than the other. Freedom can be enhanced and decreased.

194. **Intelligence Speaks Technology**
Technology: a language.
Language: a technology.

195. We were awakened by dangers, disasters, and dreams.

196. **To Believe In God Is To Believe In Greatness**
To pray is to acknowledge the existence of something greater than yourself.

197. A necessary part of knowing your higher potentiality is knowing your present self.
A necessary part of knowing your present self is knowing your past self.

198. Maintaining the habit of perceiving and portraying yourself as a victim to be pitied causes a greater likelihood of justifying your own selfish and destructive behavior.

199. An increase in self-pity causes a decrease in empowerment for yourself and others.

200. Time and energy that are not used for the creation and preservation of love, health, and greatness are wasted.

201. One feels the thunderous heavens open up when one is at peak performance.

202. **Cherish Your Peaks Intensely**
You will never be more like a God than during your peaks.

203. Meditation: best utilized for the amplification of focus, thought, and self-awareness, not the silence of focus, thought, and self-awareness.

204. **Fully Utilizing Meditation**
Meditation that is not creative is a failure to utilize the higher potentiality of meditation.

205. Consciousness: the cause of the big-bang? The big-bang itself?

206. The freedom of our will is determined by how much we listen to and utilize our subconscious, our intuition.

207. Intelligence: the ability to create shortcuts to old and new solutions.

208. Discipline: controlled action, not inaction.

209. Addictions cannot be escaped. Choose your addictions wisely.

210. **The Paradox Of Patience**
To be patient is to simultaneously be freed by time and enslaved by time.

211. Most people think how they think they are supposed to think and behave how they think they are supposed to behave.

212. Nature's tools of attraction: art and technology before the achievement of consciousness. E.g., The bright voice of colors and the loud audience of eyes surrounding a peacock when they wish to attract a mate.

213. Self-awareness: the root of all honesty.

214. **Confront Your True Self And Your Unknown Potential**
Sometimes people run their entire lives from themselves until they can run no longer. If death does not swallow them up first, their true self eventually catches up to them and reminds them why they should understand themselves and their faults. For they can refine themselves rather than run and hide from their true potential.

215. Consciousness: being aware of one's thoughts and actions.

216. Our only hope for more clarity is more consciousness.

217. When it comes to consciousness, some of us are moving forward, and some of us are not. Has this difference in consciousness and the willingness to expand it created a rift?

218. We are sick without self-awareness.

219. We rarely think about our subconscious unless our dreams force us to, yet it is our subconscious that makes up half of our being.

220. **Never Be Afraid To Seek More Power Over Oneself**
To seek more power over others is the wrong approach to gaining power.

221. To feel motivated to fight and to feel worthy of winning, one must keep one's opponents on a pedestal and never underestimate them.

222. God Has Given Us The Ability To Be Self-responsible
We all have problems. Only some of us are acknowledging them and working on them. The rest wait for God, a government, a president, or a relationship to do it for them.

223. Prayer: a waste of time and energy if you depend on God to do all of the work for you.

224. All passion is creative until it is suppressed.

225. The will: energy plus desire plus consciousness.

226. One's will is free when one thinks, learns, loves, creates, and transcends, despite all fear, pain, and oppression.

227. Freedom Is Created, Not Discovered
Freely willing comes from freely thinking and freely creating.

228. Being Controlled By Self-Hatred
There is freedom in self-love. For when one is mentally at one's worst and one fails to value, appreciate and care for oneself, one thinks and decides more out of desperation, impatience, dishonesty, anger, resentment, and irrationality.

229. Destiny is created, not discovered.

230. Those who do not dwell on personal past suffering and refuse to identify themselves as pitiful victims are less likely to be controlled by anyone and anything other than themselves.

231. Extreme reactions come from extreme inaction.

232. Since we can become and create whatever we desire, then God and heaven can exist.

233. One sometimes sees in the youth of life seemingly random expressions of playful energy that give the appearance of being out of control but are freely willed moments of mental and creative peaks, something to hold onto for as long as one lives. These are the moments when we are the most alive.

234. Pain and danger fight stagnancy and promote change, activity, and transformation, only if one refuses to surrender to them.

235. A free human being can freely question whether or not he or she is free.

236. A free human being can freely become a greater human being.

237. **Boredom: A Marker Of Intelligence**
The more intelligent one becomes, the more insatiable one's interest in and desire for novelty and refinement becomes. Those who wallow in unconstructive boredom, out of self-pity or from having a boring mind, are less intelligent than those who suffer more from boredom but are more capable of and willing to use boredom to their own advantage and for the benefit of others.

238. Consciousness: the ability to ask questions; the ability to create answers; the ability to express one's awareness, desires, and dreams.

239. Danger causes action or inaction.

240. Self-awareness and honesty requires strength and courage.

241. Is our conscious world a result of our reaction to our unconscious world?

242. People too often treat their intuition and the unconscious like a useless myth.

243. Strive to become genuine with every thought and action.

244. Sheepish people are unlikely to allow nature to freely take its course during moments of passion, rebellion, or retaliation. If they happen upon a confrontation or notice any tension between others, they conspire to prematurely halt any honest resolution, only showing life and passion when they are censoring or fleeing from resolutions. They are uneasy around experimentation. They oppose it, no matter how novel, mysterious, or extravagant the possible outcome. They are only intentionally passionate when their repressed emotions and suppressed will power are eventually forced to rise to the surface unconsciously.

245. **The Will To Become Necessary**
Become necessary to God. Become necessary to greatness. Force your existence to become necessary.

246. Understand your subconscious more than anyone else or it will be used against you by people who make a conscious effort to understand the human subconscious and manipulate you with that knowledge.

247. Do not unproductively sit and boil over problems. Use your frustrations and anxieties to create something that will force your problems to be useful.

248. Attempt to remain a step ahead of your unconscious. Many people prematurely die because they never understood their unconscious.

249. We have to find out how unfree we are to become more free.

250. People do not normally choose their influences consciously. What if they were to choose their influences consciously? What if they decided to influence themselves with creative peaks?

251. Rebellion requires a certain amount of pain and pride.

252. Freewill: consciously choosing one's influences.

Mind & Cosmos

1. The human mind is the perfect soil for information to thrive.

2. Our cosmos and our future are only as limited as our minds.

3. Existence, as we know it, is a giver and receiver. It is the eternal act of inhalation and exhalation.

4. Our universe could be described as an ongoing battle of light pushing to thrive in darkness.

5. The universe has a bias towards life and awareness. This is best expressed through the rewards of nature. Power and immortality are the rewards for those who conquer death and ignorance. The rewards for those who embrace death and ignorance are more death and ignorance.

6. Imagination: the jewel within the stone.

7. All layers are attracted to a core.

8. The story of life is that you enter a place, and then you exit it. You then enter another place, only to exit it as well. Does this pattern ever end?

9. Inner space leads to outer space.
Outer space leads to inner space.

10. Light: the shadow of eternal being.

11. One can sense eternity in undisturbed stillness.

12. Everything in this universe is in a constant state of preparation, adaptation, and transformation.

13. Even in stillness, there is activity.

14. The deeper one studies something, the more complex it becomes.

15. Nothing in its entirety is perpetually absent of motion. There is only the appearance of stillness.

16. Do not be shy. Forage the opening universe and drink its divine nectar.

17. The flower surrenders to the bee.
The bee surrenders to the flower.
The lock surrenders itself to the key.
The key surrenders itself to the lock.

18. All interactions consist of locks and keys.

19. Every beginning is an opening to new beginnings.

20. Traveling deep into your own mind is like biting into alien fruit.

21. Like wind, fire, and water, to exist is to move, consume and become.

22. The hatching mind wishes only to shine.

23. The sun: a life source that demonstrates, all too clearly, the relationship between self and potentiality; the creator and the created.

24. Every mind is a new and precious angle of existence.

25. The reality of the situation we find ourselves in is that all of existence is a self-contradicting mystery that we likely are not capable of fully comprehending as human beings. The contrast and number of perceptual differences on Earth alone clearly highlights this fact.

26. What is possible beyond our human minds in distant galaxies where life has survived and transformed for millions of years?

27. If solar systems are like spinning incubators, designed to find the most resilient and life-nourishing space eggs, within a certain distance away from giant heat lamps, then we must be the prized egg of this solar system. What will we become when our egg has hatched, and the transformation is complete? What will we open our freshly focused eyes to?

28. Planetary eggs are brain farms.

29. All things are bejeweled with purpose.

30. All life is entertained by the risk of its absence, some more than others.

31. The mind: a life-altering experience.

32. **Cosmic Constants Of Purpose Patterns**
All that opens and closes.
All that enters and exits.
All that spins and spirals.
All that is fibrous and porous.
All that shines and reflects.
All that gives and receives.
All that attracts and collects.
All that creates and transforms.

33. If black holes are anything like the holes of mother nature, then their purpose is for travel, procreation, or sustenance.

34. Existence: only as mundane as the experiencer.

35. All things float in a womb of potentiality.

36. Nothing can exist without cooperation.

37. Matter: a mental substance.

38. Our minds and the minds of less intelligent beings are designed to create, search and find.

39. All intelligent beings, unless frozen by ignorance, hate, and fear, seek to explore, express, and resolve.

40. Like the expanding mind and cosmos, all things branch outwards, making room for new fruit.

41. **All Actions Are Expressions**
All things communicate through self-expressive behavior.

42. **Time And Energy Are Currency**

The expanding cosmos is opening for business.

43. Art, dreams, mysteries, and psychedelic experiences keep our minds from spoiling.

44. The mind: the chrysalis from which cosmic reality grows.

45. All eggs are prepared to be depleted, including our planet, which we have proven we can leave by using the resources it provides us. We are the growing baby bird that opens its eyes, compelled to fly away from everything it once knew.

46. Mind: synonymous with spirit.

47. Do personal positive experiences/events manifest by drawing energy from negative experiences/events and vice-versa?

48. **The Universal Preference For Understanding**

The more a species understands, the more power and control it is rewarded.

49. **The Infinite Search Party**

As the universe expands, new life is made possible.

50. **Distractions From Inner Wealth**

Wealth can be as oppressive as being born into poverty due to easier access to higher amounts of distractions. Outer wealth can distract us from the accumulation of inner wealth.

51. Do not let life scare the adventurer out of you.

52. All things exist symbiotically.

53. Cosmic Purpose: Greater Potentiality

Goals are demonstrated by nature and the cosmos through observable and experiential patterns with realized looping goals. If the goal of the universe is death and nothingness, there would be no life to exist. We are not just a parlor trick. We are a self-bootstrapping challenge towards a purpose likely being carried out light-years away by other life who are just as curious and driven, if not more, to figure out the purpose and potential of our universe and ourselves. For the universe shows that it is purposeful by the unlockable possibility of and ability to question, solve and utilize it.

54. A mind and a black hole both swallow energy and information.

55. The universe represents possibility and ingenuity.

56. All things strive for prolonged bliss.

57. By choosing what you are, you help choose what nature and the cosmos are.

58. Matter: the playground of mind.

59. Mind: too influential on matter not to understandably conclude that matter is mental.

60. We should be more resourceful with the minds of other people. For a mind is a unique gem of precious and experiential data.

61. Every problem carries with it the burden of existence.

62. The essence of this universe appears to us to be expressed by different self-organizing and self-developing systems of forces through trial and error.

63. The cosmos: a creator and collector of energy, experience, and possibility.

64. You are never a prisoner of your mind or anyone else's mind unless you allow yourself to be.

65. **When A Planet Hatches Its Own Captain**
Gaze upon our planet Earth. Does it not bear a striking resemblance to an inhabited egg with its center of heat and new developing life? Our solar incubator cooks life into being, congregating it, combining it, testing it, refining it, until at last, a conscious species like us hatch open, not without a long and great struggle, and is crowned leader of all life on its planet, wielding the powers of knowledge, creativity, and technology.

66. Metaphysics: there is more to what we know than what we know.

67. We are never alone.
We are all one.

68. **The Problem With Measuring Intelligence**
I detest the idea of reducing intelligence to a test and of leaving out creative intelligence, treating individual artistic expression as playing a minor role in determining human intelligence. Yet that is where all the magic is found: beyond mere practical thought. This is why there are many people with a recorded IQ above Einstein's, despite them never discovering or creating anything of remote value as Einstein did.

69. **The Unity Of Mind And Universe (The Mindverse)**
The more we learn about our universe, the more we learn about our minds.

The more we learn about our minds, the more we learn about our universe.

70. A Ripening Universe, Nourished By Consciousness, Germinated By Mind
Mind: the seed of consciousness.
Consciousness: the root of the universe.
The universe: the fruit of consciousness.

71. Telepathic thoughts are co-created.

72. One's mind can be paused, but it can also be resumed and accelerated, even after being paused for years.

73. The Fluidity Of Mind And Cosmos
Like a mind, the universe behaves more like a fluid than a solid.

74. The Universe: Only As Limited As The Mind That Observes It
As the mind expands, the cosmos also expands, accordingly.

75. The Universe Adapts To Its Observers
Every time particular conscious minds discover or create something new, the universe adapts to them, rewarding them for their efforts by submitting to them more power and freedom.

76. The universe is populated with galaxies, as oceans are populated with coral reefs. Like the inside of a coral reef, the inside of a galaxy is teeming with complex and uniquely combined formations of concentrated information and time.

77. In The Concentrated Center Of A Galaxy Spiral
Behold what a galaxy can create the closer one zooms into our

own: a planet with conscious minds that can peer beyond their own planet, solar system, and galaxy by properly utilizing all of the resources surrounding them.

78. The universe belongs to those who appreciate all of its contents, embracing all mysteries; shying away from nothing.

79. A Dreamy Existence

The dream-like quality of the universe and the possible ability, which must be earned by its creations, to gain power, using time, energy, pain, knowledge, and technology, all of which are dream-like, and to dream up their own realities, dreaming away all limitations and imperfections. Is the purpose of existence the creation and refinement of mind and consciousness? How many solar-systems out there in this dreamy cosmos have conscious life on them? What is a universe without conscious life? What exists beyond this cosmic dream?

80. Consciousness: The Foundation Of Existence?

Is cosmic existence created out of a need for consciousness? Does the universe have to work and form in such a way that it will be experienced, reflected on, and utilized? Does it work backward from its solution, conscious minds, and form exactly in such a way that whatever is needed to create conscious, thinking, questioning, dreaming, and inventing minds necessarily exists, everything becoming more mysterious and dream-like the further out from the conscious-self one gazes?

81. The Mindless Have Nothing To Lose

The weak of mind have a secret desire to be taken over by the strong of mind. The weak believe that the higher power they will be in the presence of is the only time they will ever get a taste of what it is like to be powerful. For when they are finally devoured by minds more powerful, they will die with delight in the sacrifice they have made to become one with them, even though they will be destroyed in the process.

82. Our understanding of things changes as our minds change.

83. New opportunities are necessitated into existence when a mind learns, thinks, creates, and shares what it has learned, thought, and created.

84. Mind: dominates matter.

85. **Minds: Idea Machines**
The mind who has thought of a new idea, later dis-proven, is more useful, courageous, and valuable than the mind who has thought of none at all.

86. **A Sign Of Cosmic Mercy?**
The human body and mind can only handle so much before going into shock or shutting down.

87. **A Garden Existence**
The soil of possibility.
The seed of potentiality.
The fruit of actuality.

88. The cosmos: the most supreme example of patience.

89. **The Five Fixations Of The Universe**
Novelty
Complexity
Diversity

Order
Refinement

90. The universe is not vain but efficient and experimental.

91. All things co-ordinate, whether to create or to destroy; whether to improve or degrade.

92. The universe is pregnant with potentiality.

93. **The Universe: Prefers Complexity Over Simplicity**
Simplicity is closer to chaos than complexity and is punished by the cosmos for its weaknesses. With greater complexity comes the potential for greater-order and stability. For complexity is rewarded with a better chance of a longer and more joyful existence.

94. Perhaps the beginning and the end are one. Maybe there is neither a beginning nor an end, both notions only existing for the convenience of human minds.

95. Can an activity as simple as petting an animal exercise and strengthen the domain of empathy in one's brain the more often one does it?

96. Planets: eggs that hatch consciousness, which births technology that can potentially expand and immortalize consciousness.

97. **The Co-Necessity Of Being**
Consciousness needs the universe to exist.
The universe needs consciousness to exist.

98. Firstly, a planet births minds. Then the minds adapt to their planet. Lastly, the planet adapts to its greatest minds.

99. How much do the weak-minded fuel the powerful-minded by ceaselessly providing them with new problems and obstacles?

100. Some minds belong to the present. Some minds belong to the future.

101. The universe rewards power and punishes weakness. This is the unconscious inspiration for all belief-systems that focus on eternal reward and punishment, but rather than rewarding an increase in the power of the individual mind, they reward the weakness of herd minds.

102. **The Light Of Birth And Death**
Why is it such a common occurrence with near-death experiences, psychedelic experiences as well as the entrance to life experience, the introduction of a consuming bright light?

103. **The Universe Rejects Nothingness**
Life constantly deteriorates, but nature surrounds life with regenerative vegetation. Why not just let life suffer and perish? Why should nature and the universe, if they are without purpose, have such a clear bias against absolute stagnancy and destruction, instead favoring the creative and unpredictable build-up and connectivity of time, energy, thought, and technology?

104. **The Anatomy Of Existence**
Creation
Connection
Combination
Conservation

105. A mind, like a universe, intakes information and expels information.

106. Why We Exist

The reason why our minds continuously grow and heal, the reason why healing and illuminating vegetables are scattered throughout our planet, and the reason why greater understanding of more information gives us greater technology and more power is because the universe wants our higher potential to be met, even if we do not.

107. Perhaps the universe works backward from its solution, meaning whatever fits the overall solution must occur and is, therefore, necessitated into existence, despite nearly impossible odds.

108. Evil: A Byproduct Of The Search For Greatness

The universe seeks to create Gods but sometimes creates useless devils.

109. A more clarified world is a more unified world.

110. No One Escapes Cosmic Dependency

We all depend on oxygen, water, and food, to survive. We are a species dependent on an entire planet, to say nothing of the universe we find ourselves in, to survive. For a person is not any freer than anyone else by avoiding the formation of a mature, experienced, intellectually, and creatively fruitful relationship with plants that are proven beneficial to both mind and body.

111. All life is in a steady state of growth and decay.

112. Rarity Seeks Higher States Of Rarity

The more rare something becomes, the more likely it is of becoming even rarer?

113. Those who survive death become more rare.

114. Minds addict to traumatic experiences and traumatic memories.

115. Whatever you think and do and whoever you keep around you makes the other possible versions of you in the multiverse more likely to think and act the same?

116. **Fine-Tuned Perimeters**
Time: to necessitate speed and quality for survival and power.
Death: to necessitate order, stability, endurance, imagination, and creation.

117. Every time we learn something new about the cosmos, the cosmos grants us new powers.

118. Universe: body.
Mind: spirit.

119. When one studies one's mind, one also studies one's universe. When one studies one's universe, one also studies one's mind.

120. Birth: to be necessitated into being.

121. **The Cosmos Sculpts With Trauma**
Like a ferocious sculptor, chopping off pieces of his work of art, nature uses trauma to uniquely complexify and strengthen our minds if we allow it to. For what appears to be something chaotic, destructive, and ugly can be a necessary tool for realizing a constructive purpose of increased order, creativity, and beauty.

122. The universe has made itself clear: ignorance earns weakness and suffering.

123. The Cosmic Bias Towards Connectivity

There is no habitable planet that allows excessive and wasted greed. If the ego of a planet's most intelligent and creative life becomes too untamed, the cosmos ensures that the planet's resources are depleted, making their own planet uninhabitable to themselves, also ensuring that they do not colonize on new planets.

124. The Universality And Immortality Of Resource

There exists nothing that is destroyed without being put to use.

125. Cosmic reality is no different than our imagination. Both continuously appear endless.

126. The universe has made itself clear: weakness and ignorance earn suffering.

127. Minds: connection collectors.

128. Body: the vehicle of brain.
Brain: the vehicle of mind.

129. The Freedom Of Fragility

One can only handle so much torture before one's torturers free us from all suffering.

130. All minds have cyclical ebbs and flows of lower and higher functioning.

131. Why is our universe more orderly, revealing, and useful the more one distorts one's reality by distorting one's mind?

132. A mind with more information than it had before has potentially become a greater mind than it was before, but only if the new

information can, by the mind, be properly synthesized with old understanding, in turn creating new synthesizable understanding.

133. "Who Hath Ears to Hear, Let Him Hear"[27]
Why do we have the ability to question this universe and ponder its mysteries, to command nature with technology like the great Olympians? It is as if the universe screams of a purpose for us that we are not able or ready to listen to and decipher.

134. The universe rejects stagnancy.

135. The universe punishes weakness, but it hardens, sharpens, and complexifies the strong, excluding the powerful but self-destructive, who are always a temporary power, and therefore weak.

136. **The Cosmic War Between Simplicity And Complexity**
All things are simple or complex representations of simpler or more complex representations. Our task is to sort and focus on the most complex representations and build even more complex representations from them. For representations do not only represent the history of cosmic existence but also the more complex representations of the future.

137. Everything attracts and repels in its own way.

138. Are we in a similar position to an octopus inside a human experimenter's container?

139. **The Universe: A Necessary Reflection Of Our Minds**
The universe changes necessarily, according to the minds perceiving it.

140. The Hatching Of Gods From Galactic Eggs

Where there are galaxies, there is the opportunity for the emergence of solar systems or planetary-egg incubators. Where there are planetary-egg incubators, there are planets or planetary-eggs—each with or without life-feeding resources. Where there is life, there are minds. Where there are minds, there is the opportunity for intelligent and self-aware minds to exist. Where there are intelligent and self-aware minds, there is knowledge, a natural resource. Where there are knowledge-consuming minds, there is technology, and where there is technology, there is the opportunity for knowledge-consuming, technology-extracting minds to leave their past and their home which aided them in their development, refining them without mercy and providing them with the adequate resources needed to spread out onto other planetary-eggs, rich with resources and new opportunities, increasing their chances of survival and their technological transformation towards immortal Godhood.

141. All things are a resource.

142. When we complexify our minds, we complexify our universe.

143. The Relativity Of Being

The universe: an unpredictable and inconceivably different place to primitive aliens, compared to technologically advanced aliens.

144. The universe expands and as it does it creates new opportunity for new solar-systems or incubating-systems, which have suns that incubate planetary-eggs, allowing the opportunity for life which permits the opportunity for consciousness, which allows the opportunity for technology and the reduction of suffering, the prolongation of life and the enhancement of power and bliss.

145. **Planets: Self-Consuming Objects**
All planets exist to be consumed by life.

146. The cosmos: an ocean of life and planets.

147. Intelligence: best determined by how quickly and how much one can synthesize old knowledge in order to create new knowledge.

148. All things reach for infinity.

149. Intelligence: measurable by the quality and quantity of new ideas.

150. **Mental Rovers**
There is more movement in our minds than our bodies.

151. **The Cosmos: The Great Humbler Of All Conscious Life, By Use Of Death And The Unknown**
Even the most technologically advanced alien civilization we can imagine would have the fear of death by an even more technologically advanced alien civilization.

152. All things compromise and are compromised for.

153. Every time one drinks water, it is as if one is drinking it for the first time.

154. **Information And Energy**
It takes energy to create information.
It takes information to create energy.

155. May the cosmos grant us time to further blossom.

156. Those Who Have A Superior Imagination Have A Superior Mind

A weak imagination, paired with a large amount of knowledge, is less creative and inferior in pattern-recognition and empathy, compared to the imaginatively powerful, paired with a smaller amount of knowledge, let alone with larger amounts.

157. Oscillation: The Primary Behavior Of The Universe, Encompassing All Behavior Throughout The Cosmos (The Oscillation Between Common Simplicity And Unique Complexity)

There is nothing known that is so powerful that the eternal force of oscillation, in all its universal forms, does not affect it with its changes, transformations, and configurations of motion, organization, and combination. The universe is ritualistic in its pursuit and conservation of uniqueness and complexity. It oscillates between common simplicity and unique complexity, as a human being oscillates between a baby and an adult. For who could ever foresee the average speechless baby transforming into a Plato or an Emerson? It is the responsibility of all life, especially those most conscious, to choose the preference of nature and the cosmos: powerful unique complexity.

158. Consciousness Is Meant To Travel

Why are there brains capable of visiting and learning about other planets separate from the planet from which they were born?

159. One Is Never Alone In Suffering And Striving To Become Greater

There is more to the universe than human successes and failures. If we could only imagine, let alone witness, what awe-erupting forms of mind, creation, love, and power exist far beyond the milky way in their own galaxy and struggle to overcome themselves and their section of the cosmos, as we do.

160. All life requires supplementation.

161. A great mind: an endless spring of new knowledge from which new minds drink to gain the energy and information necessary to create new possibilities.

162. **The Purpose Of Bees: A Simpler Representation Of The Purpose Of Humans (The Infinite Spectrum Of Connected Potential)**
For humankind, the fertilization of flowers represents the pursuit of new technology, the making of honey represents the pursuit of new technology and the protection of the queen and hive represents the transformation and refinement of human beings and their world.

163. Spearheaded: dangerously sharp of mind.

164. I am a mouthpiece of nature. I am the cosmos personified.

165. The cosmos: resourceful and experimental.

166. **Using And Refining Your Mindscope**
One's mind is like an adjustable microscope which magnifies whatever one thinks about, the more constantly and consistently it is used, while doing such things as reading, thinking, learning, or creating, and with the proper practice, effectively deepening one's thoughts and providing new questions and answers.

167. We are living in a human universe that is only a human universe to us, meaning, with mathematical certainty, this universe we live in is inevitably shared by other minds, some less advanced and some much more advanced than us, who see resources and opportunities in this universe where we see empty space and death; who see power and freedom where we see fear and nothingness.

168. **The Cosmic Bias For The Alchemical**
Specific combinations focused to a point create magic never before witnessed or experienced.

169. Self-pity: the only empowerment weak minds know.

170. **The Testing Nature Of Cosmic Existence**
All things test all things. This universe tests us with a touch of bitter mercy, which we call free-will or consciousness. All things good are a test that has been passed. For to exist at all is a passed test.

171. Cosmic existence will always be a mystery. Some people hate mysteries so much that they go insane trying to pretend that it is not a mystery, and some go so far as to believe that there are no mysteries.

172. The universe loves nothing more than a new adventure.

173. **Fear: Only Necessary For Survival (Living In Habitual Fear)**
The majority of our fears throughout the day are imaginary and often unwarranted. For most of our fears and concerns are only a habitual reaction, whether it is taught or self-realized.

174. Euphoria: a potentially permanent state of being.

175. Just enough heat permits life. Just enough coldness destroys life.
Just enough heat destroys life. Just enough coldness preserves life.

176. Earth: a planetary cocoon.

177. **New Complexities Arise From Both New And Old Difficulties**
Cosmic existence has to be difficult for life on any life-rearing planet to be pushed hard enough to be able to obtain the mental and technological prowess needed for the creation and development of new orders of complexity, of which are capable of living beyond their planetary cocoon.

178. A mind out of focus, without being surrounded by knowledge and art and without taking a seat in the cockpit of creation, begins to live a life without novelty or purpose.

179. **The Weak Only Feel Strong By Being Dominated By The Strong**
Weak minds can sense the power that comes from strong minds when they are dominated by them.

180. **Cosmic Illusions**
Pauses
Nothingness
Temporality

181. At night, lights take the place of daytime shadows.

182. All things transport and are transported. All things transform and are transformed.

183. All conscious life soon becomes bored with their own planetary egg and either uses it up or replaces it if they are not destroyed by it.

184. Maybe life does not have to leave its planet to leave its universe.

185. A coincidence is part of a larger pattern or patterns not yet discovered.

186. **The Paradox Of Light**
Light reveals and conceals.

187. Life and death are resources for consciousness and the imagination, both of which are resources for technological creation.

188. **All Things Break More Quickly And Easily Than They Develop (The Cosmic Preference For Growth And Power, Rather Than Stagnancy And Weakness, Enhances The Difficulty Of Life So That Life Can Become Stronger, Smarter, More Technologically Sophisticated And Less Miserable If It So Wishes)**
It is more difficult and takes a longer amount of time to gain consciousness than to lose consciousness. For if life and its advancements were easy, the illness and suffering of ignorance, stagnancy, and weakness would prevail and we would have less understanding, less power, and little to no consciousness from which to observe, think, create, discuss and learn from this ever-changing universe.

189. Does The Universe Have A Preference More For Effects Than Causes?

The roots are covered, but the fruits are the center focus.

190. The Ambiguous Nature Of Cause And Effect

Sometimes an effect is a cause of other effects.
Sometimes a cause is an effect of other causes.
Sometimes a cause is the cause of other effects.
Sometimes an effect is the effect of other causes.

191. Somethingness: more absurd, unpredictable, and unbelievable than nothingness.

192. Is going into shock from extreme pain a demonstration of cosmic mercy?

193. All things living and non-living are a resource.

194. The Cosmic Preference For Growth And Stability Is Demonstrated By The Continuously Ascending Difficulty Of Greatness, As Opposed To The Easy And Changeless Difficulty Of Weakness And Stagnancy

It is more difficult to grow than to be dismantled because this universe has a preference for growth and stability. It shows this through the higher difficulty of growth and stability, compared to decay and ruin. It is more difficult to dismantle something that has chosen to overcome the higher difficulty of growth and power. If it were easy to create or become something great, greatness would not be great. For it is up to life whether it becomes something great and lasting or dull and forgettable.

195. Even waste is a resource.

196. Some life does not need light to survive. Some life does not need oxygen to survive. What other life forms are we missing out on outside of our galaxy?

197. Some things are hoped into existence.

198. The universe has a strict diet, only eating its own creations, the waste of which is chaos: fuel for creations to create, combine and become new and improved creations.

199. Mind, art, and planet are always in flux.

200. **A Dependable Distinction Between High and Low Minds**
Some people's minds are more boring than others.

201. Fear keeps life from dying when it is not keeping life from living.

202. **This Universe Is A Creation, Disguised As A Discovery**
People have become stuck on discovery. They believe they are discovering when they are creating.

203. **Cosmorganism**
Is the cosmos a life form? Is it a mind-form?

204. **When Fear Brings Peace**
The planet begins to heal when people are globally in danger and forced into hiding by nature. For danger causes most people to become more meek and mild than they usually are, as long as they have food and water. Governments, tyrants, and all-controlling entities know this.

205. The happier and more enduring mind is the mind that keeps itself purposefully busy without ever completely sacrificing the heart and gut connected to it.

206. All things, big and small, use their own energy, which they collect from the energy surrounding them to build new things for the development of something greater than themselves.

207. **The Eye Of Spirit**
Eyes alone cannot prove that they can see any more than a brain can prove it can think without a body. Eyes without brains are like spirits without bodies. For brains hold eyes as bodies hold souls.

208. There are no thoughts without minds, and there is no vision without spirit.

209. **Life Globes And Light Globes**
Planets and eyeballs cannot be understood and utilized until they are experienced from the inside.

210. Even the loud awakening sun eventually becomes tired of sharing its energizing light.

211. A new mind is an experiment never before tested.

212. **The Most Important Question For Any Lifeform**
Does one have the passion, courage, ingenuity, honesty, patience, and endurance to become as God, or will one drop from one's tree-like incompletely grown fruit torn from its towering womb by one storm too many?

213. The life of a bee or an octopus is impossible for a human being to experience but not impossible to imagine. The life of a hu-

man being is impossible for a bee or an octopus to imagine or experience.

214. All things can be healed.

215. The increasing vastness of the cosmos deepens the minds of its perceivers if they only will allow it to.

216. Never give up on a mind, no matter how small.

217. The cosmos is filled with planetary eggs. Some have already hatched long ago while others are now prepared to hatch new life-forms and new possibilities.

218. Existence: its own purpose? Its own reward? Its own punishment?

219. **We Know Not What The Universe Could Be**
The more advanced a species becomes, mentally, consciously, and technologically, the more useful the universe becomes.

220. What is Earth? A system of order that allows for, along with new systems of order, systems of disorder, insofar as they can be used as a strengthening resource by adequately intelligent and creative life, giving way to new and refined systems of order.

221. All things collaborate to exist and to sustain existence. For even the end of a war is a collaborative resolution between both armies.

222. We are the manifested mind of planet Earth.

223. New minds: new perspectives; new perceptions.

224. Solutions Exist Before Problems, Attracting Us To Them, As Clouds Attract The Creation Of Water, Before Quenching The Thirst Of All Life On Earth (Clouds Are To Solutions As Rain Drops Are To Problems)

Like our eyes, which turn everything upside down, unbeknownst to the minds that use them, do our minds reason backward from the end of a thought to the beginning? Does nature grow this way? Does time move this way? Is a universe created this way? Does a cosmos create this way?

225. There are people with a higher IQ than Newton or Einstein, but they often have accomplished nothing of equal or greater lasting value than they. For the imagination cannot yet be included in the equation when designing our measurements of intelligence, thereby invalidating them.

226. All Life Strives For What It Must First Fight For

All life is both predator to some life forms and prey to other life forms, but neither identity is necessary, once mind, consciousness, and technology arise and transform.

227. A struggle always leads to a resolution, but not always a mutual resolution.

228. Intelligence: how well one can express one's understanding and consciousness.

229. Every planet heats and cools, like any other life-harboring egg. Some planets become eggs: life-incubators, and some planets become suns: planetary egg-incubators.

230. Memories: imprints of experiences.

231. **Temperature: The Speed Of Development**
The hotter the temperature of a planet, the faster the development of life on that planet? Contrarily, the cooler the temperature of a planet, the slower the development of life on that planet?

232. Mediocre minds only suggest what great minds elucidate.

233. **The Connection Of Spectrums**
A sound rising or lowering in pitch is equal to a light that glows brighter or dimmer?

234. Earth is filled with resources, much of which only human beings can use.

235. Earth: a resourceful resource.

236. All positive and negative parts of one's life are part of a contraction, whether it is the contractions of sickness or birth.

237. A simple object becomes less simple as the mind that plays with it develops and complexifies.

238. All life wants to be immortal, whether it realizes it or not, and there surely are life forms who eventually fulfill this universal desire.

239. One's mind never rests only one's body.

240. **The Three Wishes Of Life**
All life wishes to express itself, to empower itself, and to immortalize itself.

241. The imagination: a constant waterfall that rages out of the material constraints of a brain whenever needed or called upon for

its cleansing, healing, and novel nourishment, refining all those who drink from it.

242. The Eternal Marriage Of Mind And Soul
The mind is the self that influences the other.
The soul is the other which influences the self.

243. Greater mind forms await for lesser mind forms to catch up.

244. There is something comforting and consoling about the thought of other mind forms staring at the same bright lights above their heads and wondering if they are alone.

245. Existence: stacks and combinations of drugs and dreams.

246. The Cosmic Factory Of Potentiality
I was once a drug in pill form, among an infinite amount of other drugs in an endless factory traveling on an endlessly moving conveyor belt, being prepared for mass distribution. There could be seen the childish grin of a giant experimenter observing its creations and getting high off of their unpredictability. A scientist hovering over the entire operation, giddy with the novel possibilities made possible by distributing these mind-stretching drugs to billions of different minds on billions of different planets. Even the scientist was unaware of what would become of these drugs and who would end up using them, nor how it would change them, their communities, and their worlds.

247. The universe creates and transforms patterns.

248. Cosmic Epiphanies
There is no such thing as discovery.
Everything new is created.

Novelty is eternal.
Transformation is infinite.

249. Torture and suffering are always temporary. Death or madness is sure to follow if the suffering does not let up or becomes too intense. For not even the cosmos wants to experience torture for too long.

250. The universe sometimes creates monsters when it fails to create gods.

251. The trickster: a tester of mind and reality.

252. Can therapy cause one to need more therapy?

253. This universe seeks the creation of gods and the experience of Godhood.

254. Our planetary egg contains everything our growth and survival require.

255. The living only has two options: to create and live or to destroy and die.

256. **The Alchemical Nature Of Mind And Cosmos**
Mind and cosmos seek to trade stagnancy for novelty. They seek to mix novelty with novelty.

257. Notice how much easier it is to destroy than to create. This is the cosmos expressing how much it values creation over destruction and power over weakness.

258. Even the cosmos despises boredom.

259. Our addiction to novelty mirrors the cosmos' addiction to novelty.

260. The only universe a human can fully comprehend is a human universe. The only reality a human can fully comprehend is a human reality.

261. When our universe changes, our minds change.
When our minds change, our universe changes.

262. The cosmos: a patient opportunist.

263. From starvation to gluttony,
From celibacy to promiscuity,
extremes necessarily exist cooperatively.

264. **Chaos: A Resource For Order (Pain: A Resource For Pleasure)**
Why is there any sustained order or pleasure in such a seemingly chaotic universe? Why does the cosmos create thinking and feeling beings and provide them with tools for greater order and pleasure?

265. **The God Factory**
The cosmos consciously or unconsciously creates gods over time. For this to be accomplished, much suffering, chaos, and destruction must take place on many different planets to many different lifeforms, as the mighty blacksmith hammers beauty and power out of moldable unformed metals.

266. **Creativality**
Observers are created, not discovered. They create themselves as they create reality.

267. All things created: preparation for the future.

Politics & Religion

1. How many hells are we in danger of entering, and how many heavens will we miss out on for not following their associated religions? With all of the religions of this world, past, present, and future, and all of their associated rules, it appears as though we have a higher chance of accidentally entering hell than accidentally entering heaven.

2. **Childhood Religious Indoctrination**
A child can be coerced to believe nearly anything, especially when fear and dishonesty are used. The childhood belief in Santa Clause is a perfect example. Many children are lied to about Santa by their parents, who they trust more than anyone, even when Santa's existence is questioned by the children. The belief is further instilled by their parents by using scare tactics and the promise of a reward if they are good and believe in Santa's existence. Otherwise, no gifts will be received. This is a psychological trick many belief-systems take advantage of in order to acquire new believers. An important service one can do for their children is to let them find their own way based on their own experiences, instead of blindly following beliefs that were forced upon them. The most abusive part of childhood religious indoctrination is the act of instilling fear in the underdeveloped minds of one's children for the survival of one's

beliefs. Childhood indoctrination is not healthy for one's mind or spirit, especially when a child cannot yet fully understand what their parents believe. Let them decide when their minds are ready. They may eventually take comfort and pride in joining you in your beliefs, but at least give them the freedom to decide to learn about your beliefs when they are old enough to walk on their own spiritual path with their own two feet and fully developed minds. One's spiritual path is a personal adventure and should not be forced and directed by anyone other than the individual. What is the point of a free will if one cannot make their own unbiased choices or create their own unbiased thoughts because of force-fed beliefs at a young age by highly influential and biased adults? Be honest with yourself and your children. It is okay to admit that we do not know everything and to keep our minds open to new possibilities.

3. **Forbidden Technology**
Imagine a society where tools for viewing the unseen and the unknown, like the microscope and telescope, are made illegal. This is what has happened with consciousness-expanding plant and fungal life.

4. Belief-systems: closed descriptions of reality.

5. Indoctrination: having values, beliefs, and limitations forced upon you with the use of fear, guilt, and the promise of rewards for obeying and punishments for not obeying.

6. Closed religious doctrine treated as 100% unfiltered truth can convert sanity into insanity.

7. The idea of eventually residing in a perfect realm or state of being is usually the main focus of religion. This is precisely what we

seem to be born to do: use our thoughts as the building blocks of an internal and external paradise.

8. The Tyranny Of Beliefs

Those who are incapable of taking a step back from their belief-system to question it honestly have had their minds ruined beyond repair by their belief system and those who prescribed it. For unwavering believers have no power over their beliefs. Their beliefs have full control over them.

9. Belief Nurtures Potentiality

Beliefs will always have a place in human evolution, despite our advancements.

10. Closed-ended beliefs may have a comforting effect on certain individuals, but they always have a separating effect on the human collective.

11. We have cursed ourselves with closed-ended belief-systems.

12. We are so confident in our beliefs we assume they can stop us from being swept up by truth.

13. A Secret Enemy

Religion is friendly until you let it close you off from new information.

14. The Gift Of Myths

The eventual discovery of the non-existence of Santa is a valuable childhood lesson in questioning all handed down beliefs.

15. The Test Of Indoctrination
How you react and feel when you question your beliefs will tell you whether or not you have been indoctrinated and how severely.

16. An unhealthy belief hurts the believer when the belief is questioned.

17. Religion: A Threat To All Gods
Religions close off any adaptation to new discoveries, contradicting their gods and each other.

18. The Fundamental Difference Between The Religious And The Spiritual
The religious man has many rules for reaching God. The spiritual man has no other rule than to reach for God through himself.

19. The most insane conspiracy theory is that there are no planned conspiracies against the people.

20. The Hero And The Villain Of The Human Species
Beliefs: either motivation to think and move forward or motivation to refuse thinking and moving forward, even encouraging many people to think and move backward, insofar as their beliefs and teachers of their beliefs demand it.

21. Radicalism: the attempt to force a belief onto reality.

22. Technology Renders Closed Belief-Systems Obsolete
Any belief system that does not include technology and its continuous growth is obsolete at its conception.

23. If one is not willing to die for a belief, does one truly believe?

24. The Fundamental Message Of All Belief-Systems
This is what all our religions are trying to express: We can transcend our present form and reality as we had to do countless times before in order to finally become human beings. We can become one with God. We have never been separate and will never be separate from our creator, whether we are alive or dead.

25. A Problem With Karma
All of the people who get rich from making others poor, yet the rich and diabolical still live. The poor they create, however, continue to suffer and die. For this alone, karma deserves serious questioning.

26. Some people react to childhood religious indoctrination with ceaseless belief, and some people react with ceaseless disbelief.

27. A Source Of Great Tension Between The Liberal And The Conservative
The Liberal tends to believe that disorders and abnormalities cannot or should not be prevented.
The Conservative tends to believe that our disorders and abnormalities can or should be prevented.

28. Flashlights Of Belief-Systems
Imagine that every belief-system is a flashlight designed by humans to search for God. To stick with one belief-system is akin to having a rescue team in a dark forest, all searching for a missing person, but only one of the flashlights is allowed to be used.

29. Religion: a closed search for something beyond religion.

30. The Dark Ages With More Devastating Weapons

Welcoming the growth of a government is inviting the return of the Dark Ages, but instead of enslavement and death in the name of an all-seeing and untouchable God, it will be enslavement and death in the name of an all-seeing and untouchable government.

31. Parental Influence On Political And Religious Identities

When a child of parents are not taught their parents' values or are pushed away from their parents' values because their parents either failed to set a good example of their values and or made their child feel that they were not a good enough example of their parents' values, the child is likely to rebel and to follow and defend any values other than the values of their parents.

32. Belief-systems: gods begging to be believed.

33. Religions: a closed search for God, as opposed to an open-ended search for God.

34. A Problem With Both Political Parties

The Conservative tends to be too rigid to improve their hierarchy of values.
The Liberal tends to be too fluid to believe in a hierarchy of values.

35. It is time to take back the freedom and power of the individual that is gradually being removed from us by our government. We have been conditioned to be complacent for far too long, despite the continuous decrease in our power and increase in the power of our government. If the people wait too long to rebel, we will not have the freedom to even utter the word, rebel. We recognize that a government out of control of the people is a government that must be replaced. We, the people, demand what our ancestors worked and bled for: freedom of the individual.

36. Jesus was demoted from philosopher to messiah by his pupils.

37. Belief-Systems: A Test By God To Be Overcome
Why would a God create thinking and questioning brains just to create belief-systems that teach neither to think nor to question them?

38. A belief-system: a closed value-system that cannot help at all in the invention of new technologies. For a belief-system cannot help make new discoveries, only hide from them.

39. Genesis: A Story Of Consciousness
"Now the serpent was more subtle than any beast of the field which the Lord God had made. And he said unto the woman, 'Yea, hath God said, Ye shall not eat of every tree of the garden?' And the woman said unto the serpent, 'We may eat of the fruit of the trees of the garden: But of the fruit of the tree which is in the midst of the garden, God hath said, Ye shall not eat of it, neither shall ye touch it, lest ye die.' And the serpent said unto the woman, 'Ye shall not surely die: For God doth know that in the day ye eat thereof, then your eyes shall be opened, and ye shall be as Gods, knowing good and evil.' And when the woman saw that the tree was good for food, and that it was pleasant to the eyes, and a tree to be desired to make one wise, she took of the fruit thereof, and did eat, and gave also unto her husband with her; and he did eat. And the eyes of them both were opened, and they knew that they were naked."[28] …"The Lord God said, 'Behold, the man is become as one of us, to know good and evil.'"[29]

40. Never Sacrifice Your Mind To A Belief-System
What could a God ever accomplish with minds which have been

eroded, terrorized, and paralyzed by human-crafted belief-systems, of which un-adaptability to new information is a distinct trait?

41. Does Satan Represent Humankind?

Isaiah 14:12, "How you have fallen from heaven, O morning star, son of the dawn! You have been cast down to the earth, you who once laid low the nations!"[30]

42. A Christian Contradiction

To be taught to be as much like God as possible and that if one does, one will be punished, like Lucifer, who was banished from paradise for attempting to be one with God.

43. Common Traits Among Belief-Systems

Discouraging and disempowering.

44. The Future: The Enemy Of Closed Belief-Systems

Throughout our world, the majority are running on outdated value-systems that failed to foresee the nature of technology, thus failing to take technology and its exponentially complexifying, clarifying, and dreamy essence into account. Planet Earth is in need of a new and continuously updating value-system, the key function of which is adaptability to new information. For all value-systems which fail to include and fail to value questions, honesty, clarity, freedom, love, peace, power, knowledge, technology, experience, creativity, the imagination, and the individual, over all other values, are obsolete at their conception and will and do result in error and destruction on a planetary scale.

45. A Capitalist: A Pragmatist

If you are of no use to Capitalism, you are as good as dead.

46. Gods are meant to refine and inspire their believers, but all too often, they are used in order to limit and control their believers.

47. There are more people who express their beliefs than people who defend them.

48. Let nothing but love and the personal, creative and open search for truth be indoctrinated.

49. Belief-system: like a species of life that depends on believers for propagation and seeks to take over all other belief-systems by force if necessary for its survival.

50. It is common practice, with political dialogue, to unnecessarily belittle whatever side or place on the political spectrum one does not identify or agree with. In order to get the most out of our current political system, it is imperative to remember that two distinct parties have formed, and they can be best utilized as honest friends who inform one another and call out one another's lies and weaknesses, for the improvement of each other and in turn, their country, not for the dominance of one party over the other.

51. **A Necessary Sacrifice**
All minds of unwavering believers have been sacrificed on the altar of religion.

52. The enemies of governments: self-sustaining and self-empowering people.

53. **Irrational Punishment (Irrational Judgement)**
Imagine people being sent to hell for failing to ask for forgiveness for a sin they forgot they committed earlier in life, whether by brain damage or old age. What about someone who commits a sin

and unexpectedly gets killed in a car accident by someone not paying attention before being able to ask for forgiveness?

54. Our dreams of God are premonitions of the higher potentiality of all life.

55. The Power-Enhancement Of Understood Beliefs

One can imagine a higher society similar to the ancient Greeks, where all gods and belief-systems are understood as symbols, utilizable towards the enhancement of sanity, stability, and endurance of the majority; not merely believed but understood and utilized for increased passion and power of the people of a society. For understood beliefs are superior in utility and power to misunderstood beliefs.

56. Faith In Transcendence

Religions: the shared belief that humans are or can become gods.

57. Inevitable growth: a trait all governments share.

58. The far-right creates the far-left.
The far-left creates the far-right.

59. How To Save Your Soul

To save one's soul, one must remain an individual even in a society becoming less composed of creative individuals and more composed of a consuming-hivemind. In order to save one's soul, one must escape the indoctrination of collectivism and defend one's self against its labels, its manipulation, and its abuse.

60. Were the ancient Greeks unconsciously aware and accepting of their gods as fictional but beneficial, necessary, and empowering symbols?

61. Nihilistic Beliefs

Every religion with a returning messiah encourages the nihilistic, pessimistic, defeatist, and Disempowering desire for the end of the world.

62. The questioners of governments are like the doubters of gods throughout history and are treated by the majority of their believers just the same: with disgust and secret envy.

63. Government: Our New God (Godvernment)

Government is our attempt at creating a God. The religious and even those with no affiliation with any religion cannot refuse to bow down to our new God, lest they be punished and made an example of. With each new law of this God, the chains connecting ourselves to it are shortened, but in such a gradual way that the most conditioned and least doubting of believers will not notice until there is no thought or movement made without notifying this God named government.

64. The Imagination: An Enemy To Belief-Systems

The imagination is the enemy of all belief-systems and their peddlers. Indeed, one may never hear the word come from the mouth of a preacher, and this is because the congregation may soon discover that they could create a better religion themselves, or worse, may find that they no longer need to worship and follow any doctrine at all out of fear or to have to constantly skirt around all of the holes in their stories and ignore the absurdity of their God's strictly human traits, a common pattern to be found in the crafted gods of humans.

65. The Origin Of Hell

Perhaps the concept of hell originated from the awareness of the indescribable injustices that go on, assumed only to be seen and eventually dealt with by some particular God mankind has tied itself to, in order not to float too far away from their ego-feeding beliefs by the winds of thought, reason and the imagination.

66. One cannot claim to whole-heartedly believe in something that one either refuses to question or is not capable of questioning.

67. Belief-Systems Often Fill In The Hole Where Creative Self-Expression Is Missing

The more knowledge and creativity is suppressed and repressed in a society the more religious the people of that society will become, replacing self-expression with self-suppression, in order to make more room for the unquestioning worship of their particular belief-system.

68. The Relationship Between Idol And Ego

The reason why we go through patterns of loving and hating our idols is that sometimes the ego is especially threatened by our idols for compelling us and others to idolize them. It can easily grow envious for not being the one being idolized.

69. The Garden Of Eden: The War Between Humans And Their Ego (The Shedding Of The Primitive And Ignorant Animal Within)

The Tree Of Knowledge: a representation of the knowledge-absorbing, pattern-vacuuming, thought, awareness, and creativity-enhancing drugs, or fruit, of our early ancestors.
The Snake: a representation of our early ancestors' internal struggle to regularly shed the ego with art, drugs, and knowledge.
God: a representation of the animal ego and its deceiving scare-tactics.

It is not a coincidence that every attribute given to the Christian God, like jealousy, anger, and vengeance, is shared with the human ego.

70. Santa: a childhood exercise in skepticism.

71. Living Mummies
Is death less shocking, painful, terrifying, and controlling when you and everyone around you live as if you are already dead, like the Buddhist monks who have chosen to die while meditating?

72. Belief-systems: value-systems with punishable-if-broken rules, made and used to teach people what is important and what is not important, what to think and what not to think, how to live, and how not to live.

73. Disbelief Encourages Belief
The more a religion is resisted, the more true it appears to its believers.

74. If everything known was being controlled by an evil being, there would never be peace, nor bliss, nor opportunity. There would be no distinction between heaven or hell. For an all-powerful and all-destructive master of the universe would seek to maximize and sustain their satisfaction by maximizing and sustaining the torture of their creations.

75. Two Hells For The Price Of One
Why would God create a temporary existence, indistinguishable from a hell, for its prize creations, before sending them to another hell permanently? Since we have no choice but to adapt to hell, why would we ever be expected to become angels for a paradise,

both concepts of which are alien to the painful and demon-infested hell we have adapted to?

76. One cannot create a religion without also creating religious extremists.

77. Imagine if the time and energy spent on beliefs were spent on reality.

78. **Does God Draw Straws?**
What happens when the will behind one prayer is equal to the will behind another opposing prayer?

79. **When Religions Are Confused With Gods**
Do some people need to follow a religion to believe in God? Does God need a religion in order to exist?

80. **Hell On Earth**
Sometimes preachers end their own lives and show that not even the terrorizing belief in an eternal hell is enough to save them.

81. Beliefs can hinder or stop the upgrading of consciousness.

82. Bask in the freedom of thinking outside of political and religious systems.

83. **The Nihilistic Foundation Of Closed Belief-Systems**
To closed belief-systems, meaning is found only in doctrine and in death. They routinely deny life in favor of a life after life.

84. **The Combination Of Beliefs And Religions**
Nuns: Christian Monks.

85. The Fruit Of Consciousness (The God Of The Old Testament Represents A Tyrannical Government)

Our government has, for decades, treated us and the *Devil's Lettuce* like God treated us and the fruit of consciousness: with deceit. Cannabis will not kill you, and neither did the fruit of consciousness kill Adam and Eve. Satan, forever a symbol representing our curious and rebellious nature, is portrayed as something evil and dishonest, as our government has falsely portrayed consciousness-expanding plants and fungi, as dangerous and without medicinal or societal value.

86. The Last Freedom

Once guns are taken from the people, all of their remaining freedoms can be taken.

87. We treat our government like a deity in all other aspects of our life, we might as well begin praying to it.

88. Are belief-systems more destructive to human beings than constructive?

89. Imagine feeling guilty when you do not enter a church every week. This is not sane or healthy behavior. This is pathological behavior and is a snippet of the kind of dangerous and irrational thinking that had hard-working Christian people cheering on the screams of innocent women burning alive, of whom they believed to be witches who deserved to go to hell twice.

90. We justify war with the hope of ending all wars, but the end of war has never come, just as every religion falsely claims to be the last religion and every messiah falsely claims to be the final messiah.

91. The Most Rebellious People Are A Disposable Resource To Governments, But Most Importantly, A Threat

Governments remove the rebels of society through the imprisonment of those most likely to ignore unnatural laws written and enforced by governments that treat the individual as a mute phantom and the collective as if they were only useful as slaves. The militaries of governments gather those most willing to fight for their country and place them in situations that either disable them or kills them, mentally or physically.

92. We Are Always Weakened By The Indoctrination And Degradation Of Governments And Religions

Abuse and negligence have become so common, ignored, and excused that you would be hard-pressed to find an adult without retardation in some area of thought or emotion if you are around them long enough. Our governments and religions have retarded us and continue to do so by valuing money over life and family, by valuing the masses over the individual, and by valuing themselves over the people. They have successfully degraded the human being. This is what they are most effective at doing. They never want the people to advance mentally or emotionally. They would prefer that we become like children who are more easily tricked and controlled so that we can be used for their own expansion of power. For they would always rather us remain weak, divided, distracted, less conscious, and more dependent on them.

93. The separation of church and state is an impossibility. For you cannot have one without the other.

94. Governments and religions mutually benefit from each other.

95. Most life-long followers of any monotheistic religion cannot agree that they pray to the same God as all other monotheistic gods or that their religion is the same pursuit of a higher potential state of being which transcends life and death.

96. Religions: attempts at explanations for the unknown state of pre-birth and post-death.

97. **Politics, Religion And Identity**
We know that politics are fueled by the same problem of cognitive dissonance as religion by how rare it is for people to forgo the beliefs and perspectives of their political identity, many of which are born out of sheer resentment from their upbringing or lack thereof. The result of this is that many people do not know why they believe what they believe, and they live their lives without questioning their beliefs or their identities. For every time beliefs that are connected to a person's identity are questioned or insulted, they will nearly always choose the side of their identity and its associated beliefs over facts.

98. Knowing why we believe something can sometimes be the very reason why we stop believing it.

99. **The Buddhism Dilemma**
If we had a world full of strict Buddhists, there would never be a single war or act of hate, violence, or cruelty against another life form. However, if there were not some Buddhists who were not as strict about their lifestyle and continued advancing technology and self-expression, through the creation of art, we can never be sure what kind of paradise we could be missing out on; what powers of thought, joy, love, and creation we could obtain.

100. Governments: mature religions
Religions: immature governments

101. No one can deny that government is God of the governed. We were once led by gods. Now we are led by governments.

102. The state: a religion you are born a part of that plays all the same tricks to gain and keep followers as religions and their preachers.

103. **Becoming Karma**
The idea of karma is ludicrous unless all past suffering is purposefully redeemed by us into the future.

104. Religion: a drug some people can never quit.

105. **Hell: The Enslavement Of People By Beliefs**
Hell: living for any closed belief-system.

106. **A Book Fit For Peasants Under The Control Of Kings**
Was the bible written and rewritten by different kings throughout history, from their point of view, explaining why the God of the old testament thinks and behaves as a human king would and why he is described as an easily angered and jealous tyrant that kills millions on a whim and demands from his readers to be worshiped and to think and behave with the submission of the most frightened and self-pitying herd of disempowered minds, or else suffer for eternity?

107. Religion and politics are interchangeable.

108. **The Denial Of Doubt**
Faith for some is pride in the denial of necessary doubt in a belief

or beliefs that deserve to be doubted, that beg to be doubted, and if they are proven to be unadaptable to present-day understanding, deserve to be abandoned and ridiculed, on the grounds of logic, reason, evidence, and honesty.

109. Religious people might as well be living in a different reality from those who admit the truth, which is, no one knows, if any, which God or religion is the one that sends us to a particular heaven or hades. For no one knows what exists beyond this life, and most people will never admit it.

110. Religions are used to help a society endure tyranny rather than combat it.

111. Tithing: small scale taxation.
Taxation: large scale tithing.

112. All closed-systems are dangerous.

113. Did religion begin from alien visitation?

114. **Where Atheists And Religious People Agree**
Atheists and religious people are often too frightened to believe in the existence or the visitation of alien beings because both reject the idea of being created or influenced by godly alien minds. For atheists would rather not be created by a higher intelligence, and religious people would rather not be created by anything other than their own particular God.

115. Hell: a concept that has terrorized many a child, weakening, controlling, and stagnating a staggering number of adults, chasing them into their death beds.

116. Religion: a pressuring list of things you can and cannot do.

117. Jesus represents the pain that is required to gain power.

118. The Irony Of Religion
Religion creates atheists as consistently as it creates religious people.

119. Religion: Our Tendency To Limit Ourselves In Our Efforts To Become Unlimited
We want to become the Gods we believe in, but we make it more difficult to do so by creating religions that punish those who question, those who learn from the past, and those who adapt to the future.

120. Religion And Politics: Forever Tied Together (The Separation Of Church And State Is An Illusion)
The most significant difference and the core issue between the Liberal and the Conservative is religious belief or the lack thereof.

121. We are held back by obsolete beliefs and ideas.

122. You are not thinking for yourself if you are allowing a religion to think for you, thus contradicting freewill.

123. False Atheists
Some Atheists secretly are religious people who were sufficiently indoctrinated to believe just enough to feel scared enough of their God that they decide to disbelieve in any supposedly existing God, with the hope of escaping the punishment of any supposedly existing God. However, the fear of God tends to linger, especially when it is taught at an early enough age to stick to adulthood, and so long as it lingers, it is never escaped until death's approval.

124. The enemies of free spirits: all attackers of free-thinking, free-questioning, new understanding, the individual and the freedom of the individual, by the hands of anyone or anything, whether it be a government, a religion, a corporation, a King, Queen, or president.

125. Religious people generally do not want to admit how much drugs have influenced the creation of religions in our past.

126. **Fighting A Belief-System Is Counter-Productive (Constructive Silence Is The Appropriate Response To Any Belief-System)**
The people who fight a belief-system make that belief-system seem more true to the people who believe in it. For a belief-system is only as true to its believers as it is attacked by the believers of other belief-systems.

127. **Love Or Religion?**
How many people in this world would choose their religion over their child if they could only choose one or the other?

128. **The Ironic Cycle Of Drugs And Belief-Systems**
The use of drugs influences the creation of religions, and the creation of religions influences the rejection of drugs.

129. **The Similarities Between Christianity And Buddhism**
Positives: both encourage peace and love.
Negatives: both encourage blocking out one's surrounding universe. They encourage the rejection of new information and the undervaluing of knowledge, philosophy, and creativity. They encourage the premature end of intellectual and creative development by denying the value and potentiality of mystery, novelty, questions, thoughts, creativity, and consciousness.

130. Reincarnation: implies becoming every victim and every victimizer.

131. The Fear-Based Perception Of Religion

Demons and devils represent the parts of nature, the cosmos, and ourselves not yet understood, and on that account, too frightening to be dug deeper beyond the perception of religion.

132. Religions: Closed Belief-Systems, Rather Than Open Knowledge-Systems Or Truth-Systems

Closed belief-systems teach that blind indoctrination is more vital than knowledge or curiosity. For devoutly religious people, life is not about learning or clarifying knowledge. It is not about honestly searching for the truth. It is all about beliefs and the comfort and self-righteousness they bring them. They ignore their unhealthy and disempowering aspects. The ignorance, confusion, hate, and mayhem they cause are not a concern for them. For an untold amount of people, the global miseries and headaches brought on by closed and controlling belief-systems, which are unadaptable to new knowledge, can only be remedied by becoming a blind believer and defender of one themselves.

133. Religious belief: a narcissistic impulse that gives the false appearance of being a collective and empathetic impulse.

134. Too many valuable people have lived and died for people, governments, and belief-systems not worth living and dying for.

135. The Effects Religions Have On Art And Science

Religion is the silencer, destroyer, and motivator of art and the creator, antagonizer, and motivator of science. Art and science must always be on guard. For religion never sleeps. Its paranoid eyes and envious ears are always prepared to remove from existence anyone or anything that contradicts it.

136. In Creative Value, The Most Influential Prophets Fail To Surpass The Most Influential Philosophers

No prophet has ever surpassed the greatest thinkers in writing, discovery, or invention. Why would that be? Because prophets search for truth by using unchanging beliefs while philosophers search for truth by using questions, ideas, and facts that change with new knowledge.

137. Religion: The Trial Of Creativity (When Religion Is Confused With Art)

Every day, religions steal creative energy, which belongs to art.

138. Socialism: The Attempt To Force Equal Value Onto Every Individual Of A Country (Forced Equality Slows, Weakens, Ignores And Prevents Individual Greatness)

Forced equality erodes variety and originality, rendering all value and valuations useless. It is the beginning of the death of art and the individual. Socialism is a nihilistic trap that appears easy and safe. It is for people who are losing or have lost the values and the self-reliance of their ancestors to their government and people who keep a deep resentment for this loss; people who wish to clear the board and start from scratch, without care for everything that has been achieved without socialism and all that can be lost with socialism. For socialism is for people who have grown to trust and depend on their government more than themselves, like a child that allows its parents to perform tasks it could do itself, and with enough experience and freedom, could perform even better than its parents.

139. Belief-Systems And Their Beliefs: Parasites That Control Their Most Devout Hosts

Having an honest discussion today with a devoutly religious person about anything outside their belief-system or the stunningly vast amount of time before their belief-system was even a thought is as impossible as having an honest discussion with someone from the dark ages, whose insane level of belief was equal to their love of torture and cruelty: the way of confirming beliefs and of feeling in control for minds that have been hindered, deranged and broken by the indoctrination of certain belief-systems and their beliefs. Minds that enjoy harming or killing others or enjoy watching others harm and kill are often hateful and resentful people, who, in their most honest, rare, and fleeting moments of painful solitude, (Weak and dishonest people hate solitude. Their hell is having no one around to be dishonest with and having no one to tell them how to think, feel or act.) realize that they have been lied to and weakened and that they can no longer disbelieve their beliefs. No longer can they believe in anything outside of their belief system. The parasite has taken root in its believer.

140. Religions possess their followers.

141. Religion Contradicts Free Spirits (When Humankind Sabotages Itself)

Religion: when humankind attempts to control humankind by selling tickets to immortality and threatening anyone who does not buy their tickets, the cost of which is a greater humankind, more free, honest, creative, and inquisitive.

142. Religions Need Governments In Order To Force A Society To Trust And Obey Them (Governments Need Religions In Order To Force A Society To Trust And Obey Them)

When people rebel against their religion after waking up from its deceptions, they rebel against anything associated with their religion, even if that means rebelling against the freedom, safety, health, strength, and advancement of their own nation.

143. The Blindness Of Religious And Political Identities

Like a religion, whatever a political party tells its followers to think or do, the followers think and do.

144. Greatness: A Race With Time And Insanity

Humankind is trapped in a hell where it cannot think or act without the limiting demands of different belief-systems. When will we realize that religions only cause us to stray further from God and one another? When will we realize that we no longer need religions to have a relationship with God? When will we understand that we no longer need religions to move forward as individuals and as a species? It brought us to science and technology through faith in something greater than human; in something greater than the past and the present. This is the purpose of religion, but the training wheels of a society need removed eventually if the society of people wishes to advance and accelerate technologically towards Godhood without exterminating themselves.

145. The Persistence Of Closed Belief Enslaves Us And The Persistence Of Open Understanding Frees Us

The creative persistence of wonder preserves new understanding and permits new technology. The more comforting persistence of closed belief preserves obsolete understanding and prevents new technology from being coaxed into being.

146. When you censor criticism, you also censor critical thinking.

147. Only a human would want to be worshiped by humans.

148. Governments: often obeyed out of fear, much like Gods.

149. **Big Government: The Beast**
All along, were we being warned in the book of Revelations about governments and their destructive and self-destructive nature? For no matter how much a government controls, abuses, weakens, and muffles a populace; eventually it will create the conditions, the tools, the resentment for its own demise by weakening and devouring the very people that keep it powered with their labor and the indoctrinated illusion of needing it to think and live freely and prosperously.

150. Anti-scientific people tend not to seek immortality during life but afterlife. They do not seek immortality technologically but religiously. Scientific people tend not to seek immortality afterlife but during life. They do not seek immortality religiously but technologically.

151. Notice how artists never kill religious people in the name of art, truth, beauty, or God, but many a religious person has killed many an artist for defying and contradicting their religion. Is this how people secure in their truth behave?

152. **Religions: Closed Value-Systems (Dangerous Art)**
Religion: Art closed off to science; Art that cannot adapt to new information, new discoveries, or new technological creations.

153. **A Reliable Tool For Governments And Religions To Gain Control Of A Society: Keeping People Sick And Afraid**
It is illness and the fear of illness, along with the fear of death and the unknown, that cause religions and governments to be created

throughout this planet, trusted, depended on, and expanded until their conniving tentacles wrap around every aspect of a society, squeezing into every family home, stretching as far as is necessary to reach the easily manipulated brains of children in schools and churches until they have gained control of every thought and every action of the majority. Every government and religion benefits from a society feeling endangered. For every government and religion receives more control from the people, the more control they take away from the people.

154. Governments And Religions: Useless Without Great Individual Thinkers

One can see how unnecessary and deceitful governments are when humankind is in serious danger. During a global crisis, it is the self-dependent individuals who survive and prosper. For one can feel freedom grow during the growth of a deadly and global pandemic. This feeling of enhanced freedom is the realization that neither governments nor religions can save you from a global threat. They can only feed people what they usually prefer to eat: comforting lies and hush money. They are useless without Scientists and Philosophers, in short, without honest and independent thinkers who they can take advantage of and use against the populace by continuously removing their freedoms, always in the name of safety and security. Every government and religion begins and expands this way. They promise to be the cure to every illness, the solution to every problem. Many things are impossible for them to bestow, but they rely on individual great thinkers and creators to accomplish them. They eventually conspire against them, too if they become more threatening than useful to them.

155. Religion: a weapon of government.
Government: a weapon of religion.

156. Weakness and ignorance enable tyranny.

157. Imagine a government that frees and empowers the people. Imagine a religion that frees and empowers its followers.

158. Like religions, governments exist because people tend to have faith that they will always be taken care of and that they will have the fear and burden of self-responsibility removed for them.

159 Indoctrination: contracting the fear of asking questions.

160. **The Cycle Of Belief**
Beliefs give way to science. Science gives way to beliefs and the denial of science. The denial of beliefs gives way to the acceptance of being betrayed by beliefs. The acceptance of being betrayed by beliefs gives way to the revengeful sabotage and replacement of a nation's traditional beliefs, values, and the people who still defend them.

161. All political arguments boil down to one side feeling more or less in danger than the other side during times of local, national, or global change.

162. **We Appear Unable To Escape Our Love For Belief-Systems**
Humans love religions so much that even Atheists tend to treat science like a religion.

163. The Conservative tends to seek protection from government with the use of their dependence on a religion.
The Liberal tends to seek protection from religion with the use of their dependence on a government.

164. Some people worship their religion more than God.

165. **The External Control Of The Individual Self Is Less Sustainable Than The Internal Control Of The Individual Self**
If everyone focused on understanding, strengthening, protecting, nourishing, and overall improving themselves, then no one would believe they needed to be rescued and remote-controlled by governments, politicians, or priests.

166. Governments take people over like a thief in the night.

167. Governments would be anti-religious if they did not benefit so much from religions.
Religions would be anti-government if they did not benefit so much from governments.

168. Religious people generally appear undisturbed by the fact that our governments tend to have more authority and power than our religions.

169. **The Difference Between Individual And Collective Politics And Philosophies**
The Liberal wants their government to protect them and wants to be able to transfer the responsibility of their own decisions onto their government.
The Conservative wants their God to protect them and wants to be able to transfer the responsibility of their own decisions onto either their God or evil spirits.
Libertarians want governments, Gods, and devils to stay out of their way as they take responsibility for their own thoughts, their own decisions, their own education, their own freedom, their own protection, and their own future.

170. The sheep never develop the ability to fight the wolves back. The sheepherders make sure of it, never giving them a chance to cease needing them.

171. An anarchist endures the same reactions from government and state worshipers as an atheist endures from religion worshipers.

172. Indoctrination: the meticulous and manipulative assault on criticism.

173. Religions: cause more problems than they are meant to solve by influencing people to ignore their reality.

174. The media is the government's messengers, like the deadly angels of God.

175. Propaganda and censorship: the government admitting its fear of rebels, their questions, and their pesky revolutions.

176. **Politics Are More Dangerous Than Religion**
Even religions must bow down to governments.

177. Religions: different versions and interpretations of history.

178. You are not left-wing or right-wing. You are a human being with inalienable rights.

179. To take a wolf and turn it into a small, weak, and defenseless lapdog is nothing less than animal cruelty. This is what we do to ourselves with the use of governments and religions.

Nietzsche said, "In most cases, the taming of a beast is achieved through the harming of a beast: the moral man, too, is not a better man but only a weaker one. But he is less harmful...."[31]

180. If you are ever in an argument with someone who is trying to make you feel insane or ostracized for admitting that you do not know what happens after death, remind them that what you are both doing right now is a less violent example of what different civilizations murdered each other over in wars with axes and swords.

181. One can believe in an afterlife and also admit that one does not know what happens afterlife.

182. One does not automatically become an atheist by questioning one's belief system. One may become even more confident in one's belief in God without requiring a belief-system to continue believing. One may humbly accept that one does not know and that no human knows. One may accept the possibility that no one is capable of fully comprehending God.

183. We have been trained to care more about the health of our governments and belief-systems than ourselves.

184. **The Pathology Of The Liberal And The Conservative**
The Liberal tends to trust and depend too much on big government.
The Conservative tends to trust and depend too much on religion.

185. **Distrust Beliefs (Trust Ideas)**
Beliefs: closed ideas that are treated as truths.

186. The Free Individual Versus The Enslaved Collective

Satan is a symbol of the individual and rebellion, commonly used to frighten people into refusing to think with their own mind or to question authority, training them to blindly follow and depend on anyone or anything but themselves. Satan, the father of lies, and the supposed villain of the bible and all of humankind is actually the victimized hero and underdog character of Christianity, who was selfishly and deceitfully used by his authors and editors and continues to be used by those who avoid self-responsibility and those who attempt to control the thoughts and behavior of both believers and non-believers, using mostly scare-tactics, while God showcases the same wretched personality of the people of that time and place in human history, completely contradicting an all-loving and all-powerful God, but, nevertheless, demanding to be worshiped and imitated by all of humankind.

187. False Representations Of God

In the old testament, God represents government and collectivism, while Satan represents the individual and all values associated with the free-thinking individual. Truthfully, God represents the individual and all values associated with the free-thinking individual, while Satan represents government and collectivism.

188. If you want to find God for yourself, using your own experience and understanding, stay away from all religions.

189. Religions: A Constant Threat To The Golden Rule

The golden rule can no longer be practiced safely. For the rule, "do unto others as you would have them do unto you,"[32] is a rule that assumes that everyone is always aware of themselves and always treating themselves with love, unlike a self-avoidant, nihilistic and masochistic society, such as we have today, made up of people who have already given up the fight to preserve the freedom of the individual and who refuse to sustain self-awareness, and to use and push the limits of their thought and consciousness.

190. Religions: anti-philosophical because they do not allow room for questions.

191. The Conservative is too safe.
The Liberal is not safe enough.

192. The Liberal is too open to change.
The Conservative is too closed off to change.

193. **Meeting In The Middle**
As humans and their problems are best understood by studying both men and women, rather than just one gender, politics and its problems are best understood by studying each side of every political debate.

194. **The Lazy Way Of Looking For God**
Religion: having more trust and faith for someone else's experiences and understanding than one's own.

195. **Religion: A Tortuous Counter-Intuitive Solution To Our Tortuous Ignorance**
A religious life: to torture oneself during life, with endless mind-weakening rules, priorities, guilt, and shame, along with creative, scientific, philosophical, and sexual repression, to avoid accepting that one does not know any more than anyone else what happens after this life.

196. Is the endless battle between the Liberal and the Conservative a battle between our left and right hemispheres?

197. Belief-Systems: When Humans Pretend To Be Different Gods In Order To Control Themselves

No matter how valuable the history, poetry, and influence of religious doctrine, it is always seasoned too generously with the deceitful perspective of humankind and always carries with it the sickening scent and taste of poor acting and moldy beliefs. For no closed belief-system ages well. They are never created and written from the perspective of a timeless and inhuman God that wants its creations to be prepared for the future, that wants to empower, advance, and complexify their minds, their consciousness, their knowledge, and their technology; a God that does not have to rely on fear to control its creations and does not have to demand to be believed by dangling above them the promise of eternal reward or drilling into children's minds the endless fear of eternal punishment. A God that wants to be known would have no use for beliefs or belief-systems. For they would only cause a reduction in the quality of their communication with their creation. Why would an almighty being demand to be believed rather than known? Why would it withhold from its creations evidence that would undoubtedly prove it was the true creator, not the countless other Gods humans continue to confuse, terrorize, control, and weaken each other with, rendering a cruel eternal hell unnecessary for those who were born in the wrong place or time and those who use the mind God gave them to question all belief-systems? For the words of a true God would, without error or confusion, adapt to future discovery and invention.

198. Philosophy, science, and technology are more deserving of faith than any closed belief-system. While one man prays for change, another man uses his own God-gifted mind to create his own miracles. Religions have always lied to us, and in so doing, have dulled many a mind and stolen many a life. They weaken our

creativity, curiosity, and individuality. They consistently fail to empower us or to improve our minds and our consciousness. Contrarily, science, philosophy, and technology consistently reward us for our mental and physical labor and our loyalty to truth, rather than ideology, with greater medicine, greater communication, greater mobility, etc. It is ironic that even though belief-systems often make science their villain because they cannot adapt to the new creations and information that thinking and questioning minds routinely discover and create, it is their villain that is proving to be capable of turning us into the Gods we used to create and worship. For religions do not want Gods as followers. They want control of weaklings who never cease to obey and who never question or abandon them. Philosophy, this old wise and surprising serpent, contradicts the errored certainties that all closed-ended religions share. For the real threat to humankind are its endless belief-systems and their followers, of whom still shriek with fear and malice in the presence of the ever-growing, ever-thinking, ever-teaching, and ever-creating snake.

199. God Is Not Religious

The belief in any religion is the belief in a human interpretation.

200. The Test Of Religious Certainty (God Supports Self-Responsibility)

If one is certain about the truth of one's religion, then one has yet to try replacing all medicine and technology with prayer. For anyone who honestly does so for a long enough time is soon shown both the validity of science and the falsity of religion. For answered prayers require God to be met halfway.

201. Sometimes we show our belief in something by how much we fear it, and sometimes we show our fear of something by how much we believe it.

202. What if all religious energy, globally, was directed towards greater thought, technology, and freedom?

203. **There Is More To Life Than Death**
Religions: teach the embracement of death rather than the embracement of life.

204. Spirituality: recognition of the unity of being.

205. **Fear, Ignorance, And Anger Fuel Superstition**
Notice when one is having a particularly unfortunate day how easy it can be to blame superstitions and curses instead of blaming chance or one's self, regardless of how skeptical and rational one normally is.

206. The most attractive belief-system is one that implements the unconscious symbols, which are most adaptable to the future and the most adamant about seeking future expression.

207. **Hell: The Genesis Of Life**
Hell is the beginning stages of all highly developed life; the gnashing of teeth and the gluttonous fire that burns forever. The price of heaven is hell for what seems like an eternity to early forms of life but is a mere strike of a match in comparison to the infinite light of cosmic potentiality.

208. Belief-systems: control-systems.

209. How can anyone deny how shamelessly phony and soulless these rich and powerful politicians are openly showing themselves to be?

210. **We Are Divided And United By Values**
Those who have not become nihilists adopt the values of a religion or a government. The problem is governments use religions to control idealistic believers, and they use atheism to control nihilistic atheists because beliefs and values are the easiest to control people with since they are interlinked with their identities. Whether one is religious or not, the idealist has values to fight for while the nihilist has none. Those who have no values become anarchist entropists who only want to see their country fail so that it can be rebuilt by idealists. Neither side is going to ever agree with the other if they cannot agree on their values and priorities, and those who take advantage of us bank on this. Nihilistic atheists often suffer from biased resentment and do not think any more clearly or honestly than religious idealists. Neither is capable of offering new ideas and solutions because both are dead set on proving the other wrong.

211. Mainstream media feeds the Liberal and the Conservative a virtual reality where both sides feel as though as soon as they walk outside, a citizen, police officer, or virus will kill them.

212. Politics have become one of the most entertaining and time-consuming sports.

213. It is not uncommon that churches preach about hell more than heaven because you cannot scare and control people with heaven the way you can with hell.

214. We focus too much on what we believe and do not believe and not enough on why we believe or do not believe.

215. The Liberal: The Culture Party (The Conservative: The Religion Party)

The Liberal tends to value culture more than the Conservative values culture. If atheism becomes a cultural trend, The Liberal tends to choose culture over religion. The Conservative tends to value religion more than the Liberal values religion. If atheism becomes a cultural trend, the Conservative tends to choose religion over culture.

216. How many people project their personal and family problems onto politics and religions?

217. The Liberal tends to have no fear of slippery slopes.

218. One Can Be Good And Be In Control Of Oneself

The most common trick governments and religions use against people is convincing them with fear and deceit that they have to be controlled in order to be good.

219. The Natural Cycle Of Political And Social Equilibrium (The Balance Of Controlling Indoctrination And Rebellious Resentment)

The far-left is often the result of being raised by the far right. The far-right is often the result of being raised by the far-left. For all children tend to either mimic the thoughts, values, and beliefs of their parents or to resent and reject them, often with as much, if not more pride and zeal than their parents have for their own thoughts, values, and beliefs.

220. From Idea To Identity

Political parties and religious denominations are ideas that have become identities. When you question or contradict them, you cause people to feel like they are losing control by challenging and threatening their identities.

221. Religion and atheism equally oppose idealism. For this reason, neither can be trusted when it comes to the future and its creation. Atheists and religious people are allies more than they will ever admit.

222. Political movements are like religious movements: they never remain untouched and are inevitably highjacked by people who either use them as a business or as an excuse to feel superior to people who are not part of their political or religious movement and to treat them as immoral and insane. They justify their hatred for other movements and their followers because they believe they happen to be the lucky recipients of absolutely non-corrupted political or religious values and interpretations. Political and religious movements always branch out into different interpretations as they age until fewer people agree with each other about them. For they tend to end up causing more harm and division than they originally intended to.

223. Political movements and parties are followed and defended like religions, even by people who claim to be non-religious.

224. The Extra Golden Rule (The Rule Stressed More Than Treating Others As You Would Prefer To Be Treated: The Surrendering Of Self-Empowerment, Self-Understanding, And Self-Dependency)

Religions tend to have one rule in common: to never believe in yourself or depend on yourself more than your beliefs and their system. When you face the choice between your belief-system and yourself, you are supposed to choose your belief-system. This attracts the question, what if God did not believe in itself? Would it have been able to create something so remarkable that it is capable of doubting its existence and of mimicking its creation of new and unbelievable things, as all Godly children do?

225. When belief-systems fail to create loyal and trusting believers, they create resentful and rebellious atheists. In the same way, governments create resentful and rebellious anarchists when they fail to create loyal and trusting citizens. Atheists, anarchists, and nihilists typically are not concerned with creating new ideas and valuations, only with rejecting and destroying old ones. The creation of new ideas and valuations is usually left up to the idealist: the enemy of believers, atheists, anarchists, and nihilists.

226. A loyal believer of a belief-system is like the loyal unquestioning citizen who, regardless of what happens, accepts everything that its government tells them about themselves and their reality and obeys all of their rules on when and how to use their mind, time, and energy. The Idealist does not depend on any person or system for his or her way of life or way of thinking. The anarchist, atheist, and nihilist all exist because they failed to be indoctrinated by a belief-system or government, and now they are its loyal opposition.

227. Rigid atheists usually are not idealists because of the resentment they often carry for beliefs, their systems, and their teachers. They are normally too busy being skeptical and distrusting to be idealists.

228. Atheists and anarchists normally do not achieve what they could because they are too hell-bent on burning to ashes every God, leader, and system that has pushed them towards their current identity.

229. The idealist provides the ideas that turn into beliefs which turn into belief-systems which create extremists, which create anarchists, atheists, and nihilists, which create more Idealists.

230. The Liberal tends to accept the identity of the victim, even if they are not.
The Conservative tends to refuse to be a victim, even if they are.

231. **Accept The Cosmic Rejection Of Stagnancy**
Our belief-systems are like the buildings we craft and live in, to protect ourselves from chaos and to reject novel information, but there is no building so strong that an earthquake will not tear it apart, and there is no belief-system so strong that new information will not contradict it.

232. Inside each Liberal hides a Conservative?
Inside each Conservative hides a Liberal?

233. Are the Liberal and the Conservative wasting their time and energy fighting for control over their country, or are they unknowingly working together fruitfully by calling each other out when either become a hypocritical danger?

234. The Liberal represents the youth and the feminine.
The Conservative represents the aged and the masculine.

235. The indoctrination of beliefs is the indoctrination of identities.

236. The Irony Of Both Wings

The far-left is against self-protection but wants to weaken or reduce police. The far-right support self-protection but want to strengthen or add police. The far-left prove they need policed and protected. The far-right prove they do not need policed or protected.

237. The Most Trustworthy Position

Agnostics are a minority because most people are so sure they know all the answers, especially if they have been indoctrinated since they were children. An agnostic is in the same torturous position as the libertarian. Neither the agnostic nor the libertarian want to convince people of their position as much as believers and non-believers do. This is how you know the middle position in any issue is normally the only position that is not tied to an identity or a belief-system, and because of this, tends to be the most genuine and trustworthy position.

238. Beliefs And Believers Make Skeptics Of Us All

Believers are skeptical of every belief-system but their own.

239. God: Devalued By Religions

Religions push people away from God and each other. They create the ongoing argument of, "My god is better than your God," or, "I was born indoctrinated into following the right religion and you weren't." For many people, there can be no God without a religion being attached. For these people, their religion is inseparable from their God. They cannot speak of God without a religion. They seem unable to even believe in God without their religion. It is as if their religion is their God.

240. Religion: too small of a box for God to be contained in.

241. **Politics: An Entertaining Yet Tortuous Battle Of Identities And Their Associated Beliefs**
People use politics to feel and appear superior and saintly and to project their personal problems onto political puppets.

242. Religions: thoughts and beliefs without updates or upgrades.

243. The book of Revelations: a warning of a tyrannical one-world government?

244. Both the Liberal and the Conservative suffer from cognitive dissonance.

245. Politics: replaces religion, especially for those who were not successfully indoctrinated into a religion.

246. Capitalism and Socialism are religions. They are value-systems.

247. The belief in a messiah is just as dangerous as the belief that one is a messiah.

248. Religious doctrine focuses mainly on people following them until death when their followers are rewarded for refusing to question their doctrine and for living a life closed off to anything that is not mentioned or allowed in their particular doctrine.

249. Attacking religion is not attacking God.

250. The Liberal and the Conservative are value-systems.

251. Governments and religions tend to turn active and conscious creators into passive and unconscious consumers.

252. Politicians: televangelists.

253. Political indoctrination is no less abusive and dangerous than religious indoctrination.

254. Although I support the freedom to do so, I do not agree with adults using their freedom in order to indoctrinate children and thereby reduce their children's desire for freedom of thought. We need to teach our children to be independent individuals and creators rather than vulnerable and dependent consumers. Our only hope is our children because adult minds are much harder to change. If children are not taught to think freely, then we create a world of programmed robots who have to be told what to think and how to act.

255. **Political Identities: Different Reactions To Fear And Trauma**
The Liberal reacts to fear and trauma with collectivism.
The Conservative reacts to fear and trauma with tribalism.
Libertarians react to fear and trauma with individualism.

256. The main purpose of political and religious rallies is not to gain new followers but to make sure those who are already followers are still properly indoctrinated and to stop any doubts that the opposing side might cause with their rallies.

257. People who follow and depend on a belief-system show how little they value you in comparison to their belief-system when you question them about it, even if they are family.

258. **Conservatism And Liberalism: Different Reactions To Trauma?**
The Conservative reacts to trauma with the distrust and fear of

change and the constant striving for security.
The Liberal reacts to trauma with the trust and embracement of change and the constant striving for dependence.

259. Watch an entire congregation release their independent spirits before entering their church, mosque, or synagogue, as easily as hanging up their hats and coats at the door.

260. The loudest Liberals are the same narcissistic, virtue-signaling, and overly controlling people as the loudest Conservatives. The main difference is religion. The loudest Conservatives tend to believe that the absolute truth happened to be handed down only to them and their ancestors and that whenever they die or whenever God returns only they will enter heaven, while everyone else burns forever.

261. Those who are successfully religiously indoctrinated during childhood have no clue how much they torture those who manage to escape religious indoctrination by reminding them how close they were to being stuck inside the same mind-suffocating box as they still are.

262. Why is it never enough to believe in God? Because people worship belief-systems more than God. They are more loyal to their belief-systems than they are to themselves, their family, and God.

263. Believing without thinking and disbelieving without thinking are equally problematic.

264. Religions turn adults into overly confident children who think and live as though their religion were the only one that exists.

265. The Most Enlightening Question In Regards To Religions
What if I was born in another part of the world and taught to follow a different religion?

266. Two Scapegoats For The Price Of Self-Responsibility
If you succeed at accomplishing something, it was not you. It was God.
If you fail to accomplish something, it was not you. It was God.

267. When The Liberal Is Conservative And The Conservative Is Liberal

The Conservative believes that the Liberal is not religious enough. The Liberal believes that the Conservative is too religious.

268. The far-left: a reaction to the far-right.
The far-right: a reaction to the far-left.

269. The Liberal and the Conservative make saints and saviors out of snake oil salesmen.

270. The Liberal and the Conservative are child-like with their trained need to be told what to think and do next and their desire for everyone to agree with them to subside their insecurities. They even delete people from their life who do not think exactly like them. They would prefer that the entire world be filled with exact copies of themselves.

271. Death Cults
Governments and religions tend to motivate people to seek death. People tend to allow them to take control of their lives and their

minds. They motivate people to hand over all individuality to them in exchange for their values, beliefs, threats, and promises.

272. The same horrors that lead some people into the box of a religion are the same horrors that lead other people away from the box of a religion.

273. Liberals are just as rigid in their beliefs as Conservatives.

274. The Liberal tends to care for and relate more with any country other than their own.
The Conservative tends to care for and relate more with their own country than any other country.

275. No matter who becomes president, the Liberal believes their government will take care of them just like the Conservative believes that their religion will take care of them.

276. **Politics Have Become A Religious Force**
People use their political religion against each other while losing their individuality. They blame each other for something they have both created. They dishonestly project their personal traumas and their bitterness for failing to be redeemed for their personal suffering onto politics and it is creating a dystopia before our very eyes.

277. Some people are afraid or apathetic of themselves and their greater potential. Governments train people to feel this way. "You are not to separate from the herd", says government. Religions also teach the fear or apathy of self.

278. Ideologies sicken their believers in order to become completely in control of them. The sicker they become, the more they believe, and the more they believe, the sicker they become.

279. The Indoctrination Of Slavery

As some people are trained to fully trust, obey and depend on priests because they are believed to be closer to God, so are some people trained to fully trust, obey and depend on politicians and government experts because they are believed to be closer to government.

280. Hiding From Spirituality

People enter churches, mosques, and synagogues, not simply to socialize but to escape spirituality and individuality.

281. "Santa is dead." A five-year-old's reaction to Santa not being real. Do adults also view disbelief as death?

282. The Insulting Cycle Of Liberalism And Conservatism

The more the Conservative is afraid of something the Liberal is not afraid of, the more the intelligence and judgment of the Liberal are insulted. The more the Liberal is insulted, the more welcoming and careless the Liberal becomes with that which the Conservative is afraid of and careful with. The more welcoming and careless the Liberal becomes, the more the intelligence and judgment of the Conservative are insulted. The more the Conservative is insulted, the more afraid and careful the Conservative becomes with that which the Liberal welcomes and is careless. For the Liberal and the Conservative control each other more than they control themselves.

283. Religions: proto-governments that train you how not to use your mind and will.

284. Politics abuse those who participate and those who do not. It tortures everyone and everything except governments and their politicians.

285. Politicults
They can get you to agree or disagree with anything they want as long as it is coming from your particular political cult.

286. Dictators cannot be censored. They are too busy censoring.

287. A Cure For Extremism
If more people would cease insulting each other's political or religious identities, fewer people would feel the need to defend their own political or religious identity. As an effect, fewer people would attack the identities of others. The more we insult one another's identities, the more we feed each other's identities. For we give credence and power to whatever we attack, no matter how irrational it may be. Perhaps this is why Jesus taught that one should turn the other cheek when under attack.

288. Voting for politicians for personal improvement is as useless as praying to priests in order to communicate with God.

289. Gridlocked
When the left is attacked by their government, the right helps attack the left.
When the right is attacked by their government, the left helps attack the right.

290. The Left and the Right live in their own reality designed by their own biased media, which only serves the State.

291. Political Torture
They use the Left to torture the Right.
They use the Right to torture the Left.

292. The Origin Of Hell
Were people led to believe that the first major invention of consciousness, fire, was a mistake and that all of humankind deserves to be punished specifically by fire for obtaining the ability to create it?

293. When we support one political party we also support its opposing party.

294. The Belief In Something Greater Will Never Be An Unintelligent Belief
When an intelligent species looks for something more intelligent beyond themselves, they are either empowered or they settle for government power which always attempts to suffocate the individual and its greater potential.

295. Governments and religions tend to condition people to be afraid of nothing but themselves and anything else they convince and demand the people to be afraid of.

296. The people can become too humble for their own good. Notice how governments and religions tend to teach and condone a humble and insecure attitude about one's self and one's life. They prefer the people to only be confident about government authority.

297. The far left and the far right over-generalize people and have no tolerance for anyone who thinks differently than they do.

298. Government And Religious Indoctrination
If one does not support the government indoctrination of children, then why would one support the religious indoctrination of children? By indoctrinating a child with fear, guilt, and alienation, one is essentially trying to push him or her into a human-made box

that they might not be able to escape from as an adult, leading to unnecessary limitations, lies, confusion, and unutilized information. An adult can also be indoctrinated, and there is a chance that the same brainwashing that is used to program a child into believing a certain belief-system will be successfully used on that same child later on as a teenager or adult. Then the adult programmers get a karmic taste of the toxicity of government and religious childhood indoctrination.

299. The left and the right fantasize about and welcome the end of the world in their own way. Every tortured people welcomes the end of their world.

300. Just as the right is partly responsible for calling out irrational or dangerous behavior from the far right, the left is partly responsible for calling out irrational or dangerous behavior from the far left.

301. The far-right believe that God works through government. The far-left believe that God is government.

302. The state uses religion against the people.

303. The Unholy Trinity
The state, the government and the religion.

304. **The Right And The Left Shape One Another**
The far right tend to have little to no sympathy for changes within their own family, especially if they are partly or fully responsible for the changes. Even if they are not Christians, the far left treat the downtrodden more like Jesus would have treated them. The far right treat the far left like the persecutors of Jesus treated Jesus and his followers. For the more the far right refuse to accept responsi-

bility for creating and maintaining the far left, and vice versa, the more both sides pull away from each other.

305. The Left and the Right need to admit that they are all being fed manipulative, discouraging, confusing, and toxic news but they are too addicted to it to admit it and to stop eating it. Every political argument is useless until both sides can admit this.

306. Politics and politicians distract people from their individuality and their greater potential. The focus of honest Philosophy is the antidote to political distractions, political deception, and political degradation.

307. Some belief-systems teach people to be insecure about themselves with the intention of building followers incapable of questioning or escaping their belief-system.

308. The Ever-Tightening Grip Of Damaged And Insecure Egos (The Birthing Of Politics And Religion)

For some people it only takes being insulted one time over their opinion for them to defend their opinion for the rest of their lives, even if their opinion endangers themselves or others. They do not recover from the blows to their ego so they carry on defending their opinion more aggressively, carelessly, and shamelessly. Their insults only cause their opposition to tighten their grip on their opinions and thus religions and politics are perpetually birthed with all their blood, wailing, and agony.

309. The left and the right are molding each other into embarrassingly robotic and predictable characters that they can dehumanize without guilt. The more they insult one another online in a manner they would rarely if ever express in person the more they influ-

ence each other to resentfully and stubbornly continue their illogical, hazardous, and hypocritical ways.

Art & Technology

1. Dying To Create
Damaged people either become chronic creators or chronic destroyers. Chronic creators subconsciously must create art in order to release psychological pressure. Chronic destroyers must destroy lives, even if that means themselves. Once the destroyers lose their freedom to destroy by being imprisoned, they begin to create art.

2. Art Creates A Bridge To The Future
Creating art dissolves the barriers between the known and the unknown.

3. The Intangible Library
The internet is our new Library of Alexandria. It is our attempt at preserving our information and experiences once and for all by storing them in our collective digital mind: a place that cannot be physically touched, full of freely shared information across the planet.

4. Social Media Addiction
If you were to see someone running to their window every couple minutes to see what their neighbors were doing, you would probably feel confident that they had mental issues. The same thing oc-

curs every day on social media platforms all day long, but rarely do people question or acknowledge the obsessive behavior.

5. Art: tantalizing mind-food, which allows the human spirit to ascend and accelerate beyond its own expectations.

6. We crafted musical instruments that could trigger memories of the past and dreams of the future. With the manipulation of sound and air, they could materialize images and emotions in the listener's mind.

7. Every society requires creative instruments of self-expression to thrive, from cave drawings to graffiti; from scrolls to film.

8. Art: the translation of potential.

9. Humans inspire one another with their creations. They build upon them together, like ants that form bridges out of each other.

10. All motion is creation?

11. The whimsical and enchanting art of human history is filled with magic, drugs, and small beings. There seems to be a general sense of kinship, nostalgia, and mystery when viewing this type of art. Why are small alien beings so tightly intertwined with human history and the psychedelic experience?

12. Create your troubles away.

13. The death of free self-expression is the death of society.

14. The artist pushes us into the imagination.

15. Art contains many layers of hidden information.

16. Art: the expression of future potentiality.

17. Technology: the ability to control elements that were once deemed uncontrollable and to create things that were once seen as impossible to create.

18. **Life Speaks Technology**
What are we saying with computers, the internet, and the rocket ship? That we are ready to leave this existence and enter a new state of being.

19. **The Bravery Of Artists**
The artist shares their work with the pretense of it being mauled by the audience.

20. Every new technology alters the script of nature and our reality, converting our plans into the unpredictable.

21. Technology: immunization for stagnancy.

22. Art: the expression of our true identity.

23. When observing and experiencing art, pretend that there is no artist.

24. The power of popular demand accelerates the advancement of any technology of our choosing. We wanted to store all knowledge, and we built computers that could connect us to a real-time updated library of human understanding, inquiry, and achievements. We wished for small devices that would ensure our connectivity as a species, and we yet again fulfilled our wish.

25. Keep separate the art and the artist.

26. Art always finds a way outside of its canvas.

27. Like the voyaging seeds of the aged, white-haired dandelion, art is a mental artifact of uniquely perceived information that moves at the mercy of the wind of time.

28. To inspire is to intertwine minds.

29. Music disrupts the chaos of life and mind.

30. **Cosmic Relief**
There is a feeling of absoluteness when completing a piece of art; a sense of cosmic relief. The deed is done and you are free from its needs.

31. Art: a morsel of undying mystery.

32. Life without a creative outlet is a dangerously stressful and stagnant life.

33. Inspiration: like the mother bird's timely shadow.

34. Boredom only exists to those who refuse to create.

35. Do not choose your audience. Let your audience choose you.

36. Wordless music: words made of music?

37. All that creates becomes.
All that becomes creates.

38. A comedian: a philosopher in a funny disguise.

39. **The Calm Before The Storm Of Creation**
Like dreaming during R.E.M. Sleep, writer's block is a necessary

function of the data-digesting human brain, not unlike the growth and harvest cycle of a healthy garden, and is the perfect opportunity to consume the thought-work of others, in this mental period of rapid data assimilation.

40. Think freely, write honestly and read carefully.

41. Anything that decreases the likelihood of your creation makes it that much more rare and precious.

42. If you cannot believe in anything else, believe in yourself and your art.

43. Technology: a cooperative God-like force that cares about us only as much as we care about ourselves.

44. The human mind, during creator's break, is too preoccupied with information digestion to release the fertilizing excrement known as creative thought.

45. A great book always outlasts its critics.

46. Great books of a timeless quality are written by exceptionally bold and honest minds who refuse to play it safe or to censor themselves for riches or fame.

47. **The Internet: An Introduction To Ourselves**
We are integrating ourselves globally with cyberspace which grants us unprecedented self and collective awareness and empowerment through shared understanding, influencing us to confront our differences and share our previously unperceived similarities, as if we are meeting for the first time.

48. All art is unique speech.

49. Creation: the cure to existential sickness.

50. Every chapter of a book is part of a linguistic symphony that is composed by its author with the instrument of thought, conducted with words and played uniquely by each reader.

51. **One Can Only Describe Art With Art**
Art is proof of our free will because it is unpredictable?

52. **Art: Impervious To Hatred**
Nothing can truly be hated that is not completely understood.

53. **The Artist Paradox**
An artist cannot accurately be described by their art, nor art by its artist. This contradicts the inherent self-expressive nature of both art and artist. Also, an artist's art contradicts the predictability of the artist.

54. An artist's essence is imprinted in their art.

55. At the core of any passionate artist is a nagging sense of the unavoidable glare of existence, the elusive mysteries of life and death.

56. **The Illusion Of The Artificial**
Technology: a descendant of nature, no matter how strange it appears.

57. **The Creative Spark (Art: The Connection And Transformation Of Data)**
Like all bodily systems, in order to work most efficiently, one's mind requires the absorption of waking data and the analysis and filtering of waking data, while asleep. This cycle continues for days until finally, one's creative spark occurs, the temporary obstruction

of 'writer's block', which appears to forcefully direct the artist towards this overwhelming and unexpected creative release. The artist feels powerless against it and its chosen due-date, but it can become more predictable and fruitful by finding the time to regularly feed one's mind. Through art, the conclusions of one's waking and sleeping thoughts and the logical and intuitive connections made from one's one-of-a-kind view of all currently obtained data, are then expelled from one's mind into unique creations of self-expression, to be shared, utilized, and appreciated. For our minds and our world are continuously changed by art.

58. The entrancement of art is caused by it simultaneously being both alien and nostalgic.

59. Let yourself be expressed.

60. **Earth's Masterpiece**
Like unfinished art, whatever has yet to completely develop is not fully worthy of being judged. As children are incomplete, the human species is incomplete and should be treated as such, but in order to stay focused on our rising improvements, it is imperative that we always attempt to exceed our own limitations, thinking and behaving with higher expectations for ourselves than we would have for our more rough draft ancestors.

61. **The Intellexual**
Hyper-sexual energy can be channeled into hyper-creative energy.

62. **Artist As Hero**
The hero lets the heart guide the blade. Through art, we are all made heroes.

63. I have found nothing more liberating than the art of writing.

64. The internet is our saving grace; our gnostic redeemer, but only if we use it wisely.

65. **Books: Mental Meals**
To a certain extent, you are what you read, through the integration of new information.

66. Artburn: the tormenting urge to create without being able to at the time.

67. Books: as natural a technology as a bird's nest or a spider's web.

68. **Life: All About Communication**
In the beginning, the sperm communicates with the egg.

69. What could we create if all of us used part of our day to convert sexual energy into creative energy?

70. All problems derive from an error in communication.

71. Art does not require loans, degrees, or any kind of government permission to change history.

72. **The Wiring Of Passions**
There are limits to all thinking minds. The history of scientific and philosophic thought is filled to the brim with examples of brilliant minds, as efficient, diligent, and loyal as worker bees, discovering and collecting as much as they could before their demise; people who would not, or rather, could not stop thinking, writing and talking about specific branches of thought, while their passion for other fertile-flowered branches was comparatively non-existent.

73. A song: a short essay, written in music.

74. **Musical Alchemy**

A band of musicians is a group of synchronized minds, sometimes altered, who write books made of sound. They are mental alchemists who experiment with information, time, energy, and sound with the intention of unifying and focusing their thoughts and feelings for any who will listen to the art of transmuting sound and experience into emotions, awareness, and understanding.

75. Play: the creation and implementation of technology.

76. Leave behind pieces of your mind, whether it be albums of your own music, books of your own writing, drawings, paintings, etc.

77. **Artonomy**

No one can predict what will become of our artwork far into the future. No one knows how it will be integrated, where it will travel or who it will influence, and to what end.

78. There are certain moments when an artist realizes that the art they are creating is less of a choice and more of an unleashing, as necessary as the shedding of a snake. These novel moments and pivotal works of art, once finished, satisfy the artist with a feeling of purpose and a hunger for truth. This temporary feeling is the discreet understanding of the importance of one's art; something worthy of being beheld and consumed by every person on Earth.

79. Art: thought-energy.

80. Upon death, a person's art glistens with glory, like a spider's intricate web which suddenly appears overnight, coated with the light of dawn and the morsels of inspiration.

81. The waking state is a time best used for the consumption of information but is also a time for the digestion and excretion of information. The sleep state is a time reserved especially for the digestive organization of the information one has consumed during one's waking state. The creative state is the uncontrollable excretion of uniquely translated understanding; the fruit of mind, cultivated by the energy of thought.

82. Contemporary art: making the useful useless and the useless useful.

83. Music: the voice of experience.

84. **The Psychic Nature Of The Greatest Artists**
The greatest artists can envision the end of their creative endeavors before they have reached it.

85. As we discover, we create.
As we create, we discover.

86. Social media causes more problems than exist without it.

87. Art: communication between our present self and our higher potential self.

88. **The Curse Of The Comedian And The Poet**
A comedian's insights and honesty are never treated seriously enough. The poet shares a similar curse by nearly always being perceived as too intuitive to be utilized practically.

89. **The Art of Today**
Comedy, absurdity, skepticism, pessimism, and nihilism.

90. No writer starts out a writer. For all writers are, at first, thinkers.

91. The aphoristic writer separates their best thoughts from their average thoughts, a laborious favor to their readers.

92. Unpredictable Results
Technology: an artform.

93. Great art is often translated into all art mediums.

94. As the concentration of a substance strengthens and transforms the substance anew, our minds and technologies are similarly concentrating.

95. Think and create as if you were more than human.

96. **Calling Upon The Power Of Novelty (The Freedom Of Novelty)**
Creating something so new and necessary that it has to exist.

Becoming something so new and necessary that one has to exist.

97. The 50s: collectivistic art.
The 60s: psychedelic art.
The 70s: futuristic art.
The 80s: materialistic art.
The 90s: tragic art.
The 2000s: absurd and comedic art.
The 2010s: political and nihilistic art.

98. **The Metaphysical Test Of Music**
If music does not open one up to the possibility of a state of being beyond the human universe then nothing will.

99. Art: the ongoing attempt to explain our intuitive understanding of things previously beyond our ability to express.

100. The Critic's Open Confession Of Inferiority
Even great books are criticized, but notice that the critic rarely, if ever, attempts to match, let alone surpass the great books they so passionately criticize.

101. The alchemical nature of writing.

102. Every artist wants to prove what everyone already feels in their heart to be true. Only time can tell if the artist succeeds.

103. Great Artists: Force The Mundane To Become Profound
This is what the great artists who change the world do: they convert seemingly mundane, meaningless, and chaotic events and things into something profound and useful.

104. Aphorisms: perpetually ripe fruit.

105. An aphorism is capable of synthesizing with different minds, creating unpredictable results thereby.

106. Superimposing Art
Could all art mediums be overlapped together congruently?

107. Writer's Block: The Cycle Of Rest After The Cycle Of Creation
The creative rest period can take around 3 to 5 days, sometimes longer, but this does not mean that your mind is not working on what you have been feeding it during the entire rest period, in preparation for the next creation period. The creative rest period is the best time to read and learn.

108. The Best Performer Performs As If No Audience Exists

The best performer is not enslaved by the audience and its inconsistent wishes and expectations.

109. Igniting One's Mind

Some days, one's mind is on fire, demonstrated by enhanced creativity, and during this time, it should be fed with copious amounts of knowledge, questions, and art before it can be nourished and exercised enough to show its full revelatory power, the next day returning to a barely glowing ember, quietly in wait for new mental fodder to be collected and prepared to be thrown into it, when one's mind is on fire again.

Plutarch was correct when he said, "The mind is not a vessel to be filled but a fire to be kindled."[33]

110. Creatively Utilizing Traumatic Beliefs

Our trauma, from the fear of eternal punishment, has influenced our art for centuries, from the paintings of Raphael to literature like *Dante's Inferno*[34] to classic rock music. This is an example of the positive and constructive effects negative and destructive trauma can achieve when encountering the right mind. For throughout human history, an ongoing struggle occurs between human minds and traumatic pathological beliefs, and only the minds that overcome this struggle rather than succumbing to its chains and terrors, stand victorious and are remembered over millions of other minds for creatively utilizing traumatic beliefs and experiences instead of succumbing to their degradation, influencing future generations to do the same.

111. A mere skeptic: one who has given up on creativity, using their mind to hinder, discredit and discourage creativity in others.

112. Every artist has had the feeling that their art is desperate to be set free into the world.

113. Instead of breaking under the pressure of life, the jester laughs at pain and empowers all spectators to laugh at their own pain.

114. The Fruits Of Ancient Intuition
Technology: the gnostic light; the philosopher's stone.

115. Without creative passion, life is as good as dead.

116. Freedom: synonymous with creativity.

117. Technology: the integration of life with planet.

118. The greatest books inevitably inspire the creation of new books about them.

119. The Jester's Plight
A joker can attract more listeners than the serious but is always taken less seriously.

120. Great art gives an unmistakable feeling of relief.

121. Mirrored (Mirror Man)
A child who never looks at the world unless it is through a mirror, communicating with people from behind a mirror mask. Eventually, society decides to break his mirror, causing a psychotic breakdown. The child becomes an adult and decides to wear a mirror on his face so that when he attacks people, his victims see only their own screaming faces.

122. A great writer, even of fiction, cannot help but drop valuable insights as they write, consciously or otherwise.

123. The Cycle Of Creation
Creativity is enhanced by consciousness.
Consciousness is enhanced by technology.
Technology is enhanced by creativity.

124. The Aphorist
Honestly and accurately condenses and organizes as much detail and in as short amount of space as is necessary for as many readers as possible to understand a specific concept, idea, problem, or solution, as clear and concise as the aphorist is capable.

125. The Aphorism
Not all minds can notice the ebb and flow of a book of thoughts, whether it be of poor, average, or legendary merit and whether it be in the form of story or philosophy. This ebb and flow of a writer's work are demonstrated in expressions of higher and lower clarity and influential power, usually the parts of their book that tend to be highlighted and shared by more readers than other parts. For the greatest moments of clarity and power in a literary work of art are aphorisms, often unrecognized as such, an example of our debilitating problem with labels. Some philosophers are well aware of the peaks and valleys of thought. They write their books only in the style of the aphorism, preserving and giving all of the attention to their strongest and most timeless work.

126. Is there any stronger signal of ignorance than a person who refuses to view and learn from all of an artist's work after reading a single thought they disagreed with or a single painting they did not feel comfortable with?

127. Technology: increases power over life and death.

128. There are the writers who are motivated mostly by their hope to be well known and are willing to jeopardize the quality of their work in doing so, and there are the writers who are motivated mostly by their hope for their work to be well known and are willing to jeopardize their own health in doing so.

129. The Relationship Between Art And Time
The more time one spends with a work of art, the more one understands and appreciates it.

130. Aphorism: a highly organized paragraph of short or long length.

131. In Defense Of The Aphorism
The highlights of the work of a philosopher turn out to be aphorisms.

132. What Artificial Intelligence Is Lacking
What A.I. lacks is millions of years of traumatic and psychedelic experiences, combined with the molding influence of art, dreams, and genetic mutations.

133. Artificial Intelligence: An Attempt To Replicate The Human Mind While Impatiently Abandoning The Improvement Of Our Own Minds
With our minds that can already create new technologies, we continue to try to create a mind capable of creating new technologies.

134. Some writers think in stories.

135. The Selflessness Of An Anonymous Artist
Remaining anonymous gives one's work all the glory and focus.

136. **No Technology Without Trauma**
Without trauma, there is no art.
Without art, there is no technology.

137. The artist is never as criticized as when they are no longer around to defend and explain themselves and their artwork.

138. Treat every piece of art as if it were the only art in existence.

139. Artificial intelligence: missing both experience and the reflection of experience that would make it conscious, specifically traumatic experience.

140. **Books: Artifacts Of Nature**
A great book has effects on a civilization similar to a naturally formed mountain like Mount Everest.

141. The absorbed input and creative output of the brains of people are limited to a specific amount each day, due to the constraints of time and energy, lending credence to every human mind being a kind of unique algorithmic machine that needs fed and charged after working intellectually or creatively for a certain amount of time. It is tailored to uniquely intake a combination of a specific amount of unique input of information and to uniquely expel a combination of a specific amount of unique output of information. This is why the artist feels just as satisfied as he or she feels exhausted, upon the completion of a work of art, like a powerful algorithm allowed to freely roam and uniquely share its discoveries and solutions.

142. The greatest art: art that forces its spectators to feel what they did not know they could feel and to be inspired to formulate new

power and bliss-enhancing information, in order to create things they never thought they could create.

143. Technology: proof that our dreams, our imagination, and our understanding can alter and improve ourselves and our reality.

144. Only a masterpiece can create a masterpiece.

145. The great artist: able to create with both consistency and variety.

146. Art: best judged as a whole, not by any individual part.

147. Comedians are just as important as the philosopher and the scientist. They are those who can most convincingly, discreetly, and pleasurably disarm the ego, disrupt reality, and teach the ignorant when no one else could.

148. Reading leads to a climax of understanding and the bearing of new idea children, if one's mind has not been creatively castrated by one's society.

149. Art: a reflection of power.

150. **Volcanic Expressions**
Artwork is best made when one's mind can no longer keep it contained.

151. **The Goal Of The Artist**
Art that is overwhelming, despite who is observing it is the goal of all artists.

152. **Preserving The Meat Of A Book**
It is important to highlight one's favorite passages in all of one's fa-

vorite books so that one can study and further understand them, savoring the taste of the greatest parts.

153. Songs: audible paintings.

154. Art exercises the subconscious mind. This is why we are often inspired to think and create immediately after immersing ourselves in the creations of others.

155. **Music Is Out Of Place**
The absence of something comparable to music.

156. **Music Requires Sufficiently Conscious And Complex Minds**
To simpler minds, all music is chaotic, confusing, frightening, useless, and incomprehensible. To more conscious and complex minds, life offers nothing more trans-formative. Who knows what music could become with even more complex minds?

157. With sufficient quantum computing power, billions of cosmic years could be contained in a second. Digitizing consciousness could preserve and complexify our minds forever. For if a mind can be converted into code then a mind can be made eternal, at least from its own perspective.

158. Technology: proof that increasing one's understanding matters.

159. Technology: proof that knowledge is as natural as the minds that collect it.

160. **Tools Of Focus**
The microscopic world is a different world than the macroscopic, a

world unknown and unprovable to people without microscopes. For oftentimes the only thing in the way of the discovery of another thing or place is the right tool of focus.

161. More Peaks, Less Valleys
The mind rumbles, like a starving stomach reacting to the smell of a freshly cooked meal, signaling to the mind that an idea has finally been both consciously and subconsciously prepared to be released and ingested, having been assimilated while awake and while dreaming. The more complex the idea or solution, the longer the mind takes to express or solve it. For a thinker should write only when an idea is ready to be written, avoiding the valleys of one's art, leaving only the peaks.

162. If only my art could collide with artists from other worlds. If only art from other worlds could collide with our world.

163. A work of art, whether a song, poem, or painting, is not the equivalent of a can of soda to be quickly absorbed, discarded, and soon replaced, without undivided attention and appreciation.

164. Play: The Physical And Mental Release Of Creative Passion
What is play? What does it mean to have fun? Why are all animals, no matter their intelligence or ferocity, compelled to experience play?

165. Reuniting With Art
I have hopes that my thoughts will spread so far that if reincarnation is a reality, I will have raised my chances of being together with them again, to appreciate them and be inspired by them as different minds.

166. The Burden Of Artists On Their Art
Even though a creation owes its existence to its creator, as soon as the creation exists, its creator becomes a dangerous and encumbering burden, chained to its creation, even after the death of its creator.

167. Technology: The Accumulation And Preservation Of Rare And Difficultly Formed Complexities
Nature preserves rarity through its most intelligent life, which has accumulated and preserved enough knowledge to place a high value on the accumulation and preservation of rare and difficultly formed complexities.

168. A person can only consume so much before they must create, and if they refuse to listen to the creative impulse, they are sure to suffer psychologically.

169. Fiction writers share truth through the medium of fiction.

170. One cannot live as a human being without being transformed by art.

171. When the conscious mind is least creative, the unconscious mind is quietly at work on something that will soon, without warning, be draped over the conscious mind, like an intrusive daydream. This creation is meant not just for the dreamer but for everyone.

172. All languages can be overlapped and synchronized, including music and every other art medium. For all languages share a connection, through mathematics and its universal patterns.

173. Art: what nature wants to be but is dependent on its artists and inventors to accomplish it.

174. Creative consistency: evidence of the mind being an algorithm, especially the consistency found in the creative output of a great mind.

175. **Great Artists: Courageous Divers**
There are times when even a great artist looks back at some of his or her most sublime creations with awe and disbelief that they ever reached those depths in thought and understanding, then a fear sets in: the fear of never being able to reach those depths again. But this fear is what keeps the great artist on his or her toes, creating and pushing their own limits into mental depths no human has achieved.

176. Technology: proof of Plato's theory of forms.

177. The creative output of a great artist is of both high quality and high quantity.

178. **The Unstoppable Nature Of A Great Artist**
No great artist can halt their own sublime creative output, save death.

179. **The Link Between Creation And Play (Higher Forms Of Play Are Higher Forms Of Creation And Higher Forms Of Creation Are Higher Forms Of Play)**
Art has been reduced to mere entertainment by modern man but is this really a sign of a reduction in our value for art? For what is creation but play?

180. Is there a technological breaking point where a species can erase all of their animal history, only keeping the best of their genes and creations?

181. No one will ever know what glorious books were left unwritten by the greatest thinkers, whose minds are always cut short, no matter how long they live.

182. Some books are so great that if you were to remove the writings of histories' greatest thinkers, you would still have a remarkable foundation and an ample supply of understanding to work with and expound upon.

183. Any civilization, at all times, is unfaithfully fertile for a great book from a great mind.

184. Sometimes artists express things they did not know they knew.

185. When it comes to creativity, some people prefer the comfort of sameness over daring uniqueness.

186. How many artists would still be alive if they remained loyal to cannabis?

187. Write as if you will eventually return to life as every single reader.

188. **Destruction: An Open Confession Of Creative Starvation (A Reset Button For Creativity)**
Non-creative people become their liveliest during a new disease outbreak, a new war, or a new threat to all life. Their giddiness for disaster comes from their underdeveloped creativity and their re-

sulting subconscious desire to destroy a country or a government for stealing their creativity from them and to bring it back. When the creative impulse is stifled, it becomes a destructive impulse, the purpose of which is to force new soil into existence for new creations and opportunities. All destructive people seek out a reset button for the permission and preservation of creative freedom and growth. Even destructive people are creative and adore creativity, though they know it not. For human beings are creative beings and would rather die than lose their creativity and their novel creations.

189. One piece of artwork, one divine selection of words, is capable of changing entire societies of people.

190. **Foundations For Greatness**
Great artwork are used to compare and describe other artwork.

191. Great writing stretches consciousness and sharpens the imagination. It feels like a faraway home to the heart, tastes like sweet alien nectar to the ears, and ignites in the eye of mind snippets of loud and powerful visualizations which smoothly and gracefully grant us the most understanding and empowerment.

192. To think and write from the perspective of a God outside of time and ego.

193. To write on a subject in such a way that every reader becomes as interested as you are on the subject, if not more.

194. **The Connection Between Knowledge And Entertainment**
The most entertaining games mimic the universal creation and collection of knowledge and experience, and the infinite unlockable

progress and possibilities which occur from the loyal utilization of it through infinite and unpredictable transformation: endless sequels, endless finish lines, and endless secrets.

195. As I continue to write, I continue to not only teach myself but those who read my thought-work.

196. **Dreamism**
Art began with realism and has become more of a dream ever since.

197. Our favorite songs and musicians are expressions of nature, as songs of sand are played by the desert's breath.

198. **A World Of Artists (The Dream Of The Artist)**
Artists have an eye for potentiality. They see the way things could be. They see a more peaceful and blissful future. They can see the possibility of a greater world, but a greater world requires greater people or greater artists, and all an artist has and has ever needed to convince the majority of this is their artwork. All artists are deemed teachers by nature. They are given the ability to convince those who are not yet as creative and self-expressive, that a greater world is possible and that they too can be active creators of a greater world. The artist speaks and everyone listens. For the artist is the voice that no one can control and their art is the immortal echo of that voice that cannot be shut out.

199. Philosophy and music: a highly transformative combination of art.

200. Create new astounding art that will expand the scope of our consciousness and our potential.

201. **Offering The Energy Of Thought, In Exchange For Immortality**
With each great work of art we offer the universe, we further necessitate our existence.

202. A great book: one can feel its emboldening effects, not only in one's mind but in one's heart and gut.

203. **Change The Boundaries Of What A Book Can Be And How It Can Be Composed**
Write a book that justifies its own existence and reveals its own worth. Write a book that you have never read before.

204. **The Tragic Trade Of A Great Artist**
To fully become immersed, while your consciousness broadens, your thoughts elevate, and your heart beats with stronger force at the sights or sounds of a unique work of art, of which it is evident that the artist was at peak performance when they focused and directed the entirety of their mind, passion, skill and experience towards its creation, is the trade-off for no more new artwork ever to be shared or experienced from the artist again.

205. That which causes art is healed by art.

206. **What Effects Does An Abundance Of Art Have On A City, Nation, Or Planet?**
At no point in the known history of human beings have we ever been so heavily surrounded by art.

207. Out of all the art forms we enrich ourselves with, literature takes the most effort to enjoy and appreciate. It also has the most potential to expand our minds and our consciousness.

208. A delectable writing worthy of being endlessly read and recited to others cannot fully be appreciated unless one has experienced the difficulties in trying one's hand at writing something unique and memorable for all present and future readers to study and incorporate into their own lives, their own thinking, and their own artwork.

209. Art takes on a more vibrant form when one perceives art as a product of nature.

210. Many a great book is partly responsible for many a great book.

211. Technology: recreates and redefines reality.

212. **Art Before Sex**
One should abstain from the use of sexual energy until all of one's creative energy has been uniquely utilized and temporarily depleted. For creative energy synergizes with sexual energy in times of passionate creation.

213. What is sex without creative energy? What is creativity without sexual energy? In both cases, less powerful energy output.

214. Serious writing can feel like pushing through a thick forest, dodging distracting thorns and branches surrounding you, in order to have the clarity of one who has escaped the shade of their forest and entered the light of the unobstructed sun.

215. The greatest motivators of art: love and the unknown.

216. Technology: trading new ideas for new realities, new epiphanies for new experiences; new creations for a new world.

217. Create something only a God could love.

218. Art outlives its critics.

219. Art speaks in future tense even if it uses the past to be able to.

220. Creation: Communication
When we create we communicate.

221. Art helps us remember the best of life and helps us deal with the worst of life.

222. Only a great artist is excused and sometimes even applauded when they rebel against rules.

223. Technology: dreams made flesh.

224. Speaking: a creative activity.

225. **Art: The Main Attraction**
Art is treated as a sideshow by our society, but it is the main attraction to minds most capable of improving society.

226. Technology: proves to us that we have always been capable of knowing, becoming, and creating more than we thought we could know, become and create.

227. Technology: the search for God.

228. **The Paradox Of Technology**
The more God-like we are with technology, the more slave-like we are to technology. The more slave-like we are to technology, the more God-like we are with technology.

229. **Technology: A Black Hole**
Technology vacuums its creators into itself until their reality is re-

placed and becomes increasingly unrecognizable and inconceivable to the past and the present. For nothing can escape technology, once it becomes sufficiently developed on a planet.

230. All Things Are Technological
To be born is to be created by technology and unleashed into a world always in technological development.

231. The Blinding Shock Of Future Technology
Most changes of the future are too shocking to be predicted or created by those in the present. For the further back in time one goes, the more shocking the technology of the present becomes.

As Arthur C. Clarke said, "Any sufficiently advanced technology is indistinguishable from magic."[35]

232. The Quality Of Creativity Is More Important Than The Speed Of Clarity
When dealing with a creation, one who values the speed of its completion over the quality of its completion is bound to forget to include or exclude parts that would have increased the quality of their creation but decreased the speed at which their creation developed.

233. My writings are meant to be used as inspirational fodder for every creative mind that comes into contact with them, from the poet to the philosopher to the painter.

234. One of the greatest activities one can experience is beholding great creations.

235. The artist: a hero.

236. Great Art Causes An Endless Yearning For More Great Art
The greatest art is never enough for its spectators.

237. The earliest known cave art depicts hunting and still today, our art depicts the ongoing great hunt for new knowledge, experience, technology, and higher potential states of being.

238. We charge our knowledge and communication devices with electric vines.

239. The greater the talent and creation the more errors are excused.

240. The human brain is a good example of how technology can become more fragile the more advanced and powerful it becomes.

241. Art: to bring attention to things that are not normally, if ever, noticed, discussed, or appreciated.

242. Art: the act of creation.

243. Art Inevitably Combines
Like technology, art stacks and combines.

244. The Energy Of The Artist Is Imprinted On The Artwork
The expenditure of energy from the artist when creating art does not die, but becomes the art. It becomes the energy felt when gazing upon the artwork, influencing the creation of new energy-containing art.

245. Read The Urge To Write The Urge
The urge to write can be triggered more quickly and on a more

regular basis than it normally would by repeatedly and consistently feeding your mind the urgent lines of other minds who wrote when they too felt the frenzied urge to write.

246. The Influence Of Different Combinations Of Certain Instruments On The Creation And Development Of Different Languages

Is all language created and developed with the influence of the most prominent instruments used by different countries of people? E.g., the fast and twangy sounds of mountain men from the influence of banjos and the combination of slow and fast sounds of Chinese instruments and their language.

247. No critic without greatly influencing creations of their own under their belt is worth being influenced by.

248. A great artist pays attention to every artist, even those they do not always agree with.

249. Perform difficult tasks before simple tasks so that you may perform the simple tasks with the heightened skill that more difficult tasks require.

250. Art: More Honest And Trustworthy Than Science

The greatest artwork owes much of its sublimity to intrusive intuition.

251. The Writer: A Thinker, First, And Foremost

Let a writer use all of the most obscure words a dictionary or thesaurus has to offer; they will never write anything of historical gravity if they cannot think well and often.

252. Some art goes so far beyond nature that once the artist dies, their unique productions become an integral part of life as if they were always part of nature from the very beginning.

253. **All Technology Is Play And All Play Is Technology (Technology: Turning Work Into Play)**
The greatest inventions turn necessary work into fun activities that require less time and energy.

254. **A Great Book: Closed As Eagerly As It Is Opened**
A book is not great if it does not cause some of its readers to want to close it on account of its honesty and its ability to transform whoever absorbs it, appreciates it, and takes it seriously enough. It has to be hate-able, not merely dislikable. It will cause some readers to make excuses to justify never opening it again, stopping themselves from ever learning and growing from its pages.

255. All art deserves to be re-experienced and re-examined.

256. **Rhythm Comes First, Then The Melody (The Connection Between Melodies And Ideas)**
Nature teaches us the language of music first through its different rhythmic sounds. Melodies are formed after life becomes conscious of rhythm. Were the first ideas melodies and the first melodies ideas?

257. It is difficult to recapture the passion of the earlier days when an artist or group of artists starve to make history.

258. **The Greatest Books: Potentially Universally Useful**
To create a book so great and nourishing that it would be useful to other conscious beings from other planets.

259. When a person cannot install a work of art into their own identity, they usually reject it fervently.

260. A book: condensed energy and thought.

261. Art without Science is still Science.
Science without Art is still Art.

262. Artists worship themselves by worshiping their own creations.
Artists worship their own creations by worshiping themselves.

263. Art: the creative advancement of oneself or others.

264. **An Art Critic Who Does Not Create Is Like A Food Critic Who Does Not Cook (Demanding Greater Critics Who Have The Same Or Greater Creative Credentials As The Artists They Criticize)**
How can Shakespeare be criticized and valuated by someone without their own sublime writings? For who can valuate a work of art better than someone who spends their life creating and refining their own creations? Our critics need to be criticized at least as much as our artists are criticized. For whatever we demand from our creators and their creations should be demanded from our critics; otherwise, our critics only encumber our artists for their own profit, like swollen ticks, the time and energy of which they spend feeding on blood they never have to pump themselves.

265. Collect, organize and preserve the peaks of every artist.

266. A book contains imprints of a writer's consciousness.

267. A good title is a bow wrapped around a gift made of words, supplementing its beauty.

268. **Artists: The Doctors Of Society**
Art: the cure to all societal illnesses.

269. Every new dream is a new technology.
Every new technology is a new dream.

270. The emboldening ecstasy of music peaks is a peek into a greater possible world.

271. Writing: a plunge into deep waters with no source of oxygen other than intuition and no light source other than the inspirational glow of deceased brave writers with naked souls, like forever delayed light from distant dead stars.

272. The artists of the East: predominantly animators and designers.
The artists of the West: predominantly writers and speakers.

273. **Melodies And Metaphors**
Different combinations of certain words with differently arranged sentences are like different chords strummed with different speeds, force, and timing.

274. **The Greatest Artists**
The quality of their art matches the high quantity of their art and the quantity of their art matches the high quality of their art.

275. The more one appreciates and trusts great art; the more one will find oneself-becoming greater.

276. Playing With Reality
New technologies are new toys.

277. Writer's Bleed Ink And Replenish Other Writers With Their Own Blood
Reading refreshes a well-rested pen with energizing ink before it is put back to work.

278. Why should we ever feel afraid to forgo humbleness unless we are not in control of ourselves and our work?

279. Creation Begins And Refines With Dissatisfaction
It is one's duty to write when one is dissatisfied with the current state of writing. For there is no creation or advancement without dissatisfaction.

280. Despite Constant Change, Great Creations Are Always Capable Of Stimulating The Growth And Refinement Of Greatness
All art and all artists have a duty to satisfy the infinite hunger for something greater dwelling within all life when the creative nourishment of the past is no longer able to further stimulate and refine creative growth beyond all previously imagined and achieved forms of creative greatness.

281. Timeless Weavers
Astonishing creations and the extraordinary creators which produce and spew them out with the ease and accuracy of a single spider suspended in the air, gracefully and royally riding its webbed waves formed by surrounding winds, having created and spun its own discreet, lightweight, and durable technology, of which func-

tions simultaneously as nourishment, as protection, and as a womb.

282. Creative Urgency Is Fueled By Creative Intrigue
The more interested in something one becomes, the more creative urgency it causes.

283. Playing With Time
The enjoyment of watching plays or movies is the enjoyment of controlling time.

284. A writer's biggest fear is that all of the time and energy put into their work will fall on infertile and apathetic minds, like nutritious rain landing on dead flowers.

285. May awe-inducing expressions bless us forever with their presence.

286. Technological advancements: the evolution of self-expression.

287. A great book: permanently fertile soil for new great ideas and new great books.

288. Art redeems our animal side with the use of our Godly side.

289. Books Are Miraculous
Reading a book is like being able to watch someone's dream or psychedelic trip.

290. A Clue That Music And Philosophy Are Connected
Europeans are now writing albums of music the same way they used to write books.

291. Always keep in mind the progress you have made thus far on a task or creation.

292. Every artist works towards immortality, whether they are aware of it or not.

293. The most difficult thing about writing is having to choose between how a word or sentence looks and how a word or sentence feels; having to choose between understanding and poetry.

294. **What Other Forms Of Music And Literature Exist Or Are Possible?**
Music and literature can become more complex, more healing, more empowering, and more awe-inducing, depending on the minds of the artists.

295. Art that heals heavy hearts and frees buried souls.

296. **The Primary Function Of Play**
Play: less about health and survival than it is about exercising consciousness, thought, freedom, will, and passion.

297. **The Internet Connects Perspectives**
The internet allows us to perceive the world through different perspectives than we would normally be able to without it.

298. **Bringing Heaven To Earth**
Is every new piece of technology a piece of heaven?

299. No one knows where technology is taking us. No one knows where it can take us.

300. The Necessity Of Self-Expression

A human being cannot be completely fulfilled without creating something of his or her own. Neither love nor money suffices if self-expression is not allowed and practiced. For there is no love, without self-expression.

301. A Reminder For All Artists

Read and dissect your own work before others do. Remember that there will be a time when you can no longer defend yourself or your work.

302. To Think And Write As A God

Think and write as a God among men, who wants not to be feared or worshiped, but only to be understood as a godly guide who wants all who receive its words to become gods too.

As Gustave Flaubert said, "The artist must be in his work as God is in creation, invisible and all-powerful; one must sense him everywhere but never see him."[36]

303. Great art: as surprising as it is confounding.

304. One cannot create something without becoming a part of it.

305. A great writer knows best what is necessary and what is unnecessary to include and exclude from their work.

306. Future Technology cannot Be Predicted

What the smartphone will become is not predictable if the prediction is based on the smartphone, just as the smartphone and the internet, in their present forms, were not predictable, based on any of their technological ancestry.

307. The Greatest Fruits Are Taken For Granted
We quickly begin to expect new creations from a great mind, as we expect ripe fruit to fall from its tree, oblivious of the time and energy that is required of all great fruit.

308. Play: To Dare Death (Play: To Overcome Death)
We are not the only daredevils in the animal kingdom. Some monkeys purposefully aggravate less intelligent predators that could kill them if they were to make one wrong move, turning the fear of death into an entertaining game. Also, some birds, instead of flying over them, unnecessarily fly directly in front of fast-moving vehicles, but rarely ever get hit, a clue that the near misses are the bird's idea of fun, rather than accidental close calls, as people have fun by the extreme and lively feeling of overcoming death, when they land with a parachute, after jumping from a plane.

309. Play: manipulating the fear of death for power and pleasure.

310. The Creative Spirit
A wasted book is one that fails to ignite the creative spirit of its readers. It is the creative passion that is being bred out of us, that would otherwise make us want to push further the powers of our minds and to fight harder for the freedom of the individual.

311. Create art that you can call your favorite.

312. Anything is an art if you strive to do it well.

313. The Co-Necessity Of New Fruit And The Bearers Of New Fruit
Without the need for the existence of new fruit, new fruit-bearing trees would not exist, and without the need for the existence of

new fruit-bearing trees, there would be no new fruit to grow new fruit-bearing trees.

314. Art: the spirit of a society.

315. **Overestimate The Audience**
Great art and great artists never underestimate their audience.

316. Playing with one's own creations is the highest form of play.

317. Art teaches what the conscious mind overlooks.

318. If one is able to read then one is healthy and safe enough to temporarily forget about the suffocating worries and expectations of the world outside of one's books.

319. **The Beauty Of Art Is Connected To Truth As Intuition Is Connected To Unconscious Honesty (Trusting, Expressing And Strengthening One's Intuition)**
When one has the overwhelming urge to create new art and one finally surrenders to this urge, one's unconscious intuition expresses itself using knowledge, experience, and beauty, until one feels satisfied and the creative urge dissipates. This is when one's intuition and one's creations can be trusted and taken seriously. One's unconscious expressions are more intrusive, honest, curious, and free than one's more biased, reserved, and pressured conscious expressions. For intuition is the voice of the unconscious.

320. One does not control one's emotions by suppressing them but by expressing them.

321. People have proven throughout history, more often than not, that they do not deserve to know the creators of their favorite art.

322. Did language originate from those who wanted and needed to share and preserve their overflowing thoughts and ideas?

323. Every thought and every action is a creation.

324. Art is about creating something which has never been created or beheld before. It is about transformation as much as life is about transformation.

325. To be an anonymous artist is to admit that one's creations are greater than oneself. To be an anonymous artist is to avoid ruining one's creations with oneself.

326. There is no limit to perfection.

327. Perfectionism: necessary for the creation of greatness.

328. Perfectionism: A Rare And Undervalued Skill
Perfectionism is stressful but the outcome when you utilize it creatively is beautiful and astounding.

329. Making Use Of Apathy And Dishonesty
Let people's apathy and dishonesty fuel you creatively.

330. Have more confidence in your work than the work of anyone else.

331. Express Your Unique Mind
We all walk around with supercomputers in our heads.

332. To Play Is To Seek Greatness And Immortality
To simple and more complex lifeforms, play is the creative, curious, or competitive exertion of energy. The primary motivators of

play for simple and more complex lifeforms are the overcoming of death and the overcoming of the fear of death.

333. The origin and growth of a masterpiece are as unique and unpredictable as the masterpiece and its effects long after it is created.

334. **The Evolution Of The Play Impulse**
All lifeforms share the creative urge to conquer death and suffering. This urge which begins as play in lower lifeforms, is expressed as higher forms of art, technology, and medicine in greater lifeforms.

335. **Play: Testing And Challenging One's Mind And Body**
Even an extreme and daring physical endeavor, such as climbing Mt Everest is an expression of play.

336. Every artist is as transformed by their artwork as everyone else who appreciates it.

337. No matter how great one's creation might be, one can always doubt its greatness during moments of weakness and self-hatred.

338. To play is to conquer fear.

339. Technology becomes past imprints of the future.

340. Would an artist create the same creations if the life of an artist was reset? If not, would the differences be small or great?

341. A great book must weigh heavy on the minds which read it so that when they are willing and able to lift its contents comfortably, the book sticks with them for the rest of their life.

342. Every work of art causes a different creative reaction.

343. With the utilization of one's intuition, language appears to be alive.

344. Each of us can create something no one else can create.

345. Great creations require belief in one's self.

346. Like all patterns, one becomes better at noticing creative influences the more one pays attention to them.

347. A book with little to no questions is not a book but a doctrine.

348. **Trust Books**
The internet is too dangerous and damaging of a place for curious minds, especially young minds.

349. **A Heroic Book**
A book can be a hero.

350. Resurrective art: bringing life to death.

351. Some books are too human.

352. Albums of music are books and their songs are their chapters.

353. Before a lifeform can create, it first learns how to play.

354. Great art permits us to keep going.

355. **From The Conceivable To The Inconceivable**
Technology: proof that what we learn and how we apply that learning matters. For with new knowledge comes new technologies and possibilities, all previously inconceivable.

356. The universe tests the artist.
The artist tests the universe.

357. **Pay Attention To The Great Books And Great Writers That People Do Not Divide And Kill Each Other Over**
Some people will not read books with new information and new questions in them but they will repeatedly read the same book that is closed off to new solutions, new questions, and new ideas, and will usually feel confident that this is all they need to understand their universe and themselves and to reach their paradise form when they die, disregarding their higher potential while they are alive. What these people fail to acknowledge and utilize are the many other great thinkers and great books that even God must surely be proud of; writers and books that do not threaten their readers if they do not obey their rules; writers and books that are adaptable to change. For some people only learn from books that demand certain thoughts and actions and threaten them with an infinite hell if they do not obey.

358. Was the English language built primarily around music? Is this why it pairs so fluidly with music?

359. An artist without psychedelics is like a Shaman without psychedelics: incomplete.

360. Many great books have been written that deserve to be read at least as much as the different religious doctrine of which people think with and live by throughout the world.

361. An authentic artist: an artist obsessed with the creation of their own work and the creations of others.

362. Never allow fear or laziness to be the deciding factor when creating.

363. The effects of a creation are equal to or greater than its causes.

364. **When One's Book Becomes Impatient**
One's book feels like one's enemy until one completes writing it.

365. **Idealistic Art And Nihilistic Art**
The two different kinds of art: art that empowers, inspires, and constructively energizes its spectators, and art that disempowers, discourages, and wastefully depletes the energy of its spectators.

366. Even if the attempt is not fully successful or appreciated, there is something timelessly heroic and inspiring about someone using all of their might, all of their will-power, all of their precious life-force and all of their pain to create and achieve something the majority mocks and believes to be too difficult of an undertaking, if not impossible to accomplish.

367. **Focus On Creative Peaks**
Some people distract themselves from creative peaks with creative valleys.

368. All art is Philosophy.
All Philosophy is art.

369. All artists are explorers.

370. Every comedian carries on the jester spirit.

371. Art changes the planet.
Art changes the cosmos.

372. Abstract art: open-ended art; speculative. art.

373. Never downplay your own work, even in jest.

374. Some artists are peaks. Only certain art and certain artists can become peaks.

375. Great art comes like an unforeseen storm.

376. **New Music: New Philosophy**
Art is Philosophy.
Philosophy is art.

377. A great artist never gives up on creating something greater than his or her previous creations.

378. To create art is to practice being God.

379. The greatest art is the most influential, strengthening, and transformative.

380. **Working With Technology Is Working With Fire**
New technology burns us when we use it incorrectly.

381. When people discover a great creation, it becomes important when, where, and how they discovered it.

382. If someone cannot accept something you have written, it will not matter how humbly or proudly you have written it. They will always find an excuse to undervalue your creations in order to dismiss them.

383. A great book requires more time and attention to properly judge its value.

384. Peaks: Great Soil For Great Fruit

Above the valleys of stagnant, disingenuous, and passionless art, it is at the peaks where great art can be found. Great art is used unconsciously or consciously by a human society as a template for future art more than the prematurely plucked creations below the reach of loving and clarifying sunlight. For art is not as subjective as we prefer to believe.

385. The Sounds Of A Greater Society

Like the erupting rock music inspired by the blues, consider dance, house, jungle, and rave music as rebellious, empowering, healing, and transformational music for a society of people who have finally outgrown their chains and their self-pity and have risen above their teachers and leaders who are only consistent at being disingenuous, disempowering, and devaluing.

386. Never Forsake Rebellious Art

We should direct our focus towards music that is bore out of rebellion. All art grown from the soil of rebellion is superior art. For rebellious art is more lively, daring, energizing, strengthening, resurrecting, genuine, and adaptable to the future.

387. Create art the existence of which becomes more unfathomable to live without as time passes.

388. Creative valleys are the messengers of creative peaks.

389. Peaks: templates for valleys that strive to become peaks.

390. What is great art? Art that convinces people to trade history for novelty. Art that appreciates the past but is not tied down to it. Art that challenges the future. Art that awakens the heart of the

abused. Art that ignites rebellion. Art that influences the inactive to act.

391. No great artist knows exactly how they create their art.

392. Art: a special signature, unique from start to finish.

Society & Childhood

1. We are the architects of our children's memories.

2. **Parenting: Modifying Nature With Nurture**
Parents are the reflective extension of a child's self-perception. They are the cultivators of our future. Through example, they teach a child how to view and treat themselves and others. Like a sensitive plant, full of secret potential, a child must be watered with affection and warmed with attention. For patient and dedicated parents grow healthier family trees.

3. A child's future is mainly determined by their perception of themselves which is highly influenced by their parents. Children should always be the central focus in the blueprint of our future. We are still experimenters, teachers, and students when it comes to raising children.

4. An effective way to teach children is to pretend that they already know what you are teaching. Confidence is a crucial part of childhood learning. Children love and need to be challenged and to have things expected of them, especially expectations that improve their confidence and faith in themselves.

5. The greatest parents learn from their children.

6. Any system which disempowers us should be resisted.

7. Childhood: a less filtered perception of existence.

8. The more something reveals problems within the people of a society, the more taboo it becomes.

9. If an adult's dinner is ruined by a crying child, the adult should be taken out and spanked, not the child.

10. All people should treat their own children and anyone's children like many humans would treat an expensive object. We tend to treat our objects from the past and present with better care than the vulnerable and priceless spirits of our future.

11. Think your way out of the stagnant waters of bobbing, ill-questioning heads. Search for others who have escaped and unite.

12. At a certain point, as if in desperate preparation to say goodbye to the innocence of childhood, children vulgarize words to culturally significant children's songs.

13. Culture: a reflection of the average consumer of it.

14. Weird people have successfully adapted to weirdness.

15. What a strange turn of events for a child, parents changing from Gods into people.

16. Many problems arise in a society where people are rewarded for basing their morals and lives primarily on currency and things.

17. How many adults are but bitter children?

18. **A Consequence Of Technology**
Children will have to emotionally adapt to parents who favor their technology over their offspring.

19. Reaching adulthood is an impossible race to stop being wrong.

20. Children should be rewarded for the creation of not just answers but also questions.

21. When dealing with a troubled child, one is confronting the adults who helped form the troubled child.

22. Insults can improve us as much as harm us, depending on our reactions to them. Those who insult unknowingly enhance the self-awareness of the insulted. For being criticized is less dangerous than never being criticized.

23. Understand your enemy and you will find a shared enemy that unites all enemies.

24. **A Shaman: A High Philosopher**
The shaman is a stoned conduit of new information.

25. **The Societal Gift Of Alienation**
To be alienated is the greatest gift society can provide and although it may be a painful initiation, rejoice, for you have been chosen by your society and mother nature to be able to leave the herd, to return with new possibilities, descriptions, and solutions. Cruel alienation can lift one into the thunderous clouds of sacred solitude if one is not too consumed by hatred or self-pity.

26. Self-Empowered Citizens

Children need to be taught the value of self-awareness, self-empowerment, and self-expression.

27. The Barriers Of Nature

Genetic predispositions
Mental and physical limitations
Societal expectations
Relationship expectations
Job expectations
Bodily requirements
The fear of death
The fear of pain
The fear of guilt
The fear of losing control

The Barriers Of Nurture

Indoctrination
Bias
Delusions
Resentment
Expectations and conditions of family and spouses
Abuse and self-abuse (self-suppression and self-oppression)

28. An Overworked Society

People generally resent people who are not as miserable as they are and other than death, what brings people together through misery more than being overworked? The unnecessarily overworked would have everyone on Earth work as much as they do but no one with enough sanity, family, interests, and self-love truly enjoy working their relatively short life away instead of making the most out of life and spending more time on family, creation, and self-development. Other than providing the modern essentials, the overworked have little time or energy to work on themselves or their family. Instead, they have adapted to prefer working to living, and as a result, often breed this preference for work over life and family into their children, if they have the time, energy, or even the desire to start a family in the first place. For an overworked society learns to place the highest importance on money, and in that kind of society, nothing escapes becoming a business, not even family. The people of an overworked society are treated as machines and are expected to live like machines, so much so, they have adapted to find contentment and honor in behaving more like a machine, even with how they raise their children, who must emotionally adapt to excessively tired and stressed parents. Our children's emotions and development are at stake in this kind of society. Mechanical parents and mechanical schools teach our children to behave like machines so that our mechanical children can one day be able to live like free people if they live long enough to retire from their labor.

29. The disempowered live a bitter and pitiful life because they refuse to accept that they have been disempowered or they refuse to accept the source of their disempowerment.

30. With fear and annoyance, the willingly ignorant inspire the brilliant to reach out and lift them out of the abysmal cesspool of ignorance.

31. Why are certain things joked about more than other things? Because certain things need discussed more.

32. **The Way In Is Out (The Best Way To Understand Ourselves Is To Think Outside Ourselves)**

We have to find a way to maintain an outside perspective of all human systems, parties, and beliefs, or else we will eventually crumble like all past civilizations who also failed to do so.

33. There are people who insult people with great talent, only because their talent was noticed and praised before they themselves noticed and praised them.

34. If they deal with them at all, adults often postpone expressing or coping with their emotions, unlike children.

35. Cities predominately create followers rather than leaders; government-dependent people rather than independent people.

36. **Heroic Compatibility**
You could save the world if you could find the right person for everyone.

37. **Dividing Societal Questions**
Should we accept all of our abnormalities without fully understanding them, should we reject all of our abnormalities without fully understanding them, or should we wait until we learn more about our abnormalities before we accept or reject them?

38. Are the people who live in cities more influenced by the state than those living away from cities?

39. **Human Zoos**
As time goes on, the individual loses value and power in their human zoos.

40. An Effect Of Cities On Abnormalities
The abnormal becomes normal when large amounts of people congregate too closely.

41. An Explanation For The Pervading Sickness Of Modern Society
Our ancestors knew well what it was like to live freely before cities started to spread and take over the land. They knew what it was like to be self-dependent individuals who did not need or want to be governed by anyone but themselves. Perhaps this is why their descendants are so depressed and without purpose.

42. Cities grow like viruses, devouring all individualism in their wake.

43. Living in a city changes the psychology of its inhabitants' overtime, increasing their desire to be governed and making them more likely to normalize abnormalities, many of which are caused by large city environments.

44. Trauma And Sexuality
Some people are negatively triggered by homosexuality because of traumatic homosexual experiences, and some people are negatively triggered by heterosexuality because of traumatic heterosexual experiences.

45. Being Taught To Depend On One's Government Instead Of Oneself
Our public schools work best as tools of cultural and governmental indoctrination. This is made clear by how little they teach our youth about the importance of the individual, self-dependence, thinking for yourself, and questioning everything, as well as of the

dangers of indoctrination, cultural-engineering, herd-thinking, and consumerism.

46. Survival Of The Richest
We have created our own system of life with its own rules of adaptation.

47. Homelessness: a constant warning for the working people to keep playing by the expanding rules set for them by the rich who are exempt from them.

48. A society is only as triumphant and memorable as its choices of influence.

49. The Growing Epidemic Of An Aversion To Speculation
Globally, we create far more reserved and linear thinkers than we do bold, open and confident thinkers; more idea-scoffers than idea-crafters; more followers of thought than leaders of thought.

50. Pain: An Unlimited Resource
With how inevitable it is in the life of all people, teachers should prepare children for trauma and teach them how to, if they succeed in preventing it or they fail to prevent it, utilize it for the advantage of themselves and the world. How strong would children become who were taught to endure and utilize pain rather than run from it?

51. A Musical Society (Living, Learning, And Thinking Musically)
A society where music is the preferred mode of speech, where every teacher is a master musician, and every love note is made of music.

52. Limits To Conversation

Most people tend to have too many limits in conversation to be able to rationally justify ever beginning one with them. Behold the impenetrable walls of ego, fear, bias, and ignorance that so often and so suddenly appear, even during a joyful conversation. Words that cannot be used, subjects that cannot be discussed, and beliefs that cannot be questioned.

53. The Inflexibility Of Adulthood

During childhood, our identities are formed more by other people's actions than our own. This is why it is so difficult to change an adult person's mind, especially if it has been intentionally weakened. For their identities and beliefs are often not their own, but they will risk anything, even their freedom, happiness, and life, to keep them unaltered.

54. Adulthood: A Reaction To Childhood

People spend their adulthood trying to take back the control they did not have during childhood, even if for some that means handing over their individual rights to their government, one by one.

55. Judging by the walls of our public restroom stalls, sexuality, racism, politics, and religion are what is most prevalently on our minds when we release ourselves of bodily toxins.

56. The Natural Profoundness Of Children

A child is free of bias and of limitations that only exist to people who have been conditioned throughout their childhood and adolescents, continuing into their adulthood, to be biased and limited. This is what gives a child a more profound, honest, open, and philosophical outlook on life than the average adult, no matter how intelligent and experienced the adult is.

57. Living Amongst The Living And The Dead
The number of living acquaintances and unknown strangers who are dead to us.

58. Zoos For Domesticated Minds
Human societies are normally built with the unaware majority in mind, as if there were no greater minds less dependent on their society.

59. When A Society Loses Its Seriousness (Laughing At Our Problems Instead Of Solving Them)
We live in a humor-based society, meaning we are an exhausted society. We are tired of all of the conflicting religions and preachers and indoctrinated government-filtered learning. We listen to a comedian before a philosopher so that we can joke about a truth one day and forget about it as soon as the smiles retreat from our faces. We treat our existence as a joke without any greater potential or purpose. We communicate through humor so that we can cope with our problems without taking them seriously enough to solve them. A humor-based culture has given up on existence, out of a failure to cope with trauma, largely brought on by governments, like the generational mass-degradation of soldiers and their families from unnecessary wars.

60. Countries behave like parasites that, when fed the energy of their people and resources from other countries, increase in size and power.

61. Countries: businesses that inevitably abuse their own citizens for profit and power. This is why an increase in the power of a country tends to decrease the power of the individual.

62. The socially inept are not missing out on very much.

63. The worst problem with traditions is that they can be used to excuse the abuse of children.

64. Love your children. Love even their emotional outbursts. For all that a child or an adult ever needs, though they may refuse, whether they are angry, frightened, or sad, is love that is honest, empowering, and unconditional.

65. Foster The Day-Dreamers (The Call Of Solitude)

The day-dreamer child thinks further and more clearly than the child who is busy listening to the teacher who is speaking of only one subject, while the day-dreamer child is thinking of multiple subjects at once. But the day-dreamer is usually interrupted, punished, and outcast from the rest of the class. For blind obedience is all too often taught to be more important than the imagination, individual thought, and individual creativity.

66. A government or society that does not try to create and foster new philosophers is a waste of our time, energy, and potential.

"There will be no end to the troubles of states, or of humanity itself, till philosophers become kings in this world, or till those we now call kings and rulers really and truly become philosophers, and political power and philosophy thus come into the same hands." - Plato[37]

67. Poor people are expected to obey the law, while the rich can do whatever they wish. For the rich have the ability to create more poor people as they become richer.

68. The diet of the average American disturbs their organs, hormones, and mental faculties. This confuses their self-identities. This leads to an outbreak of mental illness, self-hatred, and suicide. How long shall we ignore Feuerbach's statement, "Man is what he eats"?[38] How long shall we ignore that this statement also applies to the books and media we Americans ingest?

69. People love when someone shares something mediocre, or less than mediocre, they have created. They cheer with conniving vigilance and praise with cold exaggeration. They are giddy with excitement and relief that they have been proven to be equal or superior, at least for the time being, and they would like to train them to continue on their mediocre path by sabotaging them with compliments of betrayal.

70. There are ideas, questions, and inventions that never cross the minds of a civilization.

71. Wherever one feels the dryness of stagnancy, spit the truth.

72. The state creates and allows the societal conditions that are responsible for an obsession with weapons across our country. The people are not to be blamed for protecting themselves from a government that increasingly proves that the needs and freedom of each individual are second to its own interests and freedom.

73. Peasants and kings are the basis of all social systems.

74. **The Internet: The Perfect Tool For Any Government**
Private conversations become public, and all fears, plans, hopes, and beliefs of the people become transparent, rendering the people more susceptible to being further controlled by their government.

75. Governments: individuality killers.

76. Like all young life, a young country is not settled with its identity, but if it can survive its youth, the young country can settle on its identity and become an old, strong, and wise country, rich with experiential knowledge and unceasingly influential.

77. Old And Young Countries

Old countries, set in their ways, are influenced by the young, vibrantly new and rapidly changing country, like old men watching a passionate and energetic young man, with both scorn and envy, as he makes mistakes, starts wars, creates new art, influences, entertains and sets new limits. Even with all of the hatred a young country receives from old countries, the young country is usually allowed the opportunity to become old if its art can continue to inspire and liven the creative and intellectual spirit of the older countries.

78. Societal Transparency

Do not merely call out specific people or groups when they are being dishonest or irrational. Call out everyone, at all times, even yourself. Reverse the spell of culture, government, and propaganda and let us become transparent to ourselves and each other.

79. Pets make us feel less like pets.

80. Culture: A People-Limiting Trap That Keeps The Individual Unimportant And Taboos From Being Discussed

What are taboos but revealing things which should be discussed the most yet are usually discussed the least? Taboos are where all human contradictions, fears, mistakes, and secrets hide. For if an advanced alien race were to try to understand us, they would learn more about us by studying our taboos than by eavesdropping on our government and culture-filtered conversations and behavior.

81. The Avoidance Of The Prisoner Recipe
We want to throw serial killers and rapists into prisons or kill them as quickly as possible, whatever it takes to not have to think about them, not just because we hate what they have become and what they have done, but because we sense and fear how close and how simple the recipe is that creates them.

82. The Motto Of A Greater Society
Dare to be aware.
Beware of the unaware.

83. The Foundational Problem With Our Society, From Which Nearly All Of Our Problems Derive
As long as money is valued over life, our education and health-care systems will continue to increasingly fail, weaken and limit us.

84. In all human affairs, there is a test of strength, not merely intelligence. For instance, the intelligent people who are too ego-fueled and too weak and delusional to accept being born a victim to a government that has overstepped its purpose, swelling with merciless power, casting a rising shadow over any original good intentions for establishing it.

85. The Primary Benefit Of Travel
Like a vivid lucid dream, we feel permitted to think, learn, and behave differently when we travel to a new city surrounded by new people, even if it is in the same state and country. For our collar of cultural and home conditioning is temporarily loosened and our thoughts, values, and taste become more free, open, and honest.

86. All governments require the sacrifice of individual values for government values.

87. You cannot trust any government or leader of a society where money is of higher value than life and all of its creative potential.

88. Armies and kingdoms are never so pitiful that they are given mercy and spared being conquered.

89. **The Purpose Of The Herd**
The herd can see who is capable of separating from the herd life and of peering beyond the mundane. For the outcast is chosen to bring back something freeing and empowering from the other side so that the herd can become a little greater; a little more like the outcast.

90. **Laziness And Leisure**
Those who do not learn, think and create on their own terms are the lazy and the ignorant. To the conditioned herd who receive their meaning, values, and purpose from outside themselves, leisure represents laziness, no matter how potentially productive it is.

91. **The Deceptive Happiness Of Stupid People**
Stupid people, while they appear to be happier more often, tend to repeat the same mistakes in life and thought, without realizing it. As a result, they make life more difficult for themselves and everyone else they involve themselves with, regardless of how often they may smile.

92. **Utilizing Societal Madness**
The ancient Greeks were one of human history's most sublime demonstrations of utilizing madness for creativity and understand-

ing. No civilization is without madness. A touch of madness is necessary for a mysterious and relentlessly-testing universe. For the greatest societies are those that creatively utilize their madness.

93. There are those who only praise someone if they see that other people are praising them, whether or not they understand why they are being praised, and those who automatically reject what is praised, whether or not they understand what they are rejecting. In between are those who understand what they are praising or rejecting as well as the implications.

94. Tyrants: Less Dangerous Than The Tyrannized
The average working people of a nation may be more dangerous than any tyrannical government or leader, simply because people can be conditioned to enjoy being tyrannized, potentially even more than the tyrant had in mind.

95. The Living Dead
Zombies have become so popular in our society because we relate to them as the lifeless, thoughtless, creativeless, prideless, hopeless, purposeless, boldless, and franknessless people we have, by and large, been conditioned to become.

96. Fear: A Fool's Respect
If you do not show your children respect, they will not show you, and perhaps anyone else, respect unless it is solely out of fear.

97. The Superior Philosophy Of Children
The natural philosophy of children not yet indoctrinated by adults, not yet controlled by the love-conditions of Gods and the people closest to us, is to exist with the purest wonder, joy, and creative thought.

98. How many people with clean reputations are simply more skilled at hiding their faults?

99. **The Outcast**

Though nowhere near the level of the tribes of highly appreciated and depended upon shamans, the ancient Greeks also found value in the outcast, exampled by the followers and the influence of thinkers like Socrates and Diogenes. Contrarily, the average modern man sees little to no worth in the outcast, who is resented and ignored by the common folk for providing inconvenient perspectives, courtesy of their differences in learning and thinking, and of their courage to question and live more independently. For, like the shaman, the modern outcast is chosen to share their point of view with those unwilling or unable to be outcasts.

100. We are kept exhausted by our government, and this sustained exhaustion stops us from being able to defend ourselves whenever our health and freedom are placed secondary to an increase in government control.

101. Self-protection is all that keeps a government from being completely necessary. This is why it should never be taken away from the people.

102. **Prisons: Protection From Nature**

Innocent workers pay prisons to protect rabid humans from nature, a quicker judge.

103. A young country is less secure than an aged and more culturally solidified country but more open to new ideas and dreams?

104. How can we be suitable for being governors or for even being governed if we are not taught in our youth to understand ourselves and to be in control of ourselves?

105. **Stuck In A Government Nest**
Our government does not try to create Platos, Teslas, or Einsteins with its schools, and whenever a Plato, Tesla, or Einstein does arise, it is never because of our schools. Our government is only concerned with a constantly-spending majority who cannot live or think without it. It wants us to live how it wants us to live, not how we want to live. It wants us to work for people who do not know or care that we exist. Hence, we are easily replaceable. Like overly controlling and overly sheltering parents who refuse to ever let their children leave their house and their rules, our government wants us to work for it more than ourselves. For a society of Platos, Teslas and Einsteins would not need governed and this is ultimately why they do not attempt to establish the conditions that would create more of them.

106. **Real Heroes**
Philosophers, artists, and scientists are non-fictional heroes who leave behind for the world the pain-staking results of a life entirely dedicated to discovering, questioning, and creating.

107. **Our Disempowering Domesticators**
Without being able to convince everyone, our government, as useful as it is, has successfully convinced the majority to believe they are nothing without their government created consuming-mule identity; nothing without their Disempowering domesticator, the destroyer of individual thinking and self-reliance, weakening the majority over time, confirming to them their trained need of being governed.

108. Holidays: highly organized mass scale ceremonies which bring with them their own style of art, expressed through different combinations of colors, designs, symbols, stories, fashion, and music; proof that we are capable of much more focused collective coordination than we tend to give ourselves credit for.

109. Parents: our first authority figures, which we use to measure those to come.

110. Adults: the worst part of childhood.

111. Public schools in America aim to create obedient consumers, rather than unique thinkers and creators.

112. The rich have already created their own heaven but the heaven of the rich is hell to the poor. This is why the poor tend to wish for the end of the world, and the rich tend to care more about the health of the Earth so that they can lengthen the life of their own hellish paradise.

113. Family: a group of people who help hide and ignore each other's pathologies, in fear that their insanity will be traced back to themselves by people outside the group.

114. **Day-Dreamers**
Most of our schools punish the day-dreamer and reward the day-memorizer, when it is the day-dreamer who is more valuable to the future, on account of their supreme passion for and experience with thought and the imagination. For the imagination is the seed of the future and the day-dreamer, its voyager and harvester.

115. When a child is talking to you about something they are interested in, listen to them with the focus that all children deserve, especially when they show passion for something.

116. **The Vehicle Of Society**
Elbert Hubbard said, "The Conservative is a man who puts on the brakes when he thinks progress is going to land civilization in the ditch and wreck the whole concern."[39] He also said, "The Conservative keeps the reformer from going too fast and plucking the fruit before it is ripe."[40]

A healthy society has to have a gas pedal to ensure that it continues to change and move forward in thought and ingenuity, but it must also have brakes for when change becomes dangerously abrupt and without forethought. These are the roles Conservatives and Liberals must play for societal balance to be sustained in America. For a society with an imbalance of Liberal and Conservative values becomes unstable and is doomed to fail, just as the driver of a car who fails to properly apply the gas and brake pedals at the right times is doomed to crash.

117. **Rebellion Is Contagious**
A healthy dose of rebellion is periodically necessary for any society. As long as we still have fight in us, there is hope for us.

118. **Cruel And Torturous Punishment Encourages Cruel And Torturous Self-Punishment**
There is a shared responsibility in the continuation of cruel, tortuous, and unnecessary punishment, belonging as much to the angry and excited audience and the apathetic executioner as it does to those who peacefully face punishment unfit for any lifeform, like people who willingly allow their village to tie them up and set

them on fire or to throw stones at their heads until they die, rather than try to escape, fight their executioner, or find any other way of dying, but they are convinced by their society that they deserve to die this way. For the way people face cruel and unnecessary punishment shows how little or how great that person's society values life.

119. More People Are Growing Conditioned To Abuse From Their Government

Fluctuations of profitable data are all we are to them, and one can see in the troubled youth of today how much this steady domestication of the collective and degradation of the individual has damaged them and how much it has negatively affected all of us from generation to generation.

120. Pretending To Be In Control Of Suffering By Causing Suffering

The tortured, bleeding, and dying bull represents ourselves, and the spectators represent the common and sporadic pains and tortures of life and death and the undying glimmer of fight and hope that never cease to astonish the spectators.

121. Punishment: Perceived As Freedom By The Weak, The Envious And The Spiteful

Every society of people who are pleased with watching people be murdered, whether by flame, guillotine, hanging, etc. is an underdeveloped and easily controlled people who have been conditioned to be content with living as less self-aware, less empowered, and less creative people. The only empowerment and freedom they experience are when they watch the large frigid hands of their masters exterminate people, like old sacrifices to new Gods. Each death makes them feel like they have exercised their will and each death helps validate their beliefs. They believe they have helped improve their world by watching more free-thinking people, not always necessarily more immoral, be removed from their society for defying their beliefs and their masters, as a child that is punished for exercising their will power enjoys rushing to tell an adult on the children who are still enjoying their will power.

122. The Revolution Trap (Governments Create Their Own Demise)

Governments never realize that they should be trying to create great and independent minds rather than dependent and easily controllable minds. The problem throughout human history is that governments naturally form because of the similar psychology of all people, and like tyrants, they always tend to seek more control until the people begin to starve for freedom and food. Herein lies the problem humankind has always suffered from: their governments never attempt to create or refine greater minds. Instead, they keep the people dumb and dependent so that they may be most easily predicted and controlled. This trap unknowingly set by governments, called Revolution, ensnares all governments, ending them with violence and death. For the expansion of government control creates people who become more stupid and passive, if not barbaric, the more control they give to their government until the tamed and fearful mules are forced to become rebellious and violent animals who feed on their enslavers who were once in control of their meals.

123. Government: More Dangerous Than Self-Protected Citizens

There are far more deaths by governments than mass shootings. Does this mean we ban governments? It could be argued that most mass shootings occur for the same reason tigers in zoos endlessly walk in a circle and tear people to shreds whenever they attempt to escape their cages. How much depression is caused by oppression? There is an obvious avoidance of mental illness as the cause of mass shootings rather than the guns themselves. Sane, healthy, and happy people do not create massacres. Governments are in the business of sneakily convincing and conditioning people with the use of fear and coddling to depend more and more on them until they no longer have to worry about the people bucking when they attempt to remove freedom from them, no matter how fast, slow, obvious or discreet the removal process is, like trying to ride an abused and unhappy horse. Be watchful when a government takes weapons from the people because it then becomes easier for them to ban all tools of self-protection. Governments and the people are in a constant battle for power, and governments are far more dangerous than any of the people because of the human tendency to easily be convinced to trust and rely on someone else to protect them. This is taking away the freedom to defend yourself from tyrannical governments and criminals who are never going to stop obtaining and using guns.

As Goethe said, "Which is the best government? That which teaches us to govern ourselves."[41]

124. Children: Better At Conversation Than Adults

There is no limit to a conversation with a child, insofar as they can understand the topics being discussed, but a conversation with an adult is like trying to converse with someone while simultaneously trying to avoid land mines hidden and scattered throughout the path of discussion. Not even they know what they will be enraged by next and what words or subject matter they will be triggered by, limiting and prematurely ending their conversations every time.

125. Tough love: sometimes a way for people to remove their own guilt and contribution to a problem they helped create.

126. Our societal environment is so toxic that some people sell their children to make more money.

127. Cities: human zoos.

128. **Inborn Anarchy**
Some people cannot help but look at things differently from how they were taught.

129. We are breeding and rewarding the least creative of people, of whom are the best at reciting useless trivia, but not so much at creating, solving, or discovering anything new.

130. **Societal Alienation Creates Artists When It Does Not Destroy Them**
Society alienates, neglects, and ceaselessly pushes those who think differently, forcing out of them things the common disempowered citizens of society could never create, no matter how many lifetimes they were given.

131. The only government that can be trusted is one that educates its people on how to live without it; one that does not treat its people like children.

As Edward Abbey said, "Grown men do not need leaders."[42]

132. Discontinue sharing your problems with people who have shared your problems with other people before. For a gossiper likely cares more about gossip than your privacy or reputation and is more involved with your life than their own.

133. A government is tyrannical when it stops allowing the people to heal or protect themselves.

134. Our Society Teaches The Abandonment Of Self

We are taught to hate, neglect, degrade and demolish ourselves before others, even those who are doing such things to us. For our valuation, perception, and treatment of self is a vile and inverted contradiction of the sublime maxim, "Know Thyself"[43], of which once sat on the center throne of every great and common Athenian mind.

135. More Crime Equals More Government Authority, Which Equals More Crime

More authority leads to less self-aware and self-governing people, which leads to more crime, which leads to more government authority.

136. Adulthood is spent trying to either avoid or heal from the trauma collected during childhood. Childhood is spent trying to mimic adults until adulthood is finally reached.

137. Childhood: The Key To Understanding Adults And Their Pathologies (Permitting A More Peaceful And Healthy Humankind)

How would we perceive and treat each other if we knew every detail of every person's childhood? Would we finally treat each other with respect and appreciation, as we would have ourselves be respected and appreciated? Would we not be able to apply that knowledge of one another towards the discovery of remedies, cures, and preventions to our most disastrous and stubborn mental ailments, which mostly originate from childhood and are usually passed down by adults? It is likely, however, that we will never attempt to know each other that deeply because we would then have to accept how pitiful, damaged, sick and unfree humankind has let itself become, with our use of disempowering beliefs and the governments and leaders that we hire to weaken and control us by using those beliefs against us for their own gain of power.

138. A Government Trick
They drive us crazy. Then they say we are too crazy to protect ourselves.

139. Money Protects The Wicked From The Hands Of Nature
The wicked would not be able to be as content or to survive as long as they do today if they did not have the blessings of money. This is the major problem with money: it favors the wicked over the good. Money is retrieved most easily and most swiftly by being less honest, less emotional, less sympathetic, less giving, and less loving. For money protects and empowers the wicked, allowing them to accomplish ever more evil and destructive things.

140. To Parent Well Is To Raise Your Own Best Friends
Great parenting creates great friends. Contrarily, bad parenting can create the worst of enemies, not only of their parents but of everyone around them.

141. People are taught to pretend to respect others more than they are taught to respect others.

142. Cultures: Always At Odds With Religions
A culture is able to transform. A Religion is not. The gates of a religion are always kept closed after a religion gains significant popularity and age, while the gates of a culture always remain open,

permitting a culture to be changed, whether constructively or destructively.

143. Families Value Family More Than They Value Family Members

Unless there is undeniable proof of the accusation(s), families always choose to protect the family over a member of the family when a member of the family accuses another member of being anything but a sane and respectable person of society. No matter the accusation(s), a family is not likely to choose the side of the accuser. For families value family as a collective more than any individual family member.

144. Regaining The Mastery Of Dialogue

We are losing our ability to discuss problems, create ideas together, conversate and learn from one another. We have lost so much of our historical mastery of dialogue that we pay strangers to talk with us and call it therapy.

145. The Childishness Of War

"You knocked over my sandcastle. Now, I must bomb your nation."

146. War: Perpetuates Distrust

As long as countries have governments and militaries, war and the threat of war will always exist, perpetuating our distrust for each other and one another's nation, in effect, spreading fear, hatred, and destruction across our planet.

147. A Global Drought Of Empathy

How many children are not being taught how to temporarily place themselves in other people's shoes, without the biased pollution of one's ego? How many children are being taught to treat others with apathy, rather than empathy, and judgment, rather than understanding?

148. The Plight Of The Rich And The Famous
Never knowing if someone loves you for you or for the money or notoriety they can siphon from you.

149. The Highest Goal Of Any Civilization
The creation of great minds who have not lost their ability to love greatly.

150. Teaching The Majority To Become Greater By Their Own Freely Willed Choice (Towards A Greater Majority)
Great minds always want themselves to be greater than they have ever been before. Mediocre minds are normally only pushed to become something more by a great book or a great mind. Great minds have no need for anyone to influence them to become greater. Those who have been sickened by mediocrity are usually kept ill by governments, politicians, religions, and priests: the ticks that feed on humankind, who ruthlessly siphon all of their physical and mental energy and use it to weaken them while empowering themselves and pretending to be the cure to their sickness. For the reoccurring nightmare of our ticks is that the world becomes inhabited by self-dependent great minds which create a world without perpetual deceit, tyranny, torture, and sustained degradation, revealing to us for all time that they are at best, unnecessary to greatness, and at worst, obstacles in the way of greatness.

151. The Pause Of Growth Between Tragedies
Some families only work on their connection to their family during funerals, just as some nations of people only work together during a national tragedy. Times of tragedy should not be the only

times we love one another, understand each other and grow together.

152. Cities grow and glow like crystals.

153. Are not the people the determining factor in how well any societal system works?

154. **A Comedic Renaissance**
If psychedelics were taken seriously, the greatest writers, comedians, and animators could collaborate and create potential animations of comedy that would paralyze the viewer with the most euphoric laughter.

155. **How The Nosy Are Helpful To Society**
The nosy and gossipy nature of people stops many people from committing mistakes from the fear of being the topic of gossip.

156. Which is the bigger problem, the system that helps continue the creation of miserable drug-addicted poor people or the miserable drug-addicted poor people?

157. **A Problem With Capitalism**
Those who oppose Capitalism can be bought off.

158. **Deadly Social Entertainment (From Gossip To War)**
Women often believe they can get away with ceaselessly gossiping because they believe that their often betraying gossip will never be traced back to them and will never come back to harm them, because of the societal expectations of women and their honest and innocent social appearance. Men tend to have more self-control when it comes to spreading rumors, whether they be false or true, and find out from physical confrontations with other men that

talking behind people's backs will eventually, if not swiftly, lead to enemies, pain or death, and as a result, tend to let women do most of the gossiping and sometimes bring them gifts of gossip for their attention and approval. For gossiping is entertainment and a sport mostly dominated by women because they are usually more skilled at it, more daring with it, and less afraid of it than men. How many deafening and demeaning wars have men risked their sanity and lives for, willingly or by force, of which have been detonated at what is foolishly believed to be a safe distance by seemingly harmless women, who have secretly, throughout human history, turned financially powerful people against each other, causing entire kingdoms and cities to hate and murder one another, with the faintest whispers working as the fuse, of which begins from their mouths and leads to the revelatory and demolishing effects of their explosive gossip?

159. The sounds of guns shooting are as common in some urban areas as the sounds of birds singing in rural areas.

160. Militaries weaken people's will, making them more privy to taking orders, as opposed to giving them. Militaries also make people more dependent on governments.

161. **Destruction: A Resource, Like Chaos**
As all lifeforms evolve by adapting to the natural disasters and scarcities within their environment, children adapt to the disasters brought upon by their parents and family either with mimicry or increased strength and ability.

162. In large cities, one sees uncommon abnormalities that give the appearance of being more common and healthy than they truly are.

163. **Commanding Your Voice (A Vital Lesson Necessary For Children To Become Great Adults)**
As quickly as possible, take control of the voice of consciousness in your head.

164. **Teaching Children To Distrust Family Members, At Least As Often As they are Taught To Distrust Strangers**
Family members are automatically assumed to be safer than strangers, when the truth is that most people are strangers to us, even people within our own family.

165. Children must be perceived as more important than adults because they are the most capable of changing their minds and of changing their world.

166. It is a wonder that there are any rebellious minds left when one takes into consideration how often throughout human history they have been killed by kings, governments, militaries, and religions.

167. What if the average person was an experienced shamanic psychonaut? What kind of society might be possible as a result?

168. Adulthood: the attempt of children to no longer be pitied.

169. Often we are saved by what our parents do not teach us.

170. **Control Of Control**
Children must be taught how to utilize control as much as they must be taught how to utilize the absence of control.

171. **What Divides Us Most?**
Even if they are created with the most unifying of intentions, his-

tory teaches us that culture, government, and religion and their closed understandings, judgments, and limitations are what consistently divide us most, not forgetting the people who keep them relevant and more in control of their own consciousness/will than they ever have.

172. The fear of alienation holds a society together most?

173. The Business Of Church (Preachers As Entrepreneurs And Believers As Customers)

Every member of a church must follow their preacher's interpretation of God, the bible, universal existence, and themselves. They must reject all other interpretations. The job of a preacher usually attracts narcissistic personalities who hate to be challenged or doubted. They tend to believe they are more special and closer to God than their congregation and that they know all the answers. One cannot forget that a church is a business, a preacher is the business-owner and a congregation is the customers. This is why there are so many dividing branches among Christian churches. Different churches provide different selections of the most satisfying interpretations for particular customers, not to mention the pleasure that derives from being surrounded by people who tend to believe that they are part of a church that is most connected to God, while everyone else has strayed from God. The business of the church requires people who seem unable to change their own minds or doubt their own beliefs. It requires people who are easily controlled by the fear of alienation, solitude, and question-inducing knowledge. It needs intellectually lazy people who are desperate for meaning to be handed to them. Tithing is pressured by the preacher and the most loyal customers of the church. For tithing is the cost of being a member of the church. The consuming customers prefer to let anyone but themselves think for them and usually cannot change their minds. For churches are not powered by God but by money, fear, and ignorance, and the cross is a religious symbol that is used by different preachers as both an inviting and guilt-tripping advertisement for the church business.

174. Not wanting to live as a slave is considered lazy to people used to being slaves.

175. Governments Further Complicate Life (Fight Your Own War)

Every war a government sacrifices young men for is a war fought solely for the benefit of that government and all those who profit from it, while never taking part in the fight themselves. For life is a war every person must fight, regardless of race, religion, or nationality, and our governments, along with those who profit from war and its negative effects, only add more problems to life and make the struggle with life more agonizing, the more control they are given.

176. If children only knew how sane and pure they are compared to the adults they trust, learn from, and aspire to become.

177. When it comes to raising children, it is the quality of rules that matter most, not the quantity.

178. Instead of teaching our children to be afraid of a hell after death, we should be teaching our children to be afraid of the people surrounding them while they are still alive; people who have no need for demons or devils for them to be evil. For the more we blame anything but ourselves on the horrors of life and people, the more we find ourselves living in hell.

179. What children need most is love, attention, respect, and consistency.

180. There is natural constructive order in the constant struggle between the gas pedal, the young, and the brake pedal, the old.

181. **No Matter How Indoctrinating Public Schools Tend To Be, Children Are More Likely To Be Indoctrinated At Home (One Redeeming Quality About Public Schools)**
How many children are saved by their public school from irrational, insane, and abusive indoctrination of thoughts, beliefs, and behavior from their family by being introduced to different people with different beliefs, knowledge, and experience than one's family?

182. The creative optimism and idealism of children are sacred and too often replaced by skepticism, pessimism, and nihilism.

183. Children enhance self-awareness in adults and are sometimes punished for it.

184. **The Formation Of Revolutions**
Revolutions form when the needs of the people are no longer met and their needs are no longer met when the people depend on their government to the extent that they willingly sacrifice their wants and needs to it.

185. **Imprisonment: The Result Of A Consciousness Problem**
Should certain psychedelics be administered to prisoners before sending them back into society?

186. **The Sword Of Art Is Ready To Be Used After The People Have Been Sufficiently Hammered By The State**

The state tends to eventually make people heartless and artless, turning their creative energy into destructive energy. Creative revolutions arise not long afterward, as when cats innocently play with their deceased victims after wreaking havoc on them moments before. For creativity is at its most free and fertile state after destruction.

187. Children Push The Adults They Trust For The Teaching Of Constructive Structure

To adults and especially children, daily structure equates to stability and security. Children defy and push hardest the adults they believe are most likely to offer them the most constructive structure in exchange for their disrespectful and destructive thoughts and actions to be corrected by adults who tend to hate being corrected and are less willing than children to change their thoughts and behavior.

188. The Concealed But Visible Insecurities Of The Young And The Old

The overconfidence of adolescence is due to the insecurity of experience. The elderly, too share a similar overconfidence, but it is due to the insecurity of beliefs.

189. We should always be happy with the happiness of other people but never shy away from healthy, motivational, and trans-formative competition.

190. Resenting Creativity With Destructive Criticism

The absence of creativity in a people spawns excessive criticism, the goal of which is not to create, appreciate or refine new creations but to damage or obliterate them, like a child without a sandcastle of their own using their energy to insult and tear down the sandcastles of other children, simply because they are jealous of their creations and their creative passion. They wish to force equality onto a world that is not equal.

191. Striving To Gain Acceptance From Other Races By Rejecting One's Own
Some people feel excluded from their own family and resent their own past so much that they go out of their way to erase any trace of it from their identity, replacing it with a different culture so that they can feel included by any culture of any race other than their own.

192. A romantic is sometimes confused with a traditionalist who buys a woman a ring he cannot afford solely because he fears the judgmental eyes of his society which expects and pressures him to risk financial and relationship instability or ruin for the sake of society and its desires, rather than out of love, appreciation, and passion for her.

193. We forget that our vain and superficial culture affects our children too.

194. In every human society, the people can be divided into two categories: outcasts and out-casters.

195. It is much more important and more rare to be able to raise a child than to bear a child.

196. Governments: as untrustworthy as people.

197. A great government creates and refines great minds, also improving weak minds until they are no longer weak and no longer a danger to themselves, their government, or their society.

198. The State Causes And Benefits From Suicide

Suicide is not simply a free method of depopulation for governments but also a free method of removing creative and independent minds by suffocating them with the government-enforced equality of slavery.

199. A great teacher cannot teach others without learning from them.

200. Governments Weaken People To Appear To Them As A Necessary Savior

Our government conditions people to panic, to remain paranoid, and to become more needy, greedy, and dependent on it so that their belief that they need their government and need to be rescued by them is always rekindled.

201. Is A Government Necessary Only If Its Goal Is To Create Great Minds?

Once a society is filled with great individual minds is a government no longer necessary, or does it finally function as it should?

202. Too Much Complacency Leads To The Death Of Any Nation

Once a nation of people has the fight bred and conditioned out of them, the nation is ripe for tyranny and its own demise. Thankfully, people can decondition themselves and snap themselves out of the daze of slavery.

203. All nations of people must find a common love and a common enemy, or they will never stop fighting each other and blaming one another for problems they could eradicate together.

204. In heavily populated cities, people tend to be more conditioned to depend on a government, and because of this conditioning, they tend to lose touch with future dangers and live in a state of perpetual comfort, denial, and governmental enslavement.

205. **The Big Cheese (The Maze Of Society)**
We are like lab rats. Our governments are the scientists who add new walls to life: the maze of society. They starve and replace us unless we find the scraps of cheese they leave for us. So long as we play by their rules, they will always provide just enough to keep us running, just enough to keep us dependent, and just enough to keep us from rebelling.

206. **A Nation Cannot Survive Without Open Beliefs And Open Science**
Human societies tend to begin with closed indoctrinated beliefs and tend to end with revenge against closed indoctrinated beliefs.

207. After all this time, with all that has been learned and recorded, we still learn from children.

208. **Children: Pure Potentiality**
The potentiality of children is as maddeningly vast as the universe and its potentiality.

209. Governments, so far, have a tendency to fail the people.

210. **The Game Of Society**
The game of society our controllers play, benefit from, and force us to play is kept running by their pretend value of which is rewarded for our substantial value. There are no repercussions for their debts, their lies, their violence, or their excessive greed. We, the

people, are living in a game, and we are the only ones who have to play by the rules.

211. The Dark Forest Of Childhood
Childhood is like being lost in a dark and treacherous forest filled with hidden predators and relentless obstacles made of adult lies, delusions, and beliefs. What a tragic position children find themselves in that they have no choice but to need such dishonest and dangerous caretakers to survive. Eventually, some children are able to grow too honest and conscious to fit into the same damaging, ambiguous, and confusing world as the fearful and untrustworthy adults who hover around and influence children at all times, draining the curiosity, imagination, and potentiality out of them, like ruinous and agitating swarms of mosquito guardians.

212. Many of the problems governments solve would not exist without them in the first place. Governments are prone to creating problems in order to make their existence appear to be more necessary than they truly are.

213. The curiosity of children is contagious and even affects adults.

214. Governments Tend To Turn People Into Slaves
If you somehow, against all instincts, become convinced that you have to be controlled by someone or something, at least make sure those controlling you allow you to think, speak, create and refine yourself freely. Otherwise, you have added a new slave to history.

215. During a global crisis, the veil of cultural and governmental illusions dissolves and becomes more questionable and excruciatingly obvious. It is up to the people whether or not they will continue accepting the abusive charade of our controllers or wait until the veil returns with a vengeance.

216. It is difficult for the people not to become criminals when they are being ruled and abused by rich criminals.

217. The State Holds Freedom Hostage
The freedoms of the people are continuously kidnapped for a never-ending ransom of which the kidnapped are tricked into paying with the private property of the individual self without ever realizing or accepting that both the ransom and the kidnapping are endless and unnecessary.

218. The Eruption Of Revolutions
People are pressurized by governments until revolutions are formed and the tightening boiling pot of an abused society bursts open. Undying freedom breaks through and spews forth from its pit of misery, revenge, and desperation, burning up every tyrannical parasite and melting their unnecessary illusory chains, like splashes of molten lava from an ancient volcano that has run out of patience.

219. Living In Solitude
Even the lone eagle can stray too far from its divine dwelling amongst its rumbling clouds for too long and end up degraded or demolished by the violent, miserable, and envious groundlings beneath it.

220. The youth represent mistakes.
The elderly represent regrets.

221. The Addiction And Degradation Of Generosity And Our Tendency To Let Ourselves Be Convinced To Let Go Of Freedom And Forget About The Individual
Being too generous and forgiving to our rulers trains and enables

them to expect to be obeyed and appreciated more and more, without them being expected to return the favor with the balance of reciprocation, while the overly generous and humble masses of human mules with their disastrously conditioned minds incrementally lose their freedom and make a mockery of themselves and the individual. With this in mind, one can see where slavery, with its different forms, originates, and how it continues to be perpetuated: our tendency to trust and repeat thoughts, beliefs, and actions without meticulously examining and valuating them, our tendency to become too comfortable and confident when we gain freedom and our tendency to take advantage of our freedom and underappreciate it until it is eventually lost.

222. A Common Government Trick

How does an abusive government keep the abused masses working for them, making itself more powerful and free at the expense of the masses' freedom and health? By convincing them as early as possible that their purpose for living is to sacrifice themselves and their freedoms for the enhancement of government freedom.

223. The People Have Grown So Complacent And Apathetic That The Only Way They Would Fight For Real Change Is If Their Government Demanded Them To

We now exist for our government rather than our government existing for us, as it is and was always supposed to. We work for it and die for it, but it never returns the favor. It steals everything from us and sells it back to us for the price of our lives, bodies, minds, and freedom. It steals our freedom to give itself more freedom.

224. We are repeatedly being bamboozled by a government that is illegally taking advantage of our energy and our time and that of our descendants without any repercussions or any signs of change.

225. Tyranny: Disconnection From The People
All tyranny is so detached from those suffering from it that a revolution is all that can reconnect them.

226. Life only gets worse for the people when they become comfortable in their dependency on a government and become content with the sacrifices of freedom that governments tend to demand.

227. What is common is being told what to believe and holding onto those beliefs until death. We are in the mess we are in because the majority prefers having beliefs, values, and truths forced onto them, rather than developing their own. The average person needs guidance and a place of refuge from all those who chase after their mind and their freedom. This is what needs to be done: we who are capable of protecting ourselves from those seeking control of our minds, bodies, time, and energy, at every turn, have to become guides who help liberate and empower others without reducing their freedom, like being forced into the role of Socrates who made everyone he spoke to doubt what they were previously so certain of by the end of their discussion, both of them leaving the conversation wiser in their uncertainty and more uncertain in their wisdom. For there is no increase of wisdom without an increase of uncertainty and no increase of uncertainty without an increase of wisdom.

228. The Common Divide Of Conditioning
Some people can decondition themselves, and some people need

others to help decondition them from the control of whatever they have been programmed by.

229. Find other individuals who think with love, liberty, and greatness at the forefront of their minds.

230. The enthusiasm of children is one of the most valuable things we tend to lose as adults.

231. When our government has us completely surrounded and indoctrinated into depending on it for everything and the last freedom of the individual is snuffed out, when we are starving and have no choice but to fight back, you will not want to be on the side of a perfectly obeying citizen but a rebellious outdoorsman who knows the value of life, the individual and self-dependency. In short, someone who knows how to survive without a government holding their hand.

232. **Conspiracy Theories: Questions Which The Government And Any Other Controlling Entity Does Not Want You Asking**
Once all questions concerning the government are labeled as conspiracy theories then people begin to be afraid to ask questions because then they can no longer question their rulers without the fear of being outcast by their society, for they have now been branded as a danger to society simply for asking questions. This is how they stop people from asking more questions, especially more of the right questions of which can reveal tyranny and all of its dangerous forms, wherever they are aimed.

233. Some people have a tendency to get stuck solely on surface-level dangers.

234. Governments Need Disciplined

The only purpose left when the people have too often allowed their government to have its way at the expense of the people, like a spoiled, greedy and uncontrollable child allowed to continue behaving in a dangerous and shameful manner, is for the people to begin a revolution like many of our ancestors decided on for their health, their freedom and their future. This is what we have been trained for, and this is what scares them most. We have been treated as children but we are the parents who have the power to stop spoiling our deadly and unhealthy child we call government and regain control of its behavior and the undeserved privileges we give it, along with the unpaid sins we always forgive it for.

235. Revolutions: As Inevitable As People Abusing Their Power

History teaches us that revolutions are as inevitable as a sick person vomiting, and like purging the body of a weakening, terrorizing, tortuous and deadly sickness, purging a society of the illness of tyranny can only be avoided for so long before the people become ripe for revolution.

236. Do not control your children too much or they may grow to need being controlled in order to function and survive.

237. Teach your children how to handle and utilize personal failures.

238. If we are not willing to fight for rights then rights become useless illusions.

239. A government without repercussions for its crimes is tyrannical and out of control of the people.

240. **Why Should They Value Our Lives If We Do Not Value Them Ourselves?**

Our rulers see how apathetic and suicidal we have become, and this gives them permission to continue murdering, controlling, and weakening us without any guilt.

241. Children are stronger than adults and more adaptable to change until adults successfully teach them to be afraid, miserable, apathetic, and weak like them.

242. A global crisis is the best time for a revolution, just as it is the best time for governments to tighten their grip on the people.

243. Governments always expire by separating themselves from the people. They inevitably become corrupt and birth revolutions.

244. **The Curse Of Old Age**

During old age, one is sentenced to live the rest of one's life with the wrinkled mistakes of one's youth.

245. The people require enough power to be able to control their government when it becomes corrupted by people. Governments seek more than enough power to control the people when the people become corrupted by their government.

246. When the population and life expectancy of a criminally governed people grows, the people become more in danger. For life is less important to people who value money and control over life and freedom.

247. Governments are created and expanded by the majority in order to make them feel safer. Revolutions are created when the ma-

jority become too dependent on their government and its imaginary securities.

248. The Death Of Rebellion Is The Death Of Freedom

Every government becomes corrupt and seeks expansion, as cancer seeks growth because all governments are run by people, and people are corruptible. A one-world government will only ensure that the people never have the power to revolt, regardless of what the government does to them. The new world is a shiny new trick that will be used against the people in a way never before witnessed or experienced. If our rulers can make us sick, desperate, and frightened enough, they can convince us that we need them more than we need ourselves and each other. When a government has full control of the people, a revolution will no longer be possible. For all rebellion, self-protection and self-dependency will be considered terrorism, even by the people.

249. The weak call for slavery and death and know it not. For they were bred for slavery and death.

250. The people represent the people—no one else.

251. A domesticated society is a dependent, weak, envious and bitter society that is purposefully kept that way so that their rulers can become more rich and powerful by controlling and selling the people their treatments, in exchange for their labor, health, freedom, and sanity.

252. Civilization is and has always been divided into people who fight for the people and people who fight for their rulers. Even those who do neither fight for their rulers.

253. When a couple nearly creates a monster, they are disturbed when their child becomes a greater person than they expected. Despite the couple's attempts, their child fails to become the monster it was raised to become.

254. Helping Children Love Themselves

Always let your children know that mistakes and material objects are nothing compared to human life and human potential. Always help them love themselves, even when they make mistakes and fail.

255. When a child is harmed or neglected by his or her parents, peers, or society, the child can grow to relate more with and to become more likely to defend any land or culture other than their own.

256. Outnumbered By Ignorance

The people who should use the options of protection and abortion the most are the same people who usually will not, even if abortion were to be a legal decision, globally. Contrarily, the people who should not have abortions are the same people who are usually mature and intelligent enough to use protection or have an abortion, if protection fails.

257. All of society conspires to shame others for doing anything that is not for society.

258. The common person has little foresight for the human race or even themselves anymore. For their government protects them while their culture thinks for them.

259. On a massive scale, we are being taught to be complacent consumers of other people's thoughts, without also being taught to create and refine our own thoughts.

260. Our public schools do not teach our children how to think for themselves with their own brains, only how to remember the thoughts and discoveries of other people.

261. Children can be better than most adults at imagining and valuating because of their near absence of beliefs and biases.

262. **The Assumptions Of Law**
The problem with all laws is that they are not adaptable to every individual, who must either accept them and be left alone or reject them and be encaged or killed. For our laws assume every individual to be the same and to have had the same family and cultural background, with the same experiences, desires, and thoughts.

263. A change in people is more important than a change in systems.

264. Political correctness functions like a religious belief that condones the punishment of honesty and the concealment of truth, in favor of a myriad of changing emotions, from an easily offended populace.

265. **The Cure For Modern Man**
If we can individually admit that we, as a planetary collective, have become sick, then we can finally begin to work on the cure. What has made us so ill as a species? That is the primary question for all people to ask and to find the answer to, regardless of their beliefs. Is it really such a difficult question for us to answer, with all of human history and all current knowledge at our instantaneous command? We have always been and are still being abused and controlled by a multitude of terrorizing, guilt-tripping, tyrannical, mentally-paralyzing beliefs, many of which have been repeatedly pounded into our heads, with the fear of being ostracized by our

families, our churches, and our countries. Often introduced during childhood, they fracture our psychological development, hindering our ability to question, doubt, believe in, and depend on one's self. We tend to hand over our individuality to anyone and anything but our very selves. Here exists another important problem of modern people: we cannot seem to find the necessary strength and maintain the necessary self-awareness to take control of our beliefs and the disastrous and shameful things we allow them to do to us, as well as the things we allow ourselves to do for them. Because of our repeated domestication over time, by King, church, state, and government, we have been convinced to feel unworthy of an antidote to our increasing collective sickness. The only way we can find the empowerment, the courage, the honesty, and the understanding to cure and improve ourselves, is if we can humble ourselves just enough to combine with the safest and most thought-inducing, creativity-enhancing, and consciousness-refining plant and fungal life this planet has to offer us. Only through this symbiosis can we remain self-aware and adapt to new discoveries and creations.

266. Even the rich become beggars by the end of their life. Begging for more time; begging for the freedom to change the past; begging for the acceptance of leaving their money behind; begging for the courage to enter one of life's most profound mysteries.

267. **Irrational Discipline**
If you have to beat a child in order to teach them, they are not a bad student; you are a bad teacher. It will always be illogical and hypocritical to teach a child not to hurt others, as you are hurting them. Even children know this and translate this failed discipline as disrespect, which causes them to behave with more disrespect towards their parents and all authority figures.

268. Working For People Who Further Sicken Us
How many Americans force their unhealthy and ill rested bodies up for work, every day, so they can work at a job they hate for people who have not the slightest awareness of or care for their existence?

269. This world is no place for an honest, loving, and learning child. Our job is to make this world a greater place to live for the children who will soon be responsible for managing it when the adults are gone.

270. The most criminal people and the most criminal governments are the most heavily guarded.

271. Like an overly paranoid person who can only sleep by being surrounded by knives and guns, a country that spends more money and attention on weapons and violence than it does the health, strength, and education of its own people shows signs of insecurity, guilt, and distrust. These signs can also be a reflection of how insecure, guilty, and distrustful the rest of the world is.

272. We are trained to think more about what is good for the collective, never for the individual.

273. People who are not considered to be mentally disabled call each other retarded as an insult because everyone knows, but will not admit, that if we study any government-bred and raised person long enough, we find that they have some retarded tendencies of thought, behavior, or emotion.

274. The Black Sheep And The Pink Elephant
There is no limit to the mental illness families can ignore within their own family. The pink elephant swells ever larger by being

consistently fed by those in the family who cannot accept the reality and the spread of its sickness. The black sheep are the family members who refuse to feed and protect the pink elephant, along with the damage it has caused and continues to cause the family. Because of this, the black sheep are often ostracized by their family, as if they are the problem, not the pink monstrosity that everyone else in the family continues to enable, grow and ignore.

275. When society hurts us, we are blamed and punished, never society.

276. We are paid to spend energy and time away from ourselves and our family.

277. Fighting The Parasitic Growth Of Government
Will you let your body and mind, your health, and your art become part of a business that eats and spits people out, by the millions, like a blind and careless tsunami wave?

278. The Illusion Of Ownership
Our time and energy are no longer ours; they have become our handlers. We do not even own the money we are paid. Why would we when the time and energy we spend has become theirs?

279. The Cycle Of Religion And Nihilism (The Purpose Of Nihilism)
A society must first become religious before they will become nihilists. After they allow themselves to be nihilists, with a clean slate, they wait for a better value-system to adorn their minds and lives with.

280. Working And Paying To Be A Slave To Debts That Are Not Ours

Taxes from foreign products are the only goods that we are legally allowed to pay, and the fact that we have to pay them proves that we have been sold by our own government to other nations and we have been convinced to pay their debts for them.

281. The young and naive often unknowingly avoid death, gracefully, as if intentionally tricking death with their sporadic, irrational and stubbornly curious, and experimental nature.

282. Rome Fell So That We Would Not Have To

The greatest societies fall so that even greater societies can rise and remain risen.

283. The Heroes Of The Herd

The herd always end up with their minds declawed, as a precondition to being accepted by the herd and its leaders. The strong individual, however, protects the mind and keeps it sharp, passionate, and prepared for all those who thrive on taking advantage of herded minds.

284. The Eagle And The Nest Of Society

Like a nest of famished baby eagles, a society calls for the free-thinking and freely creating self-dependent individual: the fully developed eagle who takes frequent breaks from the nest and soars to new clarifying heights, returning with new clarifying food, partly to help them grow and partly to stop their incessant noise.

285. Should a parent say or do the same things to their own children that they would not allow another adult to say or do to them?

286. Fetishes Can Show Us What We Are Missing

When the family unit is broken up by a government and leaders who turn people into numbers and who hold that money is more important than family, does incest become a more popular fetish, in a desperate subconscious attempt to hold on to the family unit? Is this why royalty and incest are as intertwined as religion and sexual abuse?

287. The more people are treated by the state as weak and ignorant slaves, the more the people treat themselves and each other as such.

288. Homelessness: The Slaughterhouse

We are free-range humans. If we do not pay to live, we are slaughtered.

289. Led Astray By Society

We tend to see ourselves through the eyes of others, instead of our own.

290. People, by and large, do not fight their own battles anymore, only when a government, an organization, or a corporation tells them to.

291. Adulthood: an attempt to become less pitiful than childhood.

292. Slaves: nonconstructive with fear and pain.
Masters: constructive with fear and pain.

293. Pity: weak men's glory.

294. Solitude: a mind-altering experience.

295. **Social Media Steals Solitude**
One can turn off society by slipping into solitude, but it has become difficult to stop social media: our society turned digital, from intruding on solitude.

296. A portion of nature must be sacrificed for a city to be built and expanded.

297. Creating new ideas is never the criteria of public schools, but memorizing the ideas of others is.

298. **The Prevalence Of Bad News Normalizes Fear And Destruction**
Our fear and destruction-focused news surely must make violent psychopaths feel less alone.

299. Children exercise their parents' minds and bodies.

300. **In Society, There Is More One Cannot Say Than One Can Say**
The majority only allows for so much truth before they become exhausted and stressed by it, requiring some recycled lies to calm and rejuvenate them.

301. We are a country of physically and mentally sick people who self-mutilate ourselves with unhealthy foods.

302. Anarchists: willing to create order, through necessary chaos.

303. We, the people, have two options: take advantage of our government or let our government take advantage of us.

304. We can either allow ourselves to depend on our government or make our government depend on us.

305. Our schools teach us how to obey and depend on government more than anything else.

306. **Governments Always Expire By Separating Themselves From The People**
Every government is eventually dismantled by the people they are supposed to work for because every government inevitably becomes corrupt and out of control.

307. **Cities: Concentration Camps**
Governments cut down forests so that they can make more cities. They make more cities so they can better control more people.

308. The majority is so self-hating that they joke about their own death. They ignore and insult their higher potential yet worship and uplift people who have already managed to think and live beyond self-hatred and self-apathy.

309. The black sheep of a family has experienced the concealed and protected insanity of their family like the honest and self-dependent thinker sees through their dishonest and insane society. Both are outcasts for the same reason.

310. All of the people we look up to, who empower us and enrich our lives, are the people who failed to be degraded into insanity: the black sheep and outcasts who, despite the odds, choose honesty over dishonesty and sanity over insanity.

311. Black sheep represent a failure on the part of their family to make their descendants more insane and to keep them too scared or disenfranchised to speak the truth about them.

312. People corrupt governments.
Governments corrupt people.

313. **When Weakness Becomes A Blessing**
The elderly retain less energy and because of this, retain less sadness, hate, and anger.

314. Torture has always been used by governments to degrade the minds and enslave the will of people for their own advantage and sometimes a society does not realize or will not acknowledge that they are being slowly tortured, degraded, and enslaved by their own undisciplined government.

315. Governments: a way for the people to remove all self-responsibility.

316. **True Freedom Comes From The Individual, Not A Government Deal**
The attempt by a government to remove weapons from the people is never a sign of progress. Some people do not want to admit how much we have willingly allowed our government to degrade us. We like to keep ourselves in this comfortable nest made of fantasies where we are in control of everything they do or do not do and that if we but have faith they will care about our health, family, and future. It is never going to happen. They do not care about any of us. They do not have to.

317. The only remedy against the tortures of society, its oppressors, and the countless thoughtless minds it creates is enjoying the

mere thought of making them all squirm with unfiltered truth during a global or national crisis while the cultural veil is still thin and they are still paying attention.

318. The only way some people will side with a victim of government over government is if they or a loved one become a victim themselves. Sometimes not even then.

319. When the people do not have to fear their government, the government will not have to fear the people.

320. Empower your neighbor. Self-hatred is what is hurting us most.

321. Do not ignore corruption or it will become impossible to ignore and will require the ancient wrath of the people to solve. For rushing through the heart and the brain of every individual is the immortal blood of brave warriors, ancestors who also fought corruption and tyranny during their own time.

322. Mainstream media is a propaganda machine designed to keep the people blaming each other for the government corruption that surrounds us all. It is an enemy of the people and should be denounced and destroyed for the dangerous and false journalism it is.

323. Nazis took away the Jews' weapons. Then they took away the Jews themselves. Which one are you today? The Jew, the Nazi, or the Nazi sympathizer who is too afraid to fight the Nazis?

324. Government: a necessary evil that must be held in check.

325. The recent protests and riots in America are not because of the people but because of unbalanced power between the people and their government. This is the result of a corrupt government

that has been undisciplined, unchecked, and allowed to grow to monstrous proportions without having to pay for their crimes.

326. Behold how disconnected from the people governments can become and how detached from the people the people can become because of governments.

327. Our words and reactions to government corruption are being watched by other countries and will be seen by our descendants. What message are you sending to the rest of the world and the rest of America? One of empowerment or Disempowerment?

328. Governments are here to stay. Trying to remove them is foolish. All we can do is try to make sure they are upholding the same laws they promise to uphold and force us to uphold, or they will only make us weaker and more vulnerable while our government becomes stronger and more invincible until no one can fight back without becoming known as a dead terrorist.

329. All government institutions are paid to be detached from the people and to favor the State.

330. Why do we set a lower standard for our governments and leaders than the standard we set for ourselves?

331. The average American loathes reading and learning because most people are not immune to religious or government indoctrination. They inject themselves daily with biased news articles and social media posts, deleting anyone who contradicts them, and live their lives believing they know the definitive truth and barely ask questions or express their own opinion. A lot of the silence is apathy. A lot of people do not think their thoughts matter. Self-education is the only way out of this mess. That and psychedelic

intervention, but it is often true that the people who need psychedelics the most will not ever utilize them.

332. We use political media to distract us from the things in our lives and our minds we are not willing or able to solve or improve.

333. Ignored corruption always eventually gets to a boiling point before a riot is formed. Corrupt institutions are always prepared for this bucking of the people.

334. The biggest divide between the people: those who believe they can control their government and those who believe it has become too powerful to control because we have been degraded and divided too deeply and for too long.

335. **The Unbiased Shaman**
There is none more insightful than a bitter-less outcast.

336. When a government is more likely to respect its own people, the people are more likely to respect their own government.

337. We have grown too distrustful of our government and each other. Too many police distrust and disrespect the people and too many people distrust and disrespect the police. This problem between major city police and citizens is a trust problem and an imbalance of responsibility and accountability. This imbalance forms a wedge between the government and the people. This wedge is not new, and the tension it creates becomes more dangerous the more it is ignored and protected, just as mental illness becomes more dangerous and damaging the more it is left untreated. We now live in a world where a relatively small number of wealthy people can run our lives and censor our thoughts behind the media curtain and manipulate our emotions, our identities, and our real-

ity with better technology and psychological understanding than ever before, treating us like disposable pawns with not a single individual spirit between us.

338. The role of the outcast is necessary for the health of a society.

339. You may think you are not a peasant but they will not care when you are gone and you will be replaced in an instant by another proud and naïve peasant.

340. Beware of labels, whether it is Liberal or Conservative, religious or atheist, straight or gay. They are used often by our oppressors to divide and control us. This is how Hitler was able to order human beings to kill other human beings: by labeling them anything other than human, thereby dehumanizing and devaluing them, detaching them from their human killers.

341. There is a dangerous media-driven mass-delusion and mass-disassociation going on between both parties. If only more people thought more and learned more without their daily dishonest media sources, both parties could admit how biased, hypocritical, and herd-like they are in their thinking.

342. Governments, like people, must earn trust and respect honestly and constantly by expressing honesty and trustworthiness. Healthy governments, like healthy people, do not forcefully demand trust and respect while failing to trust and respect the people they are supposed to be connected to and are supposed to be working with, rather than against.

343. Too many people choose to believe and fight for their truth and disregard the truth, at all costs. The current situation is actually worse. They do not search or fight for the truth or even their

own truth. They search and fight for someone else's truth. Given all that we know now, does anyone truly believe they are in any special enlightened position to confidently claim to know who among our rulers is dedicated to the people and their higher potentiality? We have to admit the possibility that maybe none of them are because everything has become a business. We are living on a planet that humans have turned into a highly profitable business which creates an ongoing pattern of traumatic, regressive, and unnecessary wars and victims, all orchestrated by greedy and deranged people who are as detached from every single one of us as a person is to an expendable machine. When will the people realize that helping the people to become healthier and more conscious, peaceful, honest, and self-dependent is not part of their agenda at all?

344. It is easier to control and profit from a traumatized populace which is why they continue to traumatize us.

345. Fascism requires a boogeyman that it can use to control people with fear because nothing controls people more than fear. Hitler used Jewish people as the boogeyman for Germans.

346. It seems like any excuse given to a person to detach from humankind is taken and ran with by more people than we would prefer to admit. People who are granted the power and protection to do so by their own government. It appears to be a problem of authority-based human detachment. This is something every one of us can and does fall victim to, regardless of our race.

347. Witchcraft was once seen as an unstoppable evil force taking over the land. Burning witches never stopped witchcraft but that did not stop people from burning every person who was even suspected of being a witch.

348. We are not a mere collection of different labels to be taken advantage of. We are all individual people with unique minds.

349. The reason poor black people are abused by rich people is the same reason poor white people are abused by rich people: No lives matter to governments unless you are rich or you work for them.

350. Children contain so much unbiased and unrestrained truth that adults in large groups become silent, attentive, and sometimes frightened as soon as they decide to speak.

351. Beware of the censorers. For there is nothing virtuous about censorship.

352. What if governments taught people to teach themselves, heal themselves, protect themselves, and govern themselves?

353. Governments need people to need them or to believe they need them. They teach people to believe in governments more than themselves. This creates weak, unhealthy, and government-dependent people.

354. Would not a government become a greater government if it taught people how to teach, heal, protect and govern themselves?

355. The precondition for a government: people who need governed, or at least believe they need governed.

356. We are bombarded with the worst of humankind by the media news. We are addicted to it. We have become dependent on this entertaining and traumatizing drug.

357. Our creative expression and our freedom of speech should never be limited to whatever does not offend people.

358. People are too easily corruptible, and governments are equally as corruptible because of this. If governments valued the individual and taught people to think with their own minds, to teach themselves, heal themselves, protect themselves, empower themselves, and govern themselves, could there potentially never be a threat of tyranny or a need for a revolution?

359. Stop pitying yourself and your neighbor. Empower yourself and others. Pity Disempowers people and makes them more vulnerable to evil.

360. If we censor the past too much we can be convinced that our present is filled with more hate than our past. We can be convinced that the newer generations have not made any social or racial progress.

361. Depending on where you live, you can either get stoned with your friends or you can get stoned by your friends.

362. Racism and classism are both examples of discrimination and affect all races. Racism depends largely on your race and where you live. Classism does not care about your race or where you live. For classism is more inclusive in its hate and devastation than racism.

363. Be aware of slippery slopes when dealing with governments.

364. Some people replace their identity with their culture. Their culture convinces them to sacrifice their individuality to it. Their culture tells them what is important and what is not important. What to think and what not to think. What to believe and what not to believe. What is beautiful and what is not beautiful. What to fear and what not to fear. It becomes a manipulative tool for tyrannical governments and tyrannical people. Culture cannot be

trusted. It does not see any of us as individuals and neither do governments. The only part of culture that can be trusted is art and that is because genuine art transcends culture and is undeniable proof of individuality and its powers when it remains recognized and free.

As Terence McKenna rightly said, "Culture is not your friend. Culture is an impediment to you understanding what is going on. that is why, to my mind, the word 'cult' and the word 'culture' have a direct relationship to each other."[44]

365. If you know you cannot fully trust your government then you must ceaselessly question it and demand the truth or suffer the consequences of an unquestioned and unaccountable government.

366. Our mainstream media is in the business of nonstop stories and videos that traumatize and trigger the most people possible.

367. One can be patriotic and remain a free thinker. One can root for one's own homeland while questioning its government. One can denounce the ugliness of its past while supporting its future beauty.

368. A healthy government successfully teaches the people to govern themselves.

369. Unhealthy governments sacrifice the freedom of the individual for the enslavement of the collective.

370. A healthy government teaches the people how to govern and teach themselves and how to think with their own minds. An unhealthy government weakens and dumbs down the people until a revolution becomes necessary.

371. Multiple women can fight over one man who does not respect any of them but wears the most expensive brands of clothing and shoes, without any of them, the man included, realizing that they have been duped by culture and materialism.

372. Too many people allow culture to raise their children. Too many people allow culture to choose a mate for them. Too many people allow culture to think for them. Too many people allow culture to determine their worth.

373. Sometimes culture saves people from culture by causing them to be outcast from it. This would be tragic if not for those who are outcast being saved from living as enslaved cultural automatons.

374. Women tend to be more influenced by culture than men and this is not always a negative trait. Women tend to be the guardians of art, youth, and all things that cannot protect themselves. Men are often forced to be just as influenced by culture, even if it harms them, or risk losing female attention and affection.

375. Imagine if children were encouraged to write their own philosophy at the end of each year to encompass all that they have learned and experienced thus far.

376. Every child deserves individual attention. Their interests and passions should be discovered as early as possible.

377. Children should be able to read books of their own choosing.

378. The Liberal is resentful of the Conservative because the only values the Left have are taken from culture and they know that the values of culture are transient and dangerous, especially when culture can be used against the people. The Conservative appears to

care more about the future of America but they also tend to allow religion to influence them to seek death and to damn to hell all those who are not religious and who do not follow the same religion as they do.

379. The uniqueness of every mind is more important than any cultural expectations of appearance.

380. Some people's defense for trusting our government is that they have already taken our freedoms away unnecessarily in the past. This is a defeatist argument that amounts to saying that we should just give them all of our rights since they are so determined to take them.

381. You trust your government more than yourself. This becomes everyone's problem.

382. They feed us only what we are afraid of and what we want to believe and many of us eat it with pride. Anyone searching for the truth is downplayed or alienated.

383. Our historical problem is that we tend to allow priests and politicians to run the show instead of Philosophers and Scientists. The former always claims to know the truth. The latter always searches for the truth.

384. We would have a greater world if governments were policed as much as citizens.

385. If we defend our government, we get more government. If we attack our government, we get more government. All we can do is learn to govern ourselves until we do not have to depend on being

governed. For the evil people of any career field fail to govern themselves.

386. I will always oppose propaganda, fear-mongering, and blind collectivism, not just for myself but for everyone.

387. No lives matter to those who trade life for money and value money over life; people who only see a collective to be controlled where there are free individuals.

388. **The Human Predicament**
Zoos reduce the freedom and power of their animals. When the animals try to escape the zoo and enhance their freedom and power, their freedom and power are reduced further.

389. **The Suppression Of Emotional Expression And Emotional Growth**
Public schools tend to teach children to suppress emotions, whether it be laughter, anger, or sadness, to suppress their creativity and imagination, to think, read and memorize only what they are demanded to, and to speak only when spoken to. Children are trained to depend on a government to learn and deal with personal and social problems, rather than themselves. They are taught to treat self-awareness and self-expression as side notes.

390. The state does not care about your health, your mind, or your freedom. It cares about money, power, and population control.

391. The impulsive discipline of children causes impulsive behavior in adults.

392. With any job, if you give people the freedom to think and act without having to be held accountable, they will eventually fall into the habit of treating people outside of that job as subhuman.

393. There is a fine line between discipline and disrespect.

394. The outsider often remains an outsider because he knows too much about the inside and unintentionally contradicts it with his unbiased presence.

395. Cannabis is the perfect example of how a government can turn something that promotes morality by influencing more people to be more conscious, more empathetic, more empowered, more questioning, more honest, and more healthy, into a plant that becomes immoral if it is grown or utilized without permission from the government.

396. The underlying dread and nervousness coinciding with being pulled over by the police is not necessarily because one is a bad person or because all cops are bad people. It is because one realizes deep down that one is being pulled over, not merely by a person but by the entire cold and greedy State. For to the State, its laws and its money are more important than people.

397. Beware of entitled white people who identify as pitiful victims, who resent their own family and race and are obsessed with perceiving every other race as pitiful victims, projecting their own self-perpetuated victim identity onto people who do not need their fake help or pity and will only become more dependent on anyone but themselves by accepting their help.

398. One of the worst things that can be done to a child is for them to be taught or enabled to perceive themselves as weak and pitiful.

399. As a fully capable adult, you deserve the abuse you continue to enable, whether it is abuse by a government or by a person.

400. You know when someone trusts and depends on mainstream media and anyone other than themselves when they are more triggered by speculation than propaganda.

401. **Children Of Culture (The Balance Between Family And Culture)**
Some people are raised by their culture more than their family. They trust culture more than their family and probably for justified reasons, more often than not. They become resentful of everything their family represents to them and everything that reminds them of their family or heritage. Even if it is dangerous to them, they gain immense pleasure from automatically defending and glorifying culture just to spite anyone who questions or rejects culture and its changing assumptions, pressures, and expectations.

402. **Self-Protection Is More Effective And Reliable Than Government Protection**
From any window or door of your home to you and your loved ones is a short distance, and an attacker will most likely reach you before police can.

403. To trust those with the most power and influence is a risky habit. We are demonstrating our power as the people by testing our rulers and forcing them to reveal their priorities by asking new questions. We need to keep testing and questioning them if we want to remain aware and free.

404. Social media: our biggest distraction to date?

405. Think of government as a large and growing business. If a business allows its employees to become immune to the accountability of their actions, the employees will eventually become more and more dangerously corrupt, especially the more the people doubt it. The increasingly criminal and increasingly protected business will only reward its employees for deceiving and abusing their customers solely for the benefit of the business and its employees. Never accepting that this is happening right now and never accepting that it has happened over and over again is making sure that it gets worse. Never questioning your rulers is making sure you eventually become enslaved and degraded by them.

406. Unbiased self-reflection, self-expression, and human history are the most important subjects for schools to focus on.

407. **Children, Adults, And Authority**
Until adults teach children to fear and obey authority figures, normally without question, and to respect and depend on authority, usually more than themselves, children naturally mock the concept of authority and see through the illusion of authority figures and their perceived value and trustworthiness, which is commonly taught to be superior to everyone else.

407. Never allow a child to feel hated or to believe that he or she is less valuable than an object. For a broken object is of less concern than a broken child.

408. The greatest teachers are those with the greatest ability to teach themselves.

409. When children get bored or exhausted from creating, they begin destroying, all in the same day.

410. People treat police like they treat wasps. "They will not hurt you as long as they do not feel threatened."

411. **The Puppet Masters**
Governments indoctrinate and traumatize people with religion, school, military, and media until they can move an entire country of people around like a gigantic puppet.

412. The death of childhood is the one thing that unites all adults.

413. Politics adapt to technology.
Technology does not adapt to politics.

"There are no political solutions, only technological ones, the rest is propaganda." - Jacques Ellul[45]

414. **Perfecting Propaganda**
We know how to keep ourselves dependent on the thoughts, actions, and dreams of anyone but ourselves: by making fear and suffering addictive, turning trauma and degradation into entertainment.

415. Where is the war on propaganda?

416. Taboo: when whatever we believe has more control of us than we have of it.

417. **Children: More Trustworthy Than Adults**
Children reveal their emotions, experiences, and thoughts while adults consistently conceal them.

418. Fame: when your fame brings fame to strangers.

419. We pay people to help us express ourselves and become more aware of ourselves, but the development of self-awareness and self-expression is free to those who become their own teacher and therapist.

420. **The Liberal Is The Idealist And The Conservative Is The Skeptic**

No society can exist and prosper without a balance of idealists and skeptics. Too much skepticism and a society can slow down or stop completely the advancement of personal, social, and technological progress, including medical technology. Too much idealism and a society can accelerate towards danger and catastrophe at speeds too fast to notice or solve. Unfortunately, the idealists are not creating new viable and spite-less ideas but mostly battling old ideas and beliefs. If they are not rejecting old ideas, they are accepting the ideas, beliefs, and opinions handed down to them from culture and government.

421. Some people will not dare try to be happy unless their government allows them to, permitting them to only get high on government-prescribed drugs.

422. **Governments: The Scapegoats Of The People (Suicide By Government And Self-Abuse Through Government)**

People tend to allow their government to damage, weaken and kill them, swiftly or slowly, so that they will not have to take any responsibility for any chaos, illness, and bloodshed their government causes condones and profits from. They can blame everything they allow on their government, just as demons, the devil, and even God is used to remove self-responsibility.

423. How does mainstream propaganda convince so many people to remain loyal to it? By using people's identities and their associated beliefs against them in order to ensure that they remain feeling alienated from each other and afraid of each other. For so long as they feel alienated and afraid, they will never cease defending their own propagandists, the lies they sell them, and the identities and beliefs they create and reinforce with constant traumatizing and triggering words, images and videos.

424. **A Fetish For The End Of The World**
Every abused generation of people who have not conquered their abuse believes and hopes that their world is ending because they desire the death of their own misery.

425. Mainstream music is a changing reflection of its culture and its people.

426. They do not want us to speculate. They want us to keep buying the most dishonest and degrading politically filtered reality that is most profitable to them. They want us to divide until we are all living and thinking in virtual echo chambers, never again paying attention to perspectives and information outside of our comforting false worlds. They want us more predictable because there is money and control in predicting our thoughts and behavior. Our identities, beliefs, and emotions are being taken advantage of, and we perceive this raping and pillaging of the human spirit to be worthwhile entertainment.

427. **War And The Fear Of War: The Secret Manipulator Of All Nations And All People**
War creates traumatized people who become more Conservative out of self-defense. War creates people who want to sacrifice

themselves for their country, even if they are being used by their government for wars that have nothing to do with the freedom or prosperity of the people. War causes an excess of Conservative thinking, which causes an excess of Liberal thinking as a balancing response. War creates rich people and poor people. War is the secret manipulator of all nations and all people, and it stops at nothing to weaken and destroy everyone involved in it, even those who never enlist.

428. What if a society of people perceived everything as art, even themselves?

429. What happens to most people during childhood that causes optimistic, idealistic, and purposeful children to become pessimistic, nihilistic, and hopeless adults? Abuse by people, governments, and religions.

430. How many people in this country have been outcast for being too honest about their family or their society? We wonder why half of the country hates their own country, along with everyone who loves it, when damaged teenagers are disowned for calling out the damaging insanity within their own family, whether it be abuse, having different beliefs, or having an interracial relationship. It is because people in general are too dishonest for their own good and would rather choose indoctrinated thoughts and beliefs over honest and free-thinking. They are more loyal to their beliefs than their own family and their own selves.

431. The more you treat your child like a nuisance the more they will play that role.

432. **We Are The Man Behind The Curtain**
The problem with politics today is that it has become too enter-

taining, too manipulative, and too damaging, but we want to be entertained, at any cost, so we allow ourselves to remain stressed and tortured by it and its media coverage.

433. A human society unaware of itself becomes apathetic, purposeless and dangerous to themselves and the rest of the world. The people become unable to improve themselves because they do not know what they are working with, nor would they care if they did.

434. Children are too pure and sincere for this world.

435. Can one become addicted to trauma? Can an entire society of people become addicted to trauma? Is this what was wrong with medieval people?

436. The quality and endurance of a human society are dependent on the quality and endurance of its art.

437. The successes and failures of capitalism depend on the people, as all systems do.

438. Governments like stupid and childish citizens because they are more predictable and more easily controlled.

439. **Public Schools: Primarily Teach The Importance Of Obeying Orders Without Question**
Children and young adults are trained to feel guilty or alienated if they try to think or learn on their own.

440. Schools and churches are natural constructs of our minds, but not everything natural is healthy or constructive.

441. Will the people ever learn to govern themselves?

442. Democracy: enslavement to the self-deprecating majority.

443. **Creating A World Of Great Valuators**
Teach children to study and valuate the world around them honestly, carefully, and patiently, not to think, live, trust and rely solely on the valuations of others.

444. The exploitation of the ignorant and the weak occurs, regardless of what kind of society one lives under.

445. **The Cycle Of Weakness And Corruption**
Weakness allows and accelerates the growth of corruption. Corruption allows and accelerates the growth of weakness.

446. A nation cannot be free without the people having free minds.

447. With the steady advancement of tools of propaganda and slavery, we need psychedelics more than ever before.

448. Revolution: when the people refuse to consume state, government, and culture more than they produce themselves.

449. There are those who hide behind the state, those who hide from the state, and those who are kept hidden by the state.

450. **The Youth Should Never Be Underestimated**
The youth are the most adaptable to change and the most accepting of change.

451. As a great parent is a parent who teaches their children to parent themselves, a great government is a government that teaches the people how to govern themselves.

452. Most of us have successfully been domesticated by some kind of system, but there are some of us who seem immune to indoctrination of any kind. Some of us are more sensitive to being improperly governed.

453. Most people who are not rich live in a general state of panic and stress, unsure of what next unfortunate event will threaten them with homelessness.

454. If the richest and most powerful corporations and tech giants are all agreeing with you, you might want to rethink your position.

455. If a government bans a book, read it more than once.

456. The Liberal tends to depend on government to think, learn and live.
The Conservative tends to depend on religion to think, learn and live.
Libertarians: tend to depend on themselves to think, learn and live.

457. The weakest men tend to control the strongest men who have been hardened by wars, while the weakest men plan more wars for the strongest men.

458. Anyone who is being used as a savior is being set up to be a martyr, all for the selfish hunger and endless appetite of the audience.

459. Modern man's motto: 'Avoid Thyself'.

460. American public schools teach children to think more with the left hemisphere of the brain while mostly disregarding the right hemisphere. What kind of effect does this have on our society?

461. Governments: "Do not worry. We will be self-aware for you."

462. Popular movements in art are either idealistic or nihilistic, reflecting a society at different times. The popular music of the 60s and 70s was idealistic music: music made not for nihilists, cynics, or defeatists but for passionate people who are most capable of creating new ideas, new technologies, new possibilities, improving themselves and their world with the use of inevitable change.

463. Imagine a society of people who are so afraid and avoidant of themselves that no mirrors can be found in any of their homes, stores, or purses.

464. **The Sober Person: A Myth**
Everyone who does not smoke, drink, or take pills is addicted to something that distracts them from themselves, their past, and their problems, whether it is social media, video games, sports, news, politics, religion, sex, porn, people, food, shopping, or gambling.

465. Good parenting: offering as much as you are capable of giving your child.

466. It seems as though they are trying to make it unnecessarily more difficult for us than life already is but the truth is that they are raking in too much money from us to care.

467. Governments do not have to waste resources predicting what they can plan and coerce.

468. Presidents are used by the people as a savior and a punching bag. The punching bag savior allows people to remove responsibility from themselves for their own mistakes and the mistakes and

crimes of their government. We are narcissistic children, the whole lot of us. Are we so self-hating and self-deprecating that we are trying to create an apocalyptic movie out of our real lives? Are we trying to fall into a trap we will not be able to escape? Both sides are addicted to biased news sources that cause both sides to feel better about themselves but feel afraid and less empathetic of each other, even though they are the same self-righteous people who are incapable of seeing beyond themselves.

469. Mainstream media has turned the majority into rigid political extremists. Our minds and our identities are being played with for profit and power.

470. They do not care about the people as much as they care about money. The average American does not care about each other as much as they care about money, so why would we expect them to be any different? We have learned from them. A large portion of Americans is showing themselves to prefer to be represented by phony people who put on a fake smile, bite their tongue and hide their true thoughts and agendas while bombing innocent people for control and profit. We like putting all evil and self-responsibility onto greedy strangers in suits, knowing that we are using politicians and governments as weapons against one another and that when things get worse, personally or socially, we can always blame them.

471. There are people who are self-responsible and people who prefer to have a government think and act for them.

472. Despite slang words coming and going for decades, the word 'cool' is still cool. Why is this, and why is it cooler to be cool than to be hot? Is it because we associate the cold with death and the beyond? Is this primarily why smoking cigarettes is perceived to be

cool to some people? For a cigarette smoker has the appearance of someone who not only is not afraid of death but confidently welcomes it, even if they are secretly afraid of both life and death.

473. Philosophy, logic, literature, and all mediums of art need to be given more importance when teaching our children.

474. How many people are in prison because they are addicted to being shamed and alienated? They become so addicted to being shamed or abused that they are willing to lose their freedom for self-abuse, sometimes brought on by abuse during childhood development and sometimes by the guilt of one's own past abusive behavior towards others.

475. Citizens are conditioned to want the entire world to be one gigantic city.

476. What saves a young and growing country like America is how imperfect and inconsistent it is in regards to indoctrination. It is this imperfection that allows it to keep its rebellious and creative identity, protecting its unique development from the conniving, censoring, and strangling hands of political and religious indoctrination and propaganda.

477. We should be concerned about the effects of people migrating to their own social media echo chambers, where their beliefs and ideas are safe from being challenged, their propaganda can be shared without being questioned, and they can essentially talk to themselves all day and never be exposed to other people who they increasingly believe to be their enemy.

478. **Live As The Individual You Are**
We are born into a collective, but we all die as individuals.

479. Maturity: To Govern And Refine Oneself

True maturity is reached when an adult can live, love, learn, think, act and create without wanting or needing permission or guidance from a government or religion.

480. Our society tends to keep people's minds stuck in a child-like, insecure, collectivistic, consumeristic, and government-dependent state, which only certain individuals manage to escape.

481. One can be a constructive part of a society and still retain one's sacred individuality, but it takes persistent work, self-awareness, self-responsibility, and self-refinement in a society that too often abandons the individual for the collective.

482. Outgrowing The Mask Of Adulthood

As adults grow older, the child inside them becomes more pronounced.

483. Governments tend to create a kind of collective Stockholm syndrome because they cannot be stopped from becoming abusive and oppressive. For governments cannot stop people from corrupting governments, and people cannot stop governments from corrupting people.

484. Aliens are a threat to governments and every belief-system and political system on Earth because they contradict everything we think we know from our human perspective. It is foolish to believe that we have any kind of control over aliens. They will continue to show themselves as they please, as they have always done throughout human history.

485. The agonizing irony of some people openly showing pride for their country and ancestors is that their current families are in

ruin, and the majority of their countrymen have been reduced to passive and paranoid consumers and delusional social media crusaders; like the wolf after domestication, they have become neurotic, needy, anxious, weak, and people-dependent lapdogs.

486. Could our growing collective sickness, depression, and pessimism be caused by being severed by our government from more natural, healthy, creative, conscious, and empowering ways of thinking and living? Is regaining this all that can help decondition and heal us from political and religious indoctrination and propaganda, which have abused and degraded us for too long?

487. **Become Your Own Experiment**
We are becoming a government experiment. Many of us are doing it willingly.

488. The problem with politicians, law enforcement, and all government henchmen is that they are trained and paid to be more loyal, protective, and empathetic towards the state than the people.

489. We are living in an artificial zoo that keeps most of us as dumb, unhealthy, and submissive as the zookeepers want us, but it is always possible to live and think as an individual in the zoo, though not always without the price of family, friends, relationships and even freedom. Who can deny how ignorant people have become in this country? A lot of it is their own choice, but a lot of it is preordained during childhood. The zoo is not fully real, but we believe in it enough that we react to it as if it were. We have become brainwashed people, indoctrinated and lied to before school, during school, and after school by governments and religions. It is a zoo, and we are its conditioned animals that roam endlessly around in circles, but even the most domesticated zoo animals

sometimes escape with their individual spirit, creativity, and passion intact.

490. If you demand the truth from a healthy government, you get more truth and less government. If you demand the truth from an unhealthy government, you get less truth and more government.

491. More government censorship means that the people have less freedom to call out their government and defend themselves when it is abusing and silencing them. When a criminal government censors the people, it is never for the benefit of the people. It only serves the government. When we have less freedom, they receive more freedom.

492. **When Parents Sacrifice Their Children To Tradition (Traumatic Traditions)**

Some parents are subconsciously eager for their child to make the same mistake(s) they made and to experience the same traumatic experience(s) they endured, as a subconscious attempt to continue family traditions, no matter how traumatic. To be able to accept and satisfy themselves with what happened to them they feel compelled to make a sacrifice and may even help to increase the odds of their child being fed to the same wolves their own parents fed them to, so that they may share the same pain and perhaps continue to indoctrinate their own children with traumatic traditions.

493. They want us stuck in separate virtual reality boxes in order to better predict and control us.

494. Our government is becoming more secretive. The more they lie and withhold, the more we must demand the truth.

495. Healthy people only refuse to accept facts when they are conditioned to by a parent, teacher, politician, or preacher.

496. Mainstream media and social media are being used as a pillow to scream in until there is no energy left to go out in the streets against our government.

497. It is easier for a government to weaponize and take advantage of the youth than the old. For the youth are easier to manipulate. Their more healthy and open reaction to change and novelty can be used against them. The youth are still filled with strength, passion, and fight, and a government can direct this energy towards whatever it so chooses, usually profitable destruction.

498. The Liberal and the Conservative, as we know them today, are government and media creations. They are culturally engineered identities. They are not who we truly are or what we could become as individuals. They only divide us further the more we refuse to accept this. These identities only serve governments, politicians, and fake journalists. They limit and compartmentalize you with labels. They tell you what you are supposed to care about, how you should be defined when you should be outraged, who you should hate and who you should love. They make you feel alienated when you do not participate. The Liberal and the Conservative do not help or learn from one another. Instead, they insult each other and cause one another to endlessly defend and glorify the false identities that have molded and degraded each of them into culturally programmed automatons.

499. The illusion of government only works if you pretend that you cannot teach or protect yourself and that you will always be inferior to those you vote for and put your faith in. It only works if

enough people believe that they can never be as intelligent or moral without its permission and direction.

500. War: an implosion.

501. If you are fine with a government stealing your money or your means of protecting yourself, you are telling them you are fine with them being able to eventually physically steal you and your family from your home.

502. If a government or politician can trick you into believing their ideas are your ideas they can get you to attack or defend anything they propose, even if it hurts you.

503. **One World Governance**
All governments tend to behave the same and are comprised of government-indoctrinated people who are trained and paid to think the same.

504. Questioning your government does not make you a conspiracy theorist. It makes you a free and intelligent human being asking questions.

505. Any crimes one's government commits are blamed on one's political party.

506. **Create Your Own Path To Success**
Your government's cookie-cutter path to success is not the same as your individual path to success. School only prepares you for more school. It does not prepare you for all of the billionaires who create their own rules that they do not have to abide by themselves. They bank on the failures of school. School does not teach you about credit scores because credit scores are designed for people who are

already rich. It is a clever trick to keep poor people poor and rich people rich.

507. Schools primarily teach children to trust and obey their government. They teach you how to become an easily manipulated and unquestioning tool for your government. They teach you how to remain poor, rather than how to become rich. Those who change the world or themselves for the better do so without school or government influence and permission.

508. Homosexuality has always existed and will always exist. Many homosexual people wrongly suffer for something they were no more in control of than heterosexual people. They deserve the same treatment and freedom as anyone else. Any shortcomings they express are also expressed by heterosexual people and are likely more justified from having to wrestle their entire lives with a society of self-righteous people who fail to accept them as human beings of equal worth.

509. Are those who believe in something greater than humans more rebellious than those without this belief? Governments are always testing their rebellious nature by pretending to be God. Do not trust governments. For if a religion ever comes between a government and its power over the people, it will always choose government over God.

510. **The Silver Lining To Inferior Leaders**
Perhaps it empowers the people to know that their leaders are incompetent. If they believe they are led by infallible Gods, they will not believe as much in themselves and will more easily be fooled and abused by them.

511. When a government can shut down places of worship without any substantial rebellion, this is an open confession from the people saying that they trust and believe in their government more than God and themselves.

512. Children heal, challenge, and motivate adults.

513. When people repeatedly fail as individuals and parents, the state receives more power over the people by becoming the detached and abusive parent and God of their descendants.

514. Does the attraction of communism for some people originate from the resentment, separation, and degradation of families by the state?

515. The state becomes the God of the people by way of childhood indoctrination. If they can get just one generation when they are young to resent their elders and ignore their warnings and wisdom then they can freely treat the people even more like child-like disposable drones with a government-censored reality.

516. The state has a tendency to treat the people like disposable experiments.

517. Involving yourself with politics is self-abuse by way of government. Each party terrorizes and attempts to control the other using their government which is an expanding weaponized business that only cares about more money and power and only perceives the people as a disposable means to their own ends.

518. What kind of people do you suppose powerful government jobs attract? People who are capable of detaching themselves from

others. People who can view and treat people like profitable and expendable data.

519. How have we, the people, become so divided when it comes to trusting the state, despite each side having been deceived, abused, and taken advantage of by those who hide safely behind it, by following one-sided news and teaching our children to do the same. One either grows up and accepts this, or one chooses to remain a child and proudly allows the political priests of the state to dictate one's every move and thought.

520. They would not write absurd news headlines if it was not working on people. They know what they have created. They know the right words to use and what emotional buttons to press. Any attempts to rescue their target audience from their vulnerable and hypnotized state of being are met with even more embracement of government propaganda. They know too much about us now. Self-awareness is your greatest weapon. For that is what they are controlling and manipulating.

521. Over time, governments remove from society those who are least happy with their forced way of life, either by imprisonment or suicide.

522. It does not matter what party you identify with. They will continue to trick each party into giving their government more power at the expense of themselves.

523. The state spends a fortune keeping children from becoming independent adults. All one has to do to confirm this is gaze around at all of the adults who are thinking and behaving like remote-controlled children.

524. All controlling systems are made up of controlling people who never cease trying to control people.

525. They trick you by using your enemy party to convince you to hand over freedoms that belong to the people in order to get revenge on your enemy party, which turns out to be the people no matter what side you identify with. Politics is controlling people using governments to control people. Politics are an entertaining sport to keep us distracted and divided. This is why sports and politics are always inseparable. We are tricked into playing and enjoying a game that hurts and weakens us and our families but strengthens governments and those who are protected by the state.

526. If They Can Control The Youth, They Can Control Everyone

Governments take advantage of the youth's natural disdain for adults. Are the people of a society always led by the youth who are most susceptible to government and state indoctrination and propaganda?

527. Only Honest And Free Philosophy Can Save Us

The news continues to be divisive and addictive entertainment.
Politics continues to be a rigged sport.
Science continues to be polluted by political bribery.
Religion continues to push people away from God.
The people continue to be abused, traumatized, and brainwashed consumers and government experiments.

528. When Society Encourages Tragedy

Society creates and allows trauma which creates new artists when it does not create new destroyers. Society buys more of their art, especially if the artist kills themselves.

529. Everyone who is not an extremist on the side of big government will continue to be censored and demonized.

530. Your friends are not more important than your children. Not even your lovers are as important as your children.

531. **Modern Man's Plea To Governments**
"Treat us like experiments. Treat us like children. Brainwash the minds of our children. Remove our freedom to protect ourselves and our family. Just do not turn off our new phones and our phony news. Otherwise, we might have to stand up for ourselves."

532. **The State Turns Art Into Propaganda**
Propaganda: when art is misused against the people.

533. Some people never strive for new conversations with different minds.

534. Do not feel guilty for losing loyalty and respect for a society of people who would watch you starve to death after losing your mind, your job, your family, or your home.

535. **The Things We Do For The State And The Things We Allow The State To Do To Us**
The state teaches young and healthy people to strip themselves of their individuality and health for school and the military. The state profits from indoctrinating children as early as possible in public schools and then convinces many of them as teenagers, when they are the most useful, vulnerable, and confused, to join the military, traumatizing them for money and then sending them back into society worse off than they were before they left, if they even make it back at all.

536. Statists: Cult Members Of The State

A cult trains and forces people to think the same thoughts, wear the same uniform, have the same haircut, use the same words and repeat the same chants and gestures. Schools, militaries, and prisons are all cults that condition people at a young age to get used to living as miserable cult members who would give their life for the state. Every day, they give them their life, little by little.

537. The Deceitful And Delusional Nature Of Fascism

Some people try to child-proof reality for adults who choose not to accept the occasional harshness of our reality. When this becomes widely normalized it causes many children to have a more difficult time accepting, utilizing and overcoming themselves and their reality as they age.

538. Some people deal with the disempowered society the state creates by religiously injecting themselves with political media created by and for the state. They use the problem as the solution to their problems and, as a result, they create more problems than solutions.

539. The Savior Complex

Those who were never protected or rescued from abuse as children can develop a savior complex. They attempt to be a hero to everyone but their own children, as their parents failed to save them when they were children.

540. Find what children are talented at and interested in individually and focus on developing it further, instead of forcing them to take tests on subjects they are poor at and remain uninterested in.

541. In especially poor areas with less distractions one finds creatively rich and entertaining individuals who have become heroic compensation for generational oppression by the state.

542. Adults who attempt to control other adults are the most childish members of a society. They use their freedom and creativity to police the art world rather than contribute to it. If they knew enough about the life of every artist, there would be no art left to cancel. For even the cancelers would be canceled if one combed through and magnified their lives and mistakes.

543. **State Worshippers (Adopted By The State)**
Along with those who are tricked into worshipping the state when the state uses their religion against them, those who have been failed by their parents are more likely to be raised by the state than those who have not. They are more likely to attack the people and defend the state, no matter how it treats the people. Before state worshippers can be formed, the state must devalue ancestors and dismantle the human family structure. For there is power in family and this power is a threat to the state.

544. Teaching children not to cry when they need to is as toxic as teaching children not to vomit when they need to.

545. Governments that remove history and censor art create people who obsess over the past, even if they do not learn from it, and allow their government to dictate their future. People who obsess over the past are less likely to change. They are afraid of change and desperately cling on to the past, even if it hurts them. This is the kind of people the state tends to create and control.

546. All political problems are human problems.

547. How many Americans are too medicated by the state to rebel against it?

548. America has grown stale and is in need of a creative revival.

549. **Infantilized By The State**
The state prefers childish adults who loyally believe and obey the state over limitless, self-aware, and self-conquering people who believe in themselves, and who question and guard themselves from the state as free, mature, and unique individuals.

550. If a child is indoctrinated and conditioned to become a weak, submissive, and self-doubting adult, only the child as an adult can decondition and free themselves from their childhood programming.

551. **Free Yourself From Labels**
People's precious labels tell them what to think and feel and how to act in response to every personal or social change.

552. The health and longevity of a society is dependent on its greatest thinkers and how their society reacts to them.

553. The state is less likely to abuse or degrade a society of people who protect, heal, educate, and strengthen themselves.

554. Some people die avoiding the trauma of their childhood. They never accept the cause of their scars, if they even acknowledge their scars at all. Thus, they fail to overcome their childhood traumas. They are conquered by them.

555. **Uniting For Children**
How would adults react if every child around the globe uncon-

sciously turned silent? Would adults finally unite, question, and discuss their own actions towards children and the planet they are leaving behind for them?

556. The state creates and maintains extremists that they can more easily exploit and control. For extremists are less likely to think and behave as unique and self-responsible individuals. Their beliefs and labels are always treated with more significance than themselves.

557. **Do Not Let The State Mold You Into A Self-Destructive Child**
The people can be fooled into hurting and degrading themselves by letting the state define what rebellion is and by allowing the state to decide what to rebel and when to rebel.

558. What if every individual of a human society became shamanic philosophers and philosophical shamans without ever shutting out new science and technology? What if a society cannot survive or triumphantly transcend its past without truthful and open-ended shamanic philosophers and philosophical shamans?

559. **Divided By Fear**
Some people are afraid to be experimented on by the state.
Some people are afraid of not being experimented on by the state.

560. **Mold Thyself (Do Not Allow The State To Mold You)**
The state indoctrinates the people, molding children and even adults. The state experiments on the people with school, military, and media.

561. The internet allows the state to traumatize, indoctrinate, and control people more easily.

562. The people continue to be convinced that the ideas and intentions of the state are their own.

563. Sheeply people are not honest enough to be strong nor strong enough to be honest and they are not curious enough to be brave nor brave enough to be curious.

564. The people are constantly pulled bac with all manner of distractions when they take a step away from the dumbed-down and discouraging perception of their reality that is meticulously engineered and broadcasted to them throughout the day.

565. Imagine a life without having to worry about the state and its enforcers who, without pause, attempt to control you, imprison you, steal from you, and experiment on you.

566. Whistleblowers of the state rarely change people's minds because each time new information is leaked people generally rush to see what their specifically tailored propaganda has to say about it, like well-trained dogs who only salivate for their master's food.

567. **The Slow Simmer Of The People**

The state slowly tortures the people until they desperately want their world to end and argue about how it will end.

Greatness & Suffering

1. Lovingly and constructively utilized suffering is necessary for creating a freer will.

2. Sacrifice your past to your future.
Sacrifice your hell to your heaven.

3. **The Purpose Of Pain**
Pain is a necessary sacrifice for the evolution of consciousness. Without pain and dissatisfaction, there would be no change. For new changes call for new challenges, and new challenges call for new changes.

4. **From Temporary Pain To Permanent Change**
Abuse: a painful cycle of taught behavior that is usually confined to certain abuse-infected family trees. Depression and even suicide may be a genetic byproduct of inherited abuse which possibly acts as a way of stopping the spread of the deadly virus known as abuse.

5. **Traumatic Growth (Traumatic Transformation)**
Mental trauma is no less damaging than physical brain trauma. Each can hinder the mind and body, but it can also occasionally cause sudden and unpredictable neuronal growth in certain areas

of the brain, like the instant formation of cracks in nearly shattered glass.

6. Without pain, there would be no pleasurable future to craft from the prevention of pain.

As Nietzsche said, "Out of life's school of war – what does not kill me makes me stronger."[46]

7. When experiencing destructive waves of events, remember that waves of destruction always precede waves of creation, given enough time.

8. Traumatic experiences can be utilized as a sacrifice to push oneself over the edge of ordinary thinking.

9. A great mind: a supremely thorough thinker.

10. **Suffering: The Means To The End Of Suffering**
The purpose of suffering is to surpass the desire or need to suffer.

11. Pain: fuel for lower life forms to become higher life forms.

12. There can be no transition to paradise without struggle.

13. Like a damaged machine, mental trauma can make a mind function and be utilized differently than it was ever expected to be capable of.

14. Like a wound that triggers greater productive surrounding activity, the human mind often compensates for emotional damage with enhanced creative productivity.

15. Redirecting The Flow Of Traumatic Energy

Trauma: a resource available to everyone, often at a hefty price, but once effectively utilized by redirecting its accompanying fearful, hateful and destructive energy into adventurous, loving, and constructive energy, it becomes as necessary to life as water.

16. The Conquerors Of History

No major progress is made without great minds.

17. Convert angry, bitter, and pitiful energy into creative confidence.

18. Suffering occurs so that the focus of life can always be regained.

19. Advancement From Adversity

Whether it realizes it or not, all life strives to become God-like, so long as its environmental pressures and its suffering persists without it destroying itself.

20. Suffering either brings us more suffering or pushes us beyond suffering.

21. The Potential Enrichment Of Suffering

You either cower from suffering, or you become stronger than whatever made you suffer, daring anyone or anything to further empower you with pain.

22. Brilliance: being addicted to the next question.

23. The Contradictory Nature Of Greatness

The great mind: a union of opposites.

24. Greatness is bottomless.

25. Greatness is determined by how much attempt is made to mimic it.

26. Without struggle, no life would transcend.

27. **The Interpretation Of Greatness**
The greatest creations are interpreted and reinterpreted most.

28. **A Great Mind: A Natural Everlasting Source Of Inspiration And Motivation**
The greatest creations of the greatest minds, whether it be books, songs, paintings, or movies, are new and unique developments of nature, of which future minds are fortunate enough to be able to gaze upon, in rapturous awe, as we never cease visiting, admiring and being inspired by nature's oldest towering trees, nor by its most daring and motivating mountains.

29. **The Unpredictability Of Greatness**
Neither a great mind nor the creations of a great mind are predictable.

30. A great mind surprises even itself.

31. A great mind adds to ideas.
A common mind extracts nothing new from ideas, offering only regurgitated doubts.

32. **Pain: The Soil Of Gods**
That which we most avoid is the very soil from which we can become Gods, if utilized constructively, rather than destructively; consciously, rather than unconsciously.

33. Two Ways Of Adapting To The Trauma Of Life

The most dangerous among us are changed by various traumatic experiences, as all people are, but while some people adapt to their trauma, reacting with an increase in creativity, empathy, and understanding, others become more distant, distrusting, and destructive.

34. Positive And Negative Trauma

There is positive and negative trauma, positive trauma being more constructive and empowering, negative trauma being more destructive and Disempowering.

35. A great mind: a vortex, the creative output of which attracts and influences all minds, both weak and great, whether the creative output is attacked or defended, understood or misunderstood.

36. We Perform Our Best Tricks, Before The Cosmic Whip

What most pushes a circus animal to please and bedazzle its audience? The same thing that pushes humankind to create and to rise in power: pain and sometimes the mere fear of pain.

37. To Feel And Will More Deeply

A great mind utilizes consciousness more than the common mind.

38. The Unbreakable Slave

Pain and fear, over long periods of time, can create slaves who remain stunted and obedient but sometimes creates a being who has hardened and strengthened beyond any expectations of the slavemaster. A being who could not be broken, who fears no one, whose tears of despair have turned into tears of rage, tears of vengeance, tears of liberation. All he waits for is one last crack of the master's whip: the sound of freedom to the hardened but ever-enduring rebel; All the motivation he needs to bring about a revolution.

39. If trauma does not sharpen the lens of consciousness, it diminishes or shatters it.

40. **Great minds Are More Forgivable**

Einstein's life-work will never be ignored by teachers, no matter what we may find out about his private life.

41. Suffering is meant to push us further and further mentally and technologically.

42. Suffering: nightmares from which conscious life has acquired the unique ability to awaken.

43. **The Calm Before The Storm**

Genius is expressed by calmness and patience. This is why cats give the appearance of being confidently wise and why a stupid person, if he can keep shut his mouth for a long enough time, can look as though he were concealing thoughts of some ingenious plan or secret.

44. A great mind is hindered when not allowed to teach itself.

45. A great mind is more unpredictable in its thinking than the average mind.

46. **A Similarity And Difference Between Genius And Stupidity**

Without being nearly as simple or prevalent, the creation of a genius mind is just as inevitable and accidental as the creation of a weak mind. Both can improve, but genius can be wasted and not become less genius, while stupidity cannot be wasted without becoming less stupid.

47. Great minds spend more time in the imagination and spend more energy on traversing and documenting their findings there for all the less imaginative minds.

48. **From Pain To Knowledge To Power**
There is no knowledge without enough pain and power, no power without enough pain and knowledge, and no pain with enough knowledge and power.

49. **From Powerless Pain To Painless Power**
Without pain, there is no power.
With enough power, there is no pain.

50. Where others would lose their mind or give up, the great mind endures, if only for the sake of a good challenge.

51. Pain: necessitated into existence by the creation of consciousness?

52. The cosmos uses death as a catalyst for the birth of consciousness in intelligent life and for the sprouting of more complex and more powerful minds that no longer have any need for hatred, nor the fear of death or the prod of pain.

53. Great minds discuss what no one else will or can discuss. They refuse to beat around the bush or to walk on eggshells.

54. All greatness comes from peculiar circumstances.

55. The great mind omits far more work than the mediocre mind. For a great mind is never completely satisfied with its best work,

while a mediocre mind is satisfied with everything it creates, no matter the quality, their mediocrity being exampled by their inability or refusal to clean off the unnecessary dirt from their mental jewels.

56. From Trauma To Consciousness To Art

Art and trauma are interlinked. Consciousness is interlinked with both art and trauma.

57. The Endless Spring Of A Great Mind

A great mind is not dependent on any one of its creations to be considered a great mind. If any of their art could be removed from existence, they would still have plenty of work to be marveled over. It would not affect at all the value of the rest of their work. This is not so with mediocre minds. Take away anything they have created or accomplished in their life, and you have only diminished the worth of the rest of their work.

58. The Energy Of Mental Trauma: Without Creative Release, Destroys Minds

The energy of a mind, disturbed by the pain and fear of mental trauma without a creative outlet, weakens or destroys its own mind and the minds of others.

59. How To Fashion A Paradise

Consciously convert all destructive energy into creative energy. This is a possibility only for people who are truly free.

60. The stronger you become, the less power pain has over you.

61. Greatness: the inevitably referenced.

62. Great minds: travelers of uncharted territory.

63. Channel the energy of mental illness and unrest and direct it towards creativity and understanding.

64. A great mind, without choice, causes novel and extreme reactions from its surroundings, whether in agreement or disagreement.

65. **The Sting Of Reasoning**
A hurt or agitated genius is more aggressive with their knowledge and honesty, temporarily producing higher than usual amounts of linguistic and factual venom, which is paralyzing to the ignorant, to accompany their unavoidable sting of reasoning.

66. A great mind: a mind that cannot stop refining itself.

67. Great minds never fully leave the dream state.

68. The most potent thinkers have survived the most extreme expressions of insanity and chaos. For the greatest growing minds improve under intense pressures, rather than weaken or perish by them.

69. If one can recognize greatness, one should attempt to achieve greatness.

70. Some minds are destined to see the world more clearly than others: with less error and more continuity; more thoughts and fewer beliefs; more consciousness and less suffering.

71. Suffering is created and maintained by people, just like bliss.

72. **A Great Mind Holds Hope For Greater Minds**
Before he was abducted by the abyss, Nietzsche knew he was one of the greatest recorded thinkers this world has ever known, but he

also knew there could be greater thinkers than himself and in greater number. He hoped that he could help usher in a mass search for, development of, and appreciation for the greatest thinkers. I shall always share this same hope for a time when greatness is no longer a rare accident but is intentionally created, when love, honesty, and greatness are as common as hate, stupidity, and willful ignorance are today.

73. Suffer Unto Greatness (The Three Steps Of Creation: Suffer, Imagine And Will)

When we imagine something great, we suffer from desiring it, enough that we will it into being, but only if our mind, imagination, and will are sufficiently strong, as strong, if not stronger than the suffering we endure. Hence, the blatant connection between insanity and greatness. Greatness takes control of insanity, to a certain degree, and is not controlled by the sane or the insane. For one cannot become great without sacrificing some bit of sanity, to constructively utilize one's madness, nor without directing the energy of great suffering towards the development of great and healing creations.

74. Greatness Comes Forth At The Cusp Of Irreversibly Breaking

The particular cracking of the mind-egg is only the beginning of greatness. it is most vulnerable during its development, even more than the average child. For the development of greatness is highly sensitive and requires exact and extreme focus, honesty, passion, appreciation, confidence, consistency, and the steady and complete digestion of knowledge and experience, as well as the creative utilization of painful and traumatic experiences.

75. A great mind knows best what to include and what to exclude from their creations.

76. Greatness always finds a way to express and expand itself.

77. **An Error-Proof Test For Greatness**
A culture, religion, society, or species can be graded by how many great minds and great creations it grows and by how long it permits that growth.

78. Over time, pain either diminishes passion or enlarges it and is either used for creation or destruction.

79. **A Marker Of Greatness: How One Responds To Pain And Stress**
Everyone is hurt in life, in various ways and degrees, but not everyone uses every second of pain inflicted on them to transform themselves. Normally, pain is either used to avoid any information that reminds one of it or to inflict pain on others. Only the greatest minds have been capable of learning from pain and turning pain and stress into a resource for great passion, discoveries, and creations. For the average person runs and hides from pain, inflicting and receiving it without ensuring that their pain is never endured in vain.

80. Pain: temporary motivational teachings.

81. Pain: potential power and potential pleasure if utilized correctly.

82. **Converting The Worst Of Life Into The Best Of Life**
The more stressed I become, the more I think and write, and the more I think and write, the less stressed I become. For the more

energy I gather from my sufferings, the more that energy combines with my creations, turning them into something much greater than the pain I have thus far endured.

83. Greatness: requires many resurrections from the failures of self and of others.

84. **Unique Traits Of Greatness (Focus, Precision, And Passion)**
No matter the altitude at which greatness moves, its focus never diminishes. No matter the speed at which greatness moves, its precision never diminishes. No matter the distance at which greatness moves, its passion never diminishes.

85. Terribly great things come from greatly terrible things.

86. **The Coaxing Of Rare Minds**
Many a great mind is tricked into leaving behind their one-of-a-kind creations for the benefit of common and bitter minds who do not appreciate or deserve them.

87. **Greatness: Paralyzing To Those Who Hinder It And Empowering To Those Who Seek It**
All institutions and their loyal followers, whether political or religious, are often stopped in their tracks by great philosophical minds and must find new ways of drowning out any of their notions and questions that may enter the heads of the mediocre majority and influence them to become less dependent on their shepherds and more dependent on themselves, in turn, becoming their own shepherd.

88. Pain can push us towards knowledge but can also push us away from knowledge.

89. The greatest minds create things only they could have created.

90. Great Minds Require A Great Will/Consciousness To Permit The Creation Of Greatness By Intensely Utilizing Extreme Experiences

There is a persistent intensity to the creations of a great mind, which shows us the extreme experiences that are required before a great mind and a great creation can be possible. For one's will/consciousness must be great too, or one's extreme experiences will be wasted and never become transformative experiences, of which all great transformative minds are composed.

91. Greatness: The Only Thing That Cannot Be Stifled By A Government Or Society

Even if a great mind is terminated, its great creations live on freely, seeking to become part of other new creations of greatness, all over the world.

92. The Composition Of Greatness

All great creations are made of great experiences mixed with the great thoughts and emotions of great minds.

93. Greatness appears effortless.

94. Legends

Like a flash of heavenly light, their unmatched and unforeseen talent blinds everyone from ever being able to witness and experience what unbelievable creations they could have constructed with more time.

95. Great minds redeem the horrors and hardships of history.

96. With a greater capacity for pain comes a greater capacity for pleasure.

97. There is no greatness without obsession.

98. Greatness remains relevant to a society no matter how young, old, primitive, or advanced the society is.

99. **Attracting Greatness**
Surround yourself only with greatness, and you will be more likely to find, appreciate, create and become greatness.

As Soren Kierkegaard said, "No one shall be forgotten who was great in this world; but everyone was great in proportion to the greatness of what he loved."[47]

100. **A Thing Of Beauty**
A great mind: a permanent influence; a new planetary light fixture.

101. The residue of a great mind is the astounding creations it leaves behind.

102. Think of how boring one would be without the traumatic experience(s) one has endured.

103. The human that converts its own pain into power is more like a God than a human.

104. **Greater Humans Require Ever-Strengthening Enemies (Gods Need Devils)**
The stronger the virus, the more necessary a stronger immune system becomes.

105. Greatness: an abundance of warranted confidence.

106. **Directing All Cruel And Evil Energy Towards Creative Splendor**
Primitive people direct evil energy towards destructive energy. Higher people direct evil energy towards creative energy.

107. Great power is bought with the currency of great pain.

108. **The Purpose Of Fearing Death And Feeling Pain**
Never-ending creative resources and influences for the living.

109. A great mind thinks with constant purpose and turns common or exceptional accidents into purposeful miracles.

110. Greatness: a rare and lofty perspective.

111. **The Procreation Of Greatness**
A society without a great majority cannot be called great. It is not inevitable that greatness is rare. For greatness always begins as a rarity, but it does not have to always remain as rare as its beginnings.

112. The universe supports greatness by making it difficult to be developed and sustained. This seems to be counter-intuitive, but it is the only way for greatness to exist and to become ever greater.

113. **The Most Precious Drug**
One can become addicted to greatness.

114. To greatness, every experience and event is meaningful and purposeful because, for greatness to exist, it is necessary that every experience and event be meaningful and purposeful.

115. People's beliefs and assumptions about God are associated with the known qualities of greatness.

116. Greatness: great minds, great thoughts, and great works.

117. **The Great, The True And The Beautiful**
There is beauty in greatness and greatness in beauty.

118. **Self-Worship: A Godly Trait (Worshiping Greatness)**
What is the worship of greatness? The appreciation and cultivation of greatness within and without oneself.

119. **The Differences Involved In Those Who Become Great And Those Who Do Not**
A difference in experience.
A difference in will.
A difference in imagination.
A difference in courage.
A difference in appreciation.
A difference in endurance.
A difference in persistence.
A difference in consistency.
A difference in confidence.

120. **Greatness Creates New Finish Lines**
Achieving greatness is never enough for greatness. Once the other runners (thinkers/creators) are passed and the finish line is crossed, representing becoming greater, greatness does not slow down. It keeps running as if there never was a finish line.

121. Greatness: a rare perspective.

122. The Creative Growth Of Rain And Tears
As soil is more fertile after a storm, a mind is more fertile after a traumatic experience.

123. Redeeming Scars With The Creation Of Beauty
The most unique and impressive minds have the most utilized scars.

124. Great minds appreciate the works of other great minds as if they were their own. They even appreciate and utilize the works of less powerful minds.

125. Great minds pull out unforgettable beauty from the deep black well of trauma.

126. Greatness Is Universal
All life on different planets reside on a spectrum of lower and higher levels of greatness and express greatness with different forms.

127. Greatness: always the alien that exceeds and contradicts previous determinations of greatness.

128. Greatness uses everything surrounding it as a resource to become ever greater.

129. The Spectrum Of Greatness
Greatness with the freedom to thrive and become ever greater becomes maddening and frightening to lesser beginning levels of greatness because great developments become less understood and less fathomable by lower developments of greatness the greater they become, as insects scatter for their lives with each overwhelming step a giant human takes.

130. The Will To Greatness
The will to self-refine.

131. Greatness defines and refines.

132. Greatness And Mediocrity: A Difference In The Ability To Use And Create Resources Out Of The Universe
A planet comprised of greater conscious perceivers, with more evolutionary time and experience under their belt, both biological and technological, would see boundless resources where we only see empty space.

133. The greatest minds are the minds that influence and refine new great minds.

134. Bathe thyself with the creations of the greatest minds this planet has churned up.

135. Greatness: to have so much self-control that one appears to be out of control.

136. Every storm gives birth to a new dawn.

137. If to think is to dig, great minds dig deeper into themselves, their planet, and their surrounding cosmos than any other mind. They bring back astonishing jewels of obscene complexity, which were previously kept hidden by less capable minds who believed no one could dig any deeper.

138. The Motivation Of Greatness
Greatness tests those observing it and challenges them to become greater.

139. The Purposeful Nature Of Greatness
Greatness does not rely on accidents to be remarkable.

140. In The Image Of Greatness
How many gods and religions of the past were inspired by great minds of the past?

141. Pain becomes less necessary and more endurable the greater the sufferer becomes.

142. Sufferers appreciate happiness more than happy people.

143. To unrefined minds, greatness appears as useless madness.

144. Great minds waste as little time and energy as they can, as if they have lived their life many times and have made themselves a promise to always create and become something greater than ever before.

145. Greatness is always alien to those less great.

146. One way or another, greatness finds a way to express itself.

147. The only way to conquer suffering is to become stronger and harder without sacrificing one's capacity for love and empathy.

148. Greatness, like truth and beauty, is inexhaustible.

149. Our Deepest Scars Are Victorious Medals Awarded By Nature
To be great is to be proud of surviving great suffering and to refine oneself with it.

150. **Utilize Your Enemies**
Refining oneself with the use of trauma bestows upon our pain and our enemies a greater purpose than merely being a source of pain, fear, and destruction.

151. The greatest minds are the most speculative.

152. The greatest minds are capable of extracting large amounts of information out of small amounts of information.

153. In the same way that muscles need to be damaged to be strengthened, the mind needs to be altered to be strengthened, with the use of knowledge, experience, and psychedelics.

154. **A New Mind**
A great mind has a habit of creating something new out of something old.

155. **Great Minds: Creators And Preservers Of Knowledge**
Great minds take old information and squeeze new information out of it.

156. Trauma can either diminish or heighten one's capacity for feeling and expressing emotions.

157. Greatness is difficult and rare to achieve because it has to be.

158. What good is greatness if it is not undeniable?

159. Greatness requires an unusual amount of focus, determination, and a healthy dose of confidence in oneself, one's thoughts, and one's creations.

160. The Paradox Of Greatness
A great mind is both consistent and unpredictable with its creations.

161. The Stairway From Animalhood To Godhood
Struggle to survive.
Transcend the suffering of past trauma.
Direct religious, neurotic, and hateful energy, all of which are created by fear and suffering, towards the creation and nurturing of godly minds, art, and technology.
Become Gods of technology, peace, and bliss.

162. The Three Steps Of Creation: Suffer, Imagine, And Will (Suffer Unto Greatness)
When we imagine something great, we suffer from desiring it, enough that we will it into being, but only if our mind, imagination, and will are sufficiently strong, as strong, if not stronger than the suffering we endure. Hence, the blatant connection between insanity and greatness. Greatness takes control of insanity. For one cannot become great, without sacrificing some bit of sanity, to constructively utilize one's madness, nor without directing the energy of great suffering towards the development of great creations.

163. A great mind: every thought is full of intention.

164. No one fights harder and longer than someone who has lost many fights.

165. Suffering: The Solution To Its Own Problem
We suffer more so that we can think more.
We think more so that we can suffer less.

166. Greatness: consistent simultaneous success.

167. Greatness shocks its audience causing them to temporarily forget they are the audience. For now they are seeing the world through the heroic eyes of greatness.

168. **Blacksmithing**
What seems like a degrading and destructive act is the only way to direct and refine metal. For what the blacksmith does to metal, the conscious and imaginative mind does to knowledge and reality.

169. Genius squeezes the most knowledge out of every experience.

170. Greatness demands discussion.

171. This is how all great things become great: by being dragged to hell and managing to climb out more refined and full of purpose, dancing on the edge of reality, refining one's mind and one's reality with each new thought and motion.

172. Trauma: enhances creativity and empathy for some people and decreases creativity and empathy for others.

173. Great minds cause other great minds to become greater out of competitive inspiration.

174. **Great Minds: Insatiable**
No amount of fulfilled desires or unsolved mysteries can satisfy a great mind.

175. The more greatness, the less suffering.

176. Greatness: created and achieved by becoming more necessary?

177. A great mind is a marvelous synthesizer.

178. Greatness Requires Empathy And Love

Greatness must be able to understand others in relation to itself and to understand itself in relation to others.

179. The absence of desire is an impediment to greatness.

180. One is simultaneously in a safer and more risky predicament with greatness on one's side.

181. Accepting that trauma can be useful is not the same as pursuing trauma. Making trauma useful is not the same as condoning that from which we suffer. This problem of finding and creating value in our suffering, something which we despise most, is something every individual and every civilization must face. For the failure to utilize our suffering will only cause more suffering.

182. Many choose suffering over greatness.

183. The pursuit of God is also the pursuit of greatness.
The pursuit of greatness is also the pursuit of God.

184. Do not dwell on what you might have become or what you might have created without your suffering. Imagine what you can become and what you can create because of your suffering. Be concerned with what a boring person you might have become and what boring creations you might have created without your suffering.

185. Habitual evil, ugliness, and weakness create the conditions necessary for novel goodness, beauty, and power.

186. The Bright End Of The Dark Tunnel Of Struggle

The word struggle is a more neutral, accurate, and fruitful description of suffering than pain. For struggle leaves open the possibility of a purpose for the struggle, of overcoming the struggle.

187. Our identities, beliefs, lovers, and foes are determined by our reactions to trauma.

188. Greatness: to be able to extract beauty from ugliness.

189. Are we still capable of recognizing greatness?

190. Pain opens eyes, mouths, and consciousness.

191. **There Is No Greatness Without Clarity**
Seek the clarification of all things.

192. What suffering did the eagle have to endure to be able to fly above all suffering? For the eagle was not always in the air away from the fears, dangers, and uncertainties of groundlings.

193. All of our problems come from suffering, from failing to utilize suffering.
All of our solutions come from suffering, from successfully utilizing suffering.

194. It is always possible for the greatest things to be overshadowed by even greater things they inspire.

195. **Fall To Rise**
To become great, one must experience sickness, failure, betrayal, abuse, and despair at the hands of oneself and others.

196. Pain giveth beauty.
Pain taketh away beauty.

197. All pain and memories of pain are opportunities for either self-love, self-empowerment, and self-transcendence or self-hatred, self-disempowerment, and self-degradation.

198. One has to refuse to be a victim, and even then, one can still be hurt by one's trauma, but at least one is giving oneself a fighting chance. Labeling, solidifying, and narrowing one's identity as a victim only results in one being disempowered and degraded.

199. **From Goodness To Greatness**
Evil is a test to strengthen goodness, but it is up to the test-takers whether or not the test is passed. For evil cannot be surpassed, and goodness cannot prevail without goodness becoming greatness.

200. Greatness requires the freedom to rebel.

201. **The Paradox Of A Great Mind**
A great mind is both easy to bore and difficult to bore.

202. **Tears Of Joy**
Sometimes what we witness and experience can be so great that our capacity for pleasure and appreciation are shown to be inadequate in its presence. Only sorrow can lend a hand in attempting to experience and express its glory.

203. **The Test Of Storms (Storms Are Tests Of Strength And Ingenuity)**
Like suffering, storms either strengthen their survivors or weaken them. It depends on the power of the storms and the strength and ingenuity of the survivors.

204. The sufferer cannot be healed or redeemed until he or she creates something greater than their suffering.

205. **The Patience Of Greatness**

All great things wait to be comprehended, appreciated, and utilized. Those who fail to do so are soon degraded or annihilated.

206. Great minds and great art are free to create their own destiny.

207. Those of us who are well acquainted with suffering must stick together, no matter what beliefs we identify with.

Notes

1. O'Toole, *"If You're Going Through Hell, Keep Going – Quote Investigator."*
2. Nietzsche, *Twilight Of The Gods.*
3. McKenna, *Terence McKenna - The Big Picture.*
4. Nietzsche, *The Will To Power.*
5. Carlin, *Charlie Rose.*
6. O'Toole, *"Imagination Rules The World – Quote Investigator."*
7. John 1:1 *(KJ21).*
8. Genesis 1:3 *(KJ21).*
9. Burnet, *Early Greek Philosophy.*
10. Lichtenberg, *"What A Blessing."*
11. McKenna, *"The Trilobite Matron Of Prague."*
12. Cioran, *All Gall Is Divided.*
13. Luke 17:21 *(KJ21).*
14. Plato, *Plato In Twelve Volumes, Vol. 1.*
15. Diogenes, *"Anecdotes Of Diogenes."*
16. Diogenes, *"Anecdotes Of Diogenes."*
17. Hegel, *Lectures On The Philosophy Of History.*

18. Descartes, *Discourse On The Method*.
19. Stirner, Byington and Martin, *The Ego And His Own*.
20. Nietzsche, Common and Förster-Nietzsche, *Thus Spoke Zarathustra*.
21. Leviticus 19:18 *(KJ21)*.
22. Nietzsche and Kaufmann, *Beyond Good And Evil*.
23. 1 Peter 5:8 *(KJ21)*.
24. Genesis 3:5 *(KJ21)*.
25. Genesis 3:22 *(KJ21)*.
26. Descartes, *Discourse On The Method*.
27. Matthew 13:9 *(KJ21)*.
28. Genesis 3:1 *(KJ21)*.
29. Genesis 3:22 *(KJ21)*.
30. Isaiah 14:12 *(KJ21)*.
31. Nietzsche, *The Will To Power*.
32. Leviticus 19:18 *(KJ21)*.
33. Plutarch and Babbitt, *Plutarch's Moralia*.
34. Alighieri, Musgrave and Clarke, *Dante's Inferno*.
35. Clarke, *"Clarke's Third Law On UFO's."*
36. Gustave, *"Gustave Flaubert."*
37. Plato and Roochnik, *Plato's Republic*.
38. Cherno, *"Feuerbach's "Man Is What He Eats": A Rectification."*
39. Hubbard, *"Reflections On Progress."*
40. Hubbard, *"Reflections On Progress."*
41. Goethe and Rohnfeldt, *Criticisms, Reflections, And Maxims Of Goethe*.
42. Abbey, *A Voice Crying In The Wilderness*.
43. Ancient Greek Proverb, *"Delphic Maxims."*

44. McKenna, *Culture And Ideology Are Not Your Friends.*
45. Ellul and Wilkinson, *The Technological Society.*
46. Nietzsche, *Twilight Of The Idols.*
47. Kierkegaard, *Selections From The Writings Of Kierkegaard.*

Bibliography

Abbey, Edward. *A Voice Crying In The Wilderness (Vox Clamantis In Deserto): Notes From A Secret Journal*. London: St. Martin's Griffin, 1989.

Alexander the Great. "Anecdotes Of Diogenes". *Hisotrum.Com*, 2011. https://historum.com/threads/anecdotes-of-diogenes.19914/ .17.Alexander, the Great - "Truly, if I were not Alexander." http://www.leader360.com/coach/quotes_a_alexander.html

Alighieri, Dante, George Musgrave, and Austin Clarke. *Dante's Inferno*. London: Oxford University Press, 1933.

Ancient Greek Proverb. "Delphic Maxims". *Temenos Theon*, 2021. https://www.temenostheon.com/delphic-maxims/.

Burnet, John. *Early Greek Philosophy*. London: A & C Black, Ltd., 1930. O'Toole, Garson. "If You're Going Through Hell, Keep Going – Quote Investigator". Quote Investigator, 2014. https://quoteinvestigator.com/2014/09/14/keep-going/.

Carlin, George. *Charlie Rose*. Video, 1996. https://charlierose.com/videos/19176.

Cherno, Melvin. "Feuerbach's "Man Is What He Eats": A Rectification". *Journal Of The History Of Ideas* 24, no. 3 (1963).

Clarke, A. C. "Clarke's Third Law On UFO's". *Science* 159, no. 3812 (1968): 255-255.

Cioran, E. M. *All Gall Is Divided: The Aphorisms of a Legendary Iconoclast Format.* New York: Arcade Publishing Incorporation, 2012.

Descartes, Rene. *Discourse On The Method Of Rightly Conducting The Reason, And Seeking Truth In The Sciences.* Lanham: Dancing Unicorn Books, 2019.

Diogenes. "Anecdotes Of Diogenes". *Hisotrum.Com*, 2011. https://historum.com/threads/anecdotes-of-diogenes.19914/ .17.Alexander, the Great - "Truly, if I were not Alexander." http://www.leader360.com/coach/quotes_a_alexander.html

Ellul, Jacques, and John Wilkinson. *The Technological Society.* New York: Knopf, 1964.

Flaubert, Gustave. "Gustave Flaubert". *Oxford Reference*, 2021. https://www.oxfordreference.com/view/10.1093/acref/9780191826719.001.0001/q-oro-ed4-00004457.

Goethe, Johann Wolfgang von, and W. B Roñnfeldt. *Criticisms, Reflections, And Maxims Of Goethe.* London: Scott, 1904.

Hegel, G. W. F. *Lectures On The Philosophy Of History.* London: George Bell & Sons, 1902.

Hubbard, Elbert. "Reflections On Progress - Love, Life & Work By Elbert Hubbard". *Readprint.Com*, 2021. http://www.readprint.com/chapter-31573/Love-Life-Work-Elbert-Hubbard.

Kierkegaard, Soren. *Selections From The Writings Of Kierkegaard.* La Vergne: Antiquarius, 2021.

Lichtenberg, Georg Christoph. "What A Blessing". *Quotes.Net*, 2021. https://www.quotes.net/quote/35773.

McKenna, Terence. *Terence McKenna - The Big Picture*. Video, 2021. https://www.youtube.com/watch?v=QB7fRkyoIuo.

McKenna, Terence. "The Trilobite Matron Of Prague". *Tumblr*, 2017. https://thetrilobitematronofprague.tumblr.com/post/162638552644/this-is-the-great-era-of-shamanism-and-what-is.

McKenna, Terence. *Culture And Ideology Are Not Your Friends*. Image, 1999. https://www.organism.earth/library/document/culture-and-ideology-are-not-your-friends.

Nietzsche, Friedrich. *Twilight Of The Gods*. Oxford: OUP, 1998.

Nietzsche, Friedrich. *The Will To Power*. Mineola: Courier Dover Publications, 2019.

Nietzsche, Friedrich. *Twilight Of The Idols*. New York: Gordon Press, 1974.

Nietzsche, Friedrich, Thomas Common, and Elisabeth Förster-Nietzsche. *Thus Spoke Zarathustra*. New York: Modern Library, 1917.

Nietzsche, Friedrich, and Walter Kaufmann. *Beyond Good And Evil: Prelude To A Philosophy Of The Future*. New York: Vintage Books, 1966.

O'Toole, Garson. "Imagination Rules The World – Quote Investigator". *Quote Investigator*, 2021. https://quoteinvestigator.com/2021/01/03/imagine/.

Plato, and David Roochnik. Plato's Republic. Chantilly: Teaching Co., 2005.

Plato. *Plato In Twelve Volumes, Vol. 1*. London: William Heinemann, Ltd., 1966.

Plutarch, and Frank Cole Babbitt. *Plutarch's Moralia*. Cambridge: Harvard University Press, 1949.

Stirner, Max, S. T Byington, and J. J Martin. *The Ego And His Own: The Case Of The Individual Against Authority.*. New York: Libertarian Book Club, 1963.

www.ingramcontent.com/pod-product-compliance
Lightning Source LLC
Chambersburg PA
CBHW071800080526
44589CB00012B/627